JUSTICE FOR OLDER PEOPLE

a volume in
Values in Bioethics
ViB
Matti Häyry and Tuija Takala, Editors

JUSTICE FOR OLDER PEOPLE

Edited by
Harry Lesser

Rodopi

Amsterdam - New York, NY 2012

Cover illustration: www.dreamstime.com

Cover design: Studio Pollmann

The paper on which this book is printed meets the requirements of "ISO 9706:1994, Information and documentation - Paper for documents - Requirements for permanence".

ISBN: 978-90-420-3490-7
E-Book ISBN: 978-94-012-0767-6

Printed in the Netherlands

CONTENTS

DEDICATION

Philip Schapiro (1918–1991), scholar and gentleman.
Sybil Schapiro, most loyal of friends.

FOREWORD

There could hardly be a more pressing set of issues today than those covered by this volume. We are at a time when, in some societies at least, intergenerational justice has moved center stage, as the baby boomers, members of the generation that has had it all, move toward retirement, while younger people regard with alarm the prospects of diminishing pension provision and a significantly longer working life in consequence.

At the same time, the science of ageing and regenerative medicine is poised to bring about changes in our expectations of how we age and the extent to which the human lifespan can be extended. These developments bring with them, however, the inevitable questions of the distribution of health resources, not only within a society but globally. Discussions of human enhancement have to face the problem of the possibility of widening existing inequalities and have the potential for distracting our attention from issues closer to home.

Arguably discussions of the more adventurous rethinking and reengineering of the ageing process are of less immediate importance than how elderly persons are treated now: the extent to which their needs for care and respect are met. The concept of human dignity, although it has been regarded as an unnecessary addition to the bioethical repertoire by some, really shows its importance in this context. Anyone who has experienced institutionalized care of their elderly loved ones has stories to tell about the importance of human dignity, and about how easily it can be threatened, especially in a situation of scarce resources, where these resources are measured not just in terms of money but also in time—the time it takes to see that someone is properly hydrated, the time to listen, the time to notice.

In the light of these considerations, it is good to see that this volume begins with a number of papers on dignity. Two other areas, in particular, are covered, of which one concerns the different aspects of the resources issue, already referred to, and the other is autonomy in ageing. The set of papers on autonomy ranges from challenges to autonomy in older people to the issue of how personal development can continue in later life. This might be regarded as a different type of "enhancement" from that which involves technological interventions to retard the ageing process or to extend the human lifespan.

Much depends on how social attitudes may change in the light of an era of austerity. Might the danger of neglect of older generations be replaced by the threat of resentment, as younger people struggle with the burden of debt in addition to reduced pensions and a longer working life? There are also issues for those in midlife who are "sandwiched" with obligations to both older and younger generations, as life expectancy increases.

There are no easy answers to these questions. One thing, however, is clear. We all, if we are so fortunate as to live long enough, get old, and we all therefore have a prudential as well as a moral interest in fairness and justice in relation to ageing. This requires an exploration of issues such as those discussed in this volume. Harry Lesser has put together a volume of thoughtful papers by a team of excellent contributors, to which I am delighted to write this Foreword.

Ruth Chadwick
Cardiff University

PREFACE

I should like this book to speak for itself, and to take this opportunity to give my warmest thanks to all the contributors for the care and thought they have given to their work and the importance of the ideas they raise. Great thanks are also due to the ViB Consulting Editor, Peter Herissone-Kelly, for his sterling work in helping me to prepare the manuscript. Finally, thanks to the *Journal of General Medicine*, in which Chapter 4 originally appeared.

Harry Lesser
August 2010, Manchester, England

Introduction

THE PRESENT SITUATION: DIAGNOSIS AND TREATMENT

Harry Lesser

1. The Right to Dignity

The authors of the papers in this collection vary considerably in age and in professional background, though they all have a connection with medicine, academia, or both. What they share is a concern for older people and a belief that, as things stand at the moment, these people are often denied what they are fully entitled to as a matter of justice, not charity. Some of the papers are mainly theoretical in orientation and others mainly practical, but those authors concerned with ethical and political theory are concerned with it because they believe that it affects practice, and that incorrect theories produce incorrect action.

Three areas in particular are investigated. The first four chapters are particularly concerned with the right of older people to dignity, or with ways in which the universal right to dignity is threatened in this particular case. The first, Peter Crome's "Older People, Care, Dignity, and Human Rights," sets the scene for this part of the book and for the book as a whole, by explaining the current situation, in the United Kingdom in particular. It sets out, first, how as a result of advances in medicine and healthcare both the numbers of older people and their proportion of the total population have rapidly increased and will increase further. Second, it explains how, even though the general health of the oldest section of the population has improved, a widespread need for care of various sorts still remains. Third, it shows how the actual care provided often falls short of what is required by the European Community's declared commitment to Human Rights, in particular threatening all too frequently the right to privacy and the right not to be treated in a degrading way (these are both aspects of the general right to dignity), and even at times the right to life.

Andrew Edgar's "Age, Dignity, and Social Policy" is concerned again mainly with the UK, and with the way in which those past "normal" retirement age have been regarded, how as a result they have been provided for, and how this has changed over the last sixty years or so. The chapter presents an analysis of various notions of dignity, and focuses on dignity as something to which all persons have a right purely by virtue of being human. It then analyses three attitudes to the protection of this right in the case of the retired. In the UK in the generation following the Second World War, the concentration was on state action and on the provision of all the material conditions for living with at least minimal dignity. This did much good, but had the drawbacks first that it concentrated almost entirely on economic conditions, and second that it treated these older people as people with nothing to give or contribute, so that many people felt like receivers of charity, although they were getting nothing to which they were not fully entitled. In the succeeding generation increasing emphasis was placed on what people could do for themselves: this encouraged self-respect, but still treated them as consumers rather than contributors, and also increased the vulnerability of those not able to pay for themselves. Most recently, a more "post-modern" attitude has emerged, recognizing that there are many ways of dealing with ageing and many positive ways in which the elderly contribute to society. This has again done much good; but the lack of any definite moral framework and the lack of emphasis on the necessary economic conditions for maintaining dignity have created further problems.

Beatriz Cardona's chapter extends the discussion to the developed world in general, particularly the United States and Australia. It focuses on problems created largely by the second of the three attitudes explained above, the emphasis on how older people continue to be responsible for their own condition. While it is obviously a good thing that people should take responsibility for maintaining their own health, and that the physical decline caused by ageing should where possible be checked or postponed, there are also four dangers. The first is the spread of the false belief that *all*, as opposed to some, of the consequences of ageing are like disease or illness, and can be removed by medical intervention. The second is the way in which the unavoidable problems of ageing are as a result made worse by feelings of guilt that one is not dealing with them as one should. The third is the increased vulnerability of older people to those selling products which allegedly prevent "ageing" (that is, the bad effects of ageing) but in fact do little or no good (medication which can do good is another matter). The fourth is the worsening of the position of those without the financial resources to look after themselves. So although emphasis on personal responsibility certainly helps in some ways to protect the dignity of the old, in other ways it works against it, and this needs to be addressed.

My own short chapter, "Loneliness in Older Patients," focuses specifically on the threat to dignity caused by the sense of loneliness and isolation. It argues that the real problem is caused not so much by physical isolation as by the failure of those around the patient, whether carers, hospital staff, friends, or family, to interact fully and wholeheartedly with them, and that when this is done the problem, though it does not disappear, is at least reduced.

2. The Right to Autonomy

The next five chapters deal with the right to autonomy. The scene is set by Caroline Dunn's "The Effect of Ageing on Autonomy." This chapter first considers the definition of autonomy, and follows Gerald Dworkin in regarding it, roughly, as the ability to make informed and reflective choices. This admits of degree, and the physical and mental effects of ageing inevitably tend to lower the degree of autonomy. But, the paper argues, these effects, even if in themselves inevitable, though taking place at very different chronological ages in different people, are made much worse than they need be, because of the way they are exaggerated, or thought to exist before they really do, as a result of negative social perceptions of older people. They are also made worse by our widespread "consumerism," which causes groups with less money, such as many of the elderly, to be automatically devalued. In addition, they can be made worse by attitudes which are in themselves positive rather than negative, such as an over-paternalistic wish to help. In this connection, the chapter goes on to discuss those occasions when there is a need to override the expressed desires of the patient in their own interest; and while this is not denied, it is suggested that there are ways of arranging things so that it can often be avoided. The final point made concerns the need to stop regarding dependence as automatically a disgrace, and to recognize that we are all interdependent.

"Autonomy for Older Patients in Bedside Medicine: Observations from a Developing Nation," by Ashish Goel, Wilma Wilson, and AB Dey, has special reference to India, but is of general relevance. Its starting-point is the same as that of the preceding paper, that the problem of loss of autonomy in older people, especially when they are hospital patients, is made much worse than it need be by the nature of the hospital environment and the assumption by carers that these people are incapable of autonomous decision making. The paper goes on to consider the external factors that affect patient autonomy and how they can be altered to improve the situation. It is recognized that these are numerous and very varied, but it is argued that the two crucial factors are the relation between physician and patient and the hospital environment. Five ways of improving these are discussed. The model of the physician-patient relationship should, where possible, be interpretive or deliberative rather than paternalistic or purely informative. The hospitals should create a patient-friendly environment. There should be a presumption that patients are competent, and, when this is doubtful, there should be proper accurate testing, and not a hasty assumption of incompetence. There must be awareness of patients' cultural and social backgrounds. Finally, and more formally, the requirement to obtain informed consent for treatment from patients should be taken seriously and maintained throughout the treatment.

My second contribution, "Intervention without Patient Consent," considers the limits of this and the question of when the expressed wishes of the patient should be overruled in the interests of their own wellbeing. I ask this question using two actual cases which are, in a sense, borderline, since the incompetence is not obvious and yet the grounds for intervention are strong. In both cases intervention took place: the reader is being asked whether she agrees, and the practitioner whether she would do the same.

Simona Giordano's "Is a Gray World Desirable?" widens the issue, by considering, after a discussion of the demographic changes and the present situation, ways in which the general autonomy of older people can be maintained. Three needs are identified: to improve the prevention of disease and disability; to promote intergenerational dialogue; and to encourage scientific research, especially genetic and cellular. There is a particular argument against the legal restrictions on these types of research that exist in some countries. There is a special emphasis on ways of preventing disease and disability, and on how this involves many factors—provision of information, improved care, a safer environment, and above all encouragement to adopt, well before old age, a healthy life style, including appropriate diet, avoidance of smoking and of excess in eating and drinking, and in particular regular physical activity and its maintenance into old age.

John Hostler's "Personal Development in Old Age" widens the issue still further, by considering not merely how threats to autonomy can be resisted but also how personal development, or change for the better, can continue in the last part of one's life. This chapter is a more theoretical one, being concerned with the definition of personal development, but it emphasizes that more precise definition may itself help toward actual achievement. Three models of personal development are considered: progression, learning, and self-realization. It is argued that all three of these, though initially vague, can, when applied to individuals, be given some definite meaning. The paper ends by considering the question of whether anyone other than the person herself or himself can judge whether a change is an improvement.

3. The Just Distribution of Resources

So, these first nine papers all consider how in old age dignity and autonomy may be preserved and increased, in a world in which the proportion of older people is markedly growing and in all probability will continue to grow, and which contains many threats to their dignity and autonomy, some inevitable but many avoidable. The individuals themselves can deal with some of these threats, for example by adopting a healthy lifestyle well before they become old; but proper handling of many of them requires that society make the appropriate resources available. This raises the question of what share of resources the oldest members of society are entitled to, given that their claims are not the only claims; and the seven final chapters are in different ways all connected with this.

Once again, the first of these chapters, Robin Attfield's "The Global Distribution of Healthcare Resources in the Twenty-First Century," sets the scene—and as the title indicates, in a very wide context—of the massive disparity in healthcare between the richest and poorest countries. Attfield argues that any credible theory of moral obligation must attach high value and high priority to the satisfaction of fundamental needs, such as life and health. From this it follows that there is an international obligation to tackle this problem. There is, as the author notes, an issue as to how far a state's first obligation is to the needs of its own citizens. But, as he then points out, whether or not this is correct, much might be done with the expenditure of a small percentage of resources, human and financial, which would not in any way threaten the life or health of the citizens of the wealthy world.

Nevertheless, it may be said, even if priority is given to meeting the most pressing needs, and even if the resources given to healthcare were larger than they are, sooner or later there will be conflicts of interest, in that resources used to meet one need will be diverted from others not obviously less important. The potential conflict between the needs of people in different parts of the world is an immensely important issue, but the concern of this book is with conflicts within a particular society. This indeed is the topic of the next chapter, Margaret Harris's "The Rival Claims of Children and Adults to Healthcare Resources: Is there a Need for Greater Coherence in our View?" Written in the form of a dialogue, the chapter discusses the problem of deciding, when resources are limited, between different sections of the population, all in genuine need. The aim is not to propose an answer but to establish a background for the following chapters by showing the difficulty and complexity of this moral dilemma.

Michael Rivlin's "Setting Limits Fairly: A Critique of Some of Daniel Callahan's Views" aims to show that one way of answering the dilemma, namely, by using age-based rationing of healthcare resources, as advocated (admittedly, not under present conditions) by Daniel Callahan, is inherently unjust. The chapter criticizes the three main arguments used by Callahan, here called the "intergenerational injustice" argument, the "accepting death" argument, and "the argument from altruism." It then goes on to make further criticisms of the view itself, arguing in particular (1) that chronological age tells us virtually nothing about a person's physical or mental condition and (2) that to discriminate against people simply because they belong to a certain group and for no other reason cannot be fair or just.

Richard Wagland's two chapters similarly criticize two arguments for age discrimination. "Social Injustice: Distributive Egalitarianism, the Complete Life View, and Age Discrimination" considers the following issue. Granted that we should prioritize meeting needs, especially in the use of healthcare resources, should we at any given time prioritize those most in need at that time, or should we try to see to it that everyone has, over their whole lives, an equal opportunity of having their needs met? The chapter argues that, apart from practical difficulties, when the implications of the second view, the "complete life view," are worked out, it can be seen that it would lead to unjust discrimination against older people.

Wagland's second chapter, "A Fair Innings or a Complete Life: Another Attempt at an Egalitarian Justification of Ageism," criticizes the "fair innings" argument, the argument that our first priority should be to enable as many people as possible to reach the currently "normal" or expected life-span (this is of course steadily rising), and that people who have passed this age have less claim on resources. The chapter considers various interpretations of the argument, and their implications, and various criticisms. Its conclusion is that the fatal criticism is the one first expressed by John Harris, in effect that people in equal need have an equal moral claim, regardless of their age.

A similar conclusion is reached in my "Triage and Older Patients." I argue, first, that the principle of triage, roughly, the principle that in an emergency priority should be given to those for whom treatment will make the greatest difference, is still a principle of justice, giving priority to those in the greatest need. I then argue that, though it is the appropriate principle to use in order to decide who in an emergency should be treated first, it is not an appropriate principle for the overall distribution of either medical or non-medical resources. Finally it is argued that triage provides no justification for discrimination on grounds of age. It provides a good ground for withholding treatment that can do no good. This does occur more often with the old than with the young, but, first, it occurs in both and, second, it never occurs simply because a person is old, but for some other reason, for example that they are already terminally ill.

Finally, Julian Hughes's "Justice, Guidelines, and Virtues" considers, with the help of a particular case discussed in detail, whether it can be morally right to override national guidelines if a doctor is convinced, or strongly suspects, that treatment not allowed by those guidelines is needed by an older patient, or very much in their interest. The conclusion is that this certainly can be right, but decisions are not easy. The chapter goes on to argue that the best framework, as regards moral theory, for considering these questions is that of virtue ethics.

So, this book endeavors to provide, first, some account of the needs of older people, especially their needs for autonomy and dignity, of ways in which these needs are not being met, and of what could and should be done to remedy this. It goes on to show that the various arguments designed to show that other needs should take precedence are invalid. We must conclude that these needs ought to be met, and things ought to change. This will require, in particular, changes in the use of resources and in social attitudes. And, as Julian Hughes reminds us, it requires a commitment by individuals, whether they are formal or informal carers, to justice and to compassion.

One

OLDER PEOPLE, CARE, DIGNITY, AND HUMAN RIGHTS

Peter Crome

1. Introduction

The fact that this subject is featuring in this volume flows from one of the greatest triumphs of humankind, the development of the world so that living well into our eighties and even nineties is no longer considered to be exceptional. The impact of the global changes in population demography ranks alongside climate change and the provision of clean water and sufficient food as major international challenges. In this chapter, three related subjects will be discussed: a summary of recent and future population demographic changes, a brief discussion of the major issues in care in the United Kingdom and their relationship to ethical principles such as equity and the requirements to do good and avoid doing harm, and finally how this impacts on dignity and human rights.

2. Demography

Longevity is not new. The Bible, perhaps exaggerating, records that Methusalah lived for 969 years and the Hebrew Patriarchs lived for over 100 years. Moses' 120 years has been surpassed in modern times by the French woman Jean Marie Lecalm who reached 123 years and who survived the lawyer to whom she sold her home in return for a life pension.

Life expectancy has been growing at the rate of approximately one and a half years per decade over the last 100 years or so and this rate of increase in lifespan shows no sign of slowing down. In the UK men reaching sixty-five lived on average for twelve more years in 1960 than was the average at the start of the century, and this had risen to 16.9 years by 2006.[1]

Life expectancies for Japan are even longer, with the number of people over seventy years increasing by 25.6% in the period 2000–2005[2] and a projected further increase of 16.7% over the following five year period in the number of those sixty-five years or older.[3]

Within the older population there will be a disproportionate rise in the "oldest old." European Union figures show that the percentage of the population over the age of eighty will rise from 3.4% in 2000 to 6.5% in 2025 and 11.8% in 2050.[4] We can expect a twenty-one-fold rise in the number of centenarians in the UK by the middle of the twenty-first century.[5] A related demographic change will be an increase in the numerical ratio of the number of retired people to the total population who are in paid employment. This will impact on the numbers of people who will able to care for those who are older and the amount of money generated through taxation to pay for pensions and care. This concept can be expressed as a dependency ratio which will rise in the UK from 20% in 2003 to 47% in 2051.[6] The factors responsible for these changes are the ageing of the baby-boom generation, lower fertility rates, and increasing life expectancy.

3. Care: Its Costs and Provision

The present standard UK pension ages of sixty for women and sixty-five for men were set in 1925 and the question of the affordability of this arrangement continues to be a lively and controversial political topic. Later retirement age, higher contributions, and lower payouts have all been suggested as part of the solution, but are not exactly vote winners. Current proposals for reducing care costs, particularly likely to affect middle-income earners, include a social insurance fund to pay for care, into which people would pay a lump sum on retirement. The state would pay for the poorest and the rich would pay for themselves. Another alternative is a "pound for pound" scheme in which the state would match each individual's contributions towards care costs. In May 2008, the then Prime Minister Gordon Brown launched a new consultation on the costs of care.

One of the questions often asked is whether these extra years of life are spent in good health or in disability. Here the answer appears to be that although there are some extra years of disability these are surpassed by extra years of healthy and active life. However it must be accepted that some old people will develop either physical or mental disabilities which will restrict their ability to live independently. For them a range of services can be provided at home—meals, alarms, help with bathing, district nursing services, and so on. Whether the help that is available matches what the person really wants is more debatable; but most (not all) people want to remain at home as long as possible, and more and more people are being supported to do this. This trend is likely to continue both for cost and for quality reasons, and new developments such as telecare, whereby sensors can be fitted up in the home to detect, for example, whether someone has fallen or had a meal, will support this further.

New types of supported accommodation are being built—extended care facilities, provided in both the private and "third" (mixed) sectors, where people retain their own front door but there is help readily available when necessary, and residents can also access communal facilities. What will happen when the whole retirement community ages and the proportion of residents with dementia increases is less clear, although in the United States many such facilities include a care home on site and such developments are also occurring in the UK.

The greater part of care at home is provided willingly by family and friends supported by the wide range of voluntary organizations, and without this provision older people's lives would be much poorer. For those with greater care needs local authority co-ordinated home care is at least potentially available. But who gets home care is an area of great contention. What is clear is that the eligibility criteria for home care are becoming tighter and tighter. Social service authorities are obliged to follow a national scheme, Fair Access to Care, in which care need is divided into four categories: critical, substantial, moderate, and low. A recent report by the Commission for Social Care Inspection (CSCI)[7] into care in six local authorities found that in one care was provided until recently only for the critical group, in one for all four groups, in one for the top three, and in the remaining three for the top two only. So in the majority of areas those with moderate needs, a description of which includes a situation in which "social support systems and relationships cannot or will not be sustained," are still not eligible for support. To quote from some of the conclusions of the report:

> people who were self-funding and facing the momentous decision of moving into a care home received little or no help from councils. At most they may be given a booklet with information on choosing a home.

In describing older people's experience the authors state:

> While few described their life in wholly negative terms most expressed a degree of resignation and acceptance of their lot. In practice this study found that self-funding people were often the most disadvantaged and isolated in the whole system. None of the people we met who were self-funding had experienced a social care assessment prior to entering a care home and most had not considered an alternative solution.

They give another case history:

> Mrs X is described as unkempt with her knickers around her knees and evidence of feces on the floor. She was not taking her medication. Mrs X was assessed as managing her own personal care and meal preparation. Case closed.

Direct payments to clients may be helpful and allow greater choice to those who receive local authority support but they are irrelevant to those who are self-funding. However, for some the only feasible solution will be transfer to a care home. This is particularly so for those who have dementia or a related illness. (Indeed, surveys show that 62% of care home residents have this condition although in many cases it is undiagnosed.[8]) Once the decision to transfer to a care home has been taken, then issues of location, cost, and quality arise. Choice will often involve a compromise, for example in deciding whether to live near your family or near your previous home. Many people will have to rely on others to make the choice for them because their physical and mental health problems limit their capacity. People in hospital may have to make rapid decisions. Some people are obliged to make choices rapidly in crisis situations. Those in hospital may be told to make a decision within forty-eight hours. Hopefully services can be instituted whereby people who no longer need acute care services can be transferred to "step-down" or intermediate care facilities and given a reasonable time to choose between homes. There is, however, general agreement that high quality care is expensive and that the system of state support can be confusing and often provides only an adequate level of care. Also, the demarcations between those who receive nursing financial support and those who do not, and those who qualify for full NHS funding and those who do not, often appear quite arbitrary.

In summary, NHS Funded Continuing Care provides for board and lodging, personal care, and nursing care to be paid for by the NHS. However, choice will be limited and is very rarely provided at home. In return for this "free" care your pension will be reduced to "pocket money" levels (£20.45 a week): in effect, only the poorest are eligible for free care. The rules covering eligibility are now national[9] and there is a system of appeals and reviews.

For those who have "nursing" needs a contribution of £101 weekly will be paid. This is often described as "free" but is better regarded as a contribution to care. Until recently nursing care was banded but this has now been abolished.

In Scotland, but not England, "personal care" is also subsidized by a payment of £145 weekly. But in return for this Scottish care home residents do not get Attendance Allowance and the nursing contribution is reduced to £65 per week (2008 figures).

There are relatively few pensioners who have an income that will cover the cost of a good quality care home, and so they will have to utilize their capital or will have to rely on family or charitable "top ups." There is no support if your capital assets are over £21,500 and only partial support if the assets are between £13,000 and £21,500. Deliberately trying to get rid of capital to avoid care home costs is unlawful, and the local authority has the power to put a charge on a property in order to recover its costs at a later stage. (There are of course certain exemptions, for example if a spouse is living in the home). The issue of being "forced to sell your home to pay for care" is also emotive, although procedures allow for people to move into care homes, and their care to be paid for by the local authority until such time as the capital has been realized.

All care homes are registered and inspected and a new body called the Care Quality Commission is being established.[10] Cleanliness, comfort, sufficient trained staff, activity, adequate food and drink, privacy, person-centered care, flexibility, and safety are just some of the components of good quality care. But things can and do go wrong. Examples from the author's personal experience of close family members' care include: kitchens closing at 6.30 pm with no food being available until breakfast; moldy food in the refrigerators; residents being given forty-eight hours' notice to quit and the family being offered no support in finding alternative accommodation; dirty bedrooms which have not been properly vacuumed; and homes closing because they are not sufficiently profitable. Inspection reports are freely available in homes and on the Internet and provide reassurance. However, the question always remains as to whether the standards being measured are the right ones. But these reports do provide information on overall quality, and highlight what could be done better, and a new star rating system is being introduced.[11] Of course there is still the problem that everyone has different views of what quality is and what we might reasonably expect from a care home.

4. Abuse

Elder abuse is defined in terms of both commission and omission. Just as in child abuse, the majority of perpetrators are close family members and abuse takes place in the home. However, it must be recognized that the special circumstances of caring for vulnerable people require special consideration. Over-medicating, physical restraint, and not attending to continence issues as a matter of urgency are all aspects of abuse that occur. There are often conflicts between the staff's "need to get everything done quickly" and the residents' need to proceed at their own pace. The physical construction of a home may not meet the demands of its client groups—many are not suitable for those with increased physical disability. People living with dementia who wander around also need specially designed facilities which allow for this without restraint. This has been recognized and many appropriate dementia units have been built. For those people contemplating a move to a care home a simple question to ask home managers is what assurance they can give that abuse does not take place in their home. A national study measuring the prevalence of abuse in care homes is about to begin.

5. Dignity

The British Geriatrics Society has been increasingly concerned that performance pressures in hospitals are compromising one of the most fundamental aspects of dignity—the necessity to ensure privacy when using the bathroom. With other organizations standards for best practice have been developed alongside a toolkit for measuring performance. The issues that too frequently arise are ignoring calls for assistance; telling people to wait; scolding those who have become incontinent; offering pads without underwear; leaving people on bedpans for excessive periods of time; not offering hand-washing facilities; and using safety concerns as a general rationale for denying choice. Best practice guidance includes ensuring toilets are adjacent to patient areas and easily accessible, clean, well-appointed, and with doors that close. All patients should be asked about their own preferences when using the toilet. Hoists, if they are necessary, must be used in a way that protects modesty. Staff should respond promptly and politely to requests for assistance. If using the toilet behind curtains is the only option, then the curtains must be closed and a notice put up. The environmental audit toolkit,[12] which has been designed to be used by lay people, asks about the width of the doors; whether a door can be opened, shut, and locked; whether the toilet flushes and how well; if toilet paper is available and who checks that it is; if the washing facilities are adequate; and if the toilets are cleaned. This approach to promoting dignity is not rocket science, and it is of course disappointing that these problems continue to be major concerns of patients and families when in hospital. Such an approach to just one aspect of dignity fits within other themes which require care to be appropriate, equitable, responsive to individual needs, kind, and respectful of human rights.

6. Human Rights

Anti-ageism legislation was the last equality issue to be placed within a statutory framework, but, disappointingly, the House of Lords has ruled that Human Rights legislation does not apply to older people living in non-publicly run care homes, even if they are funded through public funds. This now should be changing; new legislation on this issue has been promised. The first article of the Universal Declaration of Human Rights states that we are all born free, equal in dignity and human rights, and this proposition is echoed in the Charter of Fundamental Rights of the European Union and indeed in the NHS National Plan.

The European Convention on Human Rights[13] has three main articles relevant to the care of older people in hospitals and homes: the right to privacy (Article 8), the right to life (Article 2), and the right not to have degrading treatment (Article 3). In its evidence to the Joint House of Lords and House of

Commons Select Committee investigating abuses of Human Rights, some of the challenges mentioned by the British Geriatrics Society included:

- Older persons who have difficulty feeding themselves may not receive adequate nutrition as there are not sufficient members of staff appointed to feed them. If this is persistent it will come under Article 2 (the right to life).
- Older people may be placed in care homes without adequate opportunities for assessment and rehabilitation: this raises issues under Article 8 (the right to respect for private life).
- Some older persons go into long-term care without receiving a comprehensive assessment of their needs. This raises issues under Article 8 and, in extreme cases, Article 2 (the right to life).
- The conditions of some older people may be left untreated until crises arise, as it is assumed that they are in a place of safety. This raises issues under Article 2.
- Older persons in care homes may be given sedatives and tranquilizers unnecessarily or restrained physically without necessity. This can arise as a result of inadequate levels of staff or inadequate skills and training. This raises issues under Articles 8 and 3 (prohibition of inhuman and degrading treatment).
- Only 40% of general practitioners will have received any postgraduate training in the care of frail older persons with multiple pathology. This results in older frail persons in care homes receiving substandard treatment.
- Nearly half of the care homes were failing to meet national minimum standards in the way they give persons the medication prescribed by their doctors to treat their medical conditions. This raises issues under Article 8 and, in extreme cases, Article 2.

To deal with these problems, the Select Committee recommended embedding the care of vulnerable older people firmly within a legislative framework although at least one member of the Committee suggested this was all a matter of common sense!

7. Conclusions

Civilized societies must be judged by how well they care for vulnerable people, of whom older people with mental and physical health problems are a large and growing group. Although there have been many improvements in recent years there is still much to be done. Education, information, regulation, and legislation are necessary, but this will only occur if society as a whole demands it, is willing to pay for it, and affords it sufficient priority.

NOTES

1. www.statistics.gov.uk/cci/nugget.asp?id=168
2. www.stat.go.jp/english/data/kokusei/2000/kihon1/00/03.htm
3. www.stat.go.jp/english/data/kokusei/2005/kihon1/00/02.htm
4. www.euro.centre.org/detail.php?xml_id=1143
5. www.gad.gov.uk/Demography_Data/Population/Index.asp?y=2006&v=Princpal&dataCountry=england&chkDataTable=yy_singyear&subTable=Perform+search
6. www.statistics.gov.uk/CCI/nuggest.asp?ID=1272&Pos=2&ColRank=2&Rank=224
7. www.csci.org.uk/about_us/publications/lost_to_the_system.aspx
8. F.E. Matthews and T. Dening, "Prevalence of Dementia in Institutional Care," *Lancet*, 20:360 (2002), pp. 225–6.
9. www.dh.gov.uk/en/Publicationsandstatistics/Legislation/DH_078061
10. www.dh.gov.uk/en/Publicationsandstatistics/Legislation/Actsandbills/HealthandSocialCareBill/DH_080438
11. www.csci.org.uk/professional/default.aspx?page=7726&csci=2418
12. www.bgs.org.uk/campaigns/dignity.htm
13. www.hri.org/docs/ECHR50.html

Two

AGE, DIGNITY, AND SOCIAL POLICY

Andrew Edgar

1. Introduction

The purpose of this chapter is to explore the manner in which understandings of "dignity" have been articulated within social policies for older people, primarily with reference to the United Kingdom. It will be argued that the history of social policy since the Second World War reflects changing, and increasingly sophisticated, understandings of what the dignity of an older person might entail. However, the concept of "dignity" remains problematic. Its scope is broad and indefinite, and its meaning disputed. The partial or differential use of the term may serve to highlight certain concerns, but only at the expense of others. While it might be held that a recognition of the need to promote dignity may morally ground social policy, it can also be suggested that no policy can wholly encapsulate dignity as a broad and coherent whole. It will be concluded that the demand to respect the dignity of those subjected to social policy therefore ultimately represents the requirement for a continually reflective and critical approach to policy that will lead to its ceaseless revision and rethinking.

2. Varieties of Dignity

The chapter takes as its starting point a model of dignity developed by Lennart Nordenfelt (Nordenfelt, 2004). It is Nordenfelt's contention that it is not fruitful to seek a single meaning for "dignity." By drawing on its use in ordinary discourse, as well on philosophical reflection on the moral intuitions that underpin the concept, Nordenfelt proposes four morally important uses or "varieties" of dignity. The first three uses appeal to the person's experience of dignity. These are, in brief, dignity of merit, in which a person's sense of dignity rests upon the economic or social position that they occupy (for example as a mayor, a professor, or a doctor); dignity of moral stature, where a person's sense of dignity results from having lived up to her moral ideals; and dignity of identity, which comes from the capacity to articulate positive stories about yourself and the communities and groups to which you see yourself as belonging.

These three kinds of dignity may be possessed to a greater or lesser degree, and that degree will be reflected in a person's subjective sense of self-respect or esteem. More precisely, a person's sense of self-respect may be dependent upon her being credited with each variety of dignity. Denial will be a source of humiliation, embarrassment, or indignity. So, for example, a person who is demoted or loses his or her job may feel a loss of dignity (of merit); someone who has not lived up to his or her moral ideals feels humiliation; and a person who is subject to abuse or discrimination may similarly be humiliated, or made to feel worthless. This third kind of indignity further serves to stress the intersubjective nature of dignity. (Edgar, 2004) To a greater or lesser extent, my sense of self-respect and dignity will depend upon how other people perceive and judge me, or more precisely, upon how I perceive and evaluate other people's judgments of me. The point is not just that I will be hurt by abusive language or deliberate acts of discrimination. If I lose certain competencies, due say to a stroke, or if I am disfigured, I will be embarrassed or worse due to my perception of other people's evaluation of that supposed incompetence and abnormality. It may be suggested that what will count as dignity or indignity will, to a significant extent, be relative to particular moral cultures, and to the expectations that people have of themselves and others. So, for example, while being a prince may be a source of self-respect in a monarchy, it may be a humiliating anachronism within a republic.

In order to respond to the threat of relativism, Nordenfelt adds a fourth variety of dignity. This differs from the other three in that it does not relate to psychological experiences, and nor is it a matter of degree. The German term *Menschenwürde* refers to the moral status and value that comes merely from being human. It represents the fundamental moral claim that a human being has, simply as a human being, to be treated with a certain respect and consideration. *Würde* deliberately echoes Kant, and his grounding of dignity in the autonomy of the human being. (Kant, 2005, p. 97) So, while the degree of dignity that a person enjoys may vary for each of the first three kinds, the dignity that Nordenfelt seeks to capture in "*Menschenwürde*" is absolute and inalienable. It is not relative to the degree of autonomy that a particular person is capable of exercising, but is dependent only on the potential that humans as such have to be autonomous. A newborn baby, a person who is comatose, or even a human corpse, have moral worth. So, while a person may experience a loss of dignity in any of the first three senses, it is precisely because *Menschenwürde* cannot be lost that a moral wrong has thereby occurred. The humiliated person may feel no dignity or self-respect, but a moral claim is made on his or her behalf, in the name of his or her dignity as a human being.

While Nordenfelt suggests that *Menschenwürde* is often cashed out in the language of human rights (Nordenfelt, 2004, p. 78), and indeed the Universal Declaration of Human Rights (and other international rights documents, including that of the European Union) appeal to "dignity," a fundamental difference between the language of rights and that of dignity may be indicated.

The former highlights what has to be protected in order to secure the morally valuable properties and capacities of the human being—what has to be secured in order to guarantee human flourishing. Rights are therefore of instrumental value. They are tools for securing what is valuable about the human being, and as such important instruments of social policy. Dignity, in contrast, concerns intrinsic value. The language of dignity attempts to encapsulate precisely what is of value in being human, and so what rights are there to protect. But further, while a list of rights allows the reader to construct a quite precise model of what is of value in the human being, it may be suggested that *Menschenwürde* is something always to be searched for. *Menschenwürde* is always capable of exceeding our expectations. This follows from a peculiar property of at least most varieties of dignity. They are what J.L. Austin calls "trouser words." (Austin, 1962, p. 70)

To explicate Austin's metaphor: a word does not have meaning in isolation. The word does not refer to a property that we readily experience and understand. Instead, the meaning depends upon its contrast to a seemingly less important negative concept (and so the negative word "wears the trousers" and takes the dominant role). If "dignity" is indeed a trouser word, then it is understood only when it is taken from us. Only negative experiences, for example of "indignity," "humiliation," and "embarrassment," make us aware of what "dignity" might be. With the expansion of our understanding of what it is to be human and of what the good life for humans may be, we recognize indignity where it was not recognized before. This is to argue that the moral relativism inherent in the first three kinds of dignity is to be complemented by a sense of moral discovery and progress that is inherent to *Menschenwürde* (Putnam, 1998). This, in effect, is also the history of social policy. Social policy is formulated to guard against recognized sources of indignity. What counts as indignity will shift between historical periods. Yet, this shift is not wholly random, if *Menschenwürde* is understood as grounding the use of dignity, and so gesturing toward a dignity that is not yet known. The appeal to "dignity" is the condemnation of complacency in social policy.

3. Social Policy and Social Gerontology

Following Alan Walker, three broad phrases of post-war social policy concerning older people may be identified. (Walker, 1999, pp. 368–372) The period between the 1940s and early 1970s saw the consolidation and growth of the mass welfare state. In the context of full-employment and Keynesian economic policy, old age was understood predominantly in terms of retirement from economic activity. The provision of universal pensions therefore became the central element of social policy, with pensions at once guaranteeing certain welfare rights for the older person, but only by making that person largely dependent upon the state. A second period from the mid-1970s to the late

1980s saw a challenge to the idea of universal state provision of pensions. Keynesian approaches to economic policy were displaced by a neo-classicism that put greater emphasis upon the role of the free market. Early retirement became a way to manage rising levels of unemployment. Yet this also disrupted any simple association between old age and retirement (leading, for example, to the construction of a division between the "young old" (fifty to seventy-four) and the "old old" (seventy-five plus), or between "a third age" and "a fourth age" (Walker, 1999, p. 371)). The value of state pensions declined in real terms, shifting the burden of planning and preparing for retirement on to the individual (so that the state pension came to be increasingly supplemented by private pensions). A final contemporary "postmodern" stage (Polivka and Longino, 2002; Gilleard and Higgs, 2000, pp. 4–7) may be associated with a supposed "Third Way" in social democratic politics. (Giddens, 1998) Ageing now comes to be recognized as a complex and diverse cultural experience. There is no longer a single, traditional route into old age. This means that for some old age is a period of opportunity and growth, while for others it is a period of vulnerability and decline. Social policy strives to manage this complexity, at once acknowledging the positive opportunity of ageing, and seeking to safeguard against the dangers of increasing vulnerability.

These three periods may be linked to the development of social gerontology. While social policy has historically rarely drawn explicitly upon the theories of social gerontologists, broad associations and influences may be recognized, as Walker indicates. (Walker, 1999, pp. 364–368) These influences will help in the reconstruction of the senses of dignity that are implicit to much social policy. The earliest period of social policy may be seen to be couched within the assumptions of functionalist social theory, and complemented by "disengagement" theories. This is to argue, in outline, that what is most functional to both society and the individual is the effective disengagement of that individual from public social and economic activity, as he or she ages. Such an approach presumes the process of ageing to be a largely natural process (so that age is reduced to a biomedical problem (Estes and Binney, 1989)), to which the individual and society must adjust. This framework is criticized by political economy (or critical gerontology) that emerges in the work of Estes (Estes, 1979), Townsend (Townsend, 1981), Walker (Walker, 1981), Phillipson (Phillipson, 1982), and Myles (Myles, 1984). Here old age is understood as a social construct. Rather than being treated as a natural event, ageing comes to be seen as something that is managed, and so ultimately constructed, through social processes, and not least through the social policies that enforce retirement and dependency upon state pensions. (Phillipson, 1998, pp. 17–21; Gilleard and Higgs, 2000, pp. 13–19)

Political economy is challenged from the humanities and from within the social sciences. Common to both challenges is the recognition that political economy tends to reduce the older person to a more or less passive victim of social, economic, and political structures. As such, it reproduces something of the very functionalism that it sought to displace. Moral economy emerges from the humanities. Thomas R. Cole draws on E. P. Thompson's *Making of the English Working Class*, in which Thompson examined the shared moral assumptions that empowered artisans, at the end of the eighteenth century, to riot against shortages and rising food prices. (Minkler and Cole, 1991, pp. 39–40) In a line of argument that may be seen to draw on communitarian assumptions, moral economy theorists turn to the culture that gives ageing a moral meaning. Such an approach at once reinforces the rejection of a purely biomedical approach to ageing, and stresses the possibility of "successful ageing" (as opposed to the physical decline and withdrawal presupposed by functionalists). (Moody, 1998, p. 81) Age therefore ceases to be an economic problem, or even a narrowly conceived social construction, and is instead seen as a moral achievement. Successful ageing comes to depend upon the possibility of a "culture's ability to sustain morally compelling social practices and existentially vital ideals of ageing." (Cole, 1992, p. 230)

If the humanities open up the question of moral meaning, then alternatively the social sciences draw upon hermeneutics and phenomenology, and upon cultural studies and critical theory, in order to pursue the importance of "personal" meaning in ageing. (Gilleard and Higgs, 2000, p. 22) In part this serves to broaden the understanding of the cultural context of ageing beyond the relatively narrow focus of moral economy. But further, it serves to present the older person as an autonomous and reflexive social agent, and so as actively responding to the experience of age within a context of social change and cultural diversity. Within a postmodern society, ageing is understood as a matter of lifestyle choice, and so of the construction of personal and cultural identities. The agent will still draw upon the cultural resources available to him or her in order to construct this identity, and indeed an ageist culture may serve to inhibit the construction of a meaningful narrative of ageing. However, culture is no longer seen as ascribing a given meaning to the agent. Rather, it provides a diverse range of resources from which the agent selects in order to "theorize" old age and thereby to construct the reality within which they live. (Phillipson, 1998, pp. 25–6)

The politics and policies of the Third Way reflect a greater awareness of debates within social gerontology than any previous wave of policy making. (Biggs, 2001, p. 308) While the emphasis that neo-liberalism and neo-classical economics place upon the consumer, and so the individual's personal responsibility in providing for his or her old age, is not abandoned, the crisis that unbridled consumerism brings about, in the form of social exclusion, is recognized. So, in response to the analysis of the ageing process offered by political economy, targeted provision of state assistance becomes important as a complement to personal responsibility. (Gilleard and Higgs, 2000, p. 23) Perhaps more significantly, moral economy and cultural studies influence the Third Way, as Simon Biggs implies. (Biggs, 2001, pp. 307–9) In the UK, government policy in the late 1990s and first decade of the new century seeks to promote positive ageing, despite ageing having a relatively low profile for potential voters. An appeal for collective identification with inclusive national and local projects (akin to the shared moral assumptions pursued by Cole and others) is sought as a remedy to the damage done by the neo-liberal assault on the mass welfare state. In addition, ageism is recognized as a problem, akin to sexism and racism, which it is necessary for a government to tackle.

4. Post-War Policy

Dignity has not appeared in this brief narrative. Despite references to dignity in the United Nations Universal Declaration of Human Rights (in 1948), sustained and overt appeals to dignity only appear in recent policy documents, for example in the *United Nations Principles for Older Persons* (linked to the International Year of Older Persons in 1999), and in the UK "Dignity, Security, and Independence in Old Age." It may, nonetheless, be suggested that conceptions of dignity are implicit in earlier policy frameworks, beginning with the post-war welfare state.

The moral grounding of the mass welfare state, along with the complementary understanding of ageing proposed by functionalist social gerontology, may be articulated in terms of two contrasting approaches to dignity. These may be seen in the funding of pensions, and in the theory of disengagement. The introduction of a universal, non-means-tested pension within the UK welfare state in the late 1940s can readily be understood as a significant move in an attempt to secure the dignity of older people. On one level it recognizes that older people may expect to be protected from the dangers of ageing (such as poverty, homelessness, and illness). Here "dignity" functions as a "trouser word," brought into focus by fears of the indignity of poverty, homelessness, and the inability to secure adequate medical treatment. This would be coherent with the use of "dignity" by the United Nations (and in particular in articles 22 and 23). Rights, then, work as an instrument, protecting what is valuable to human existence, or more precisely, protecting the individual from specific threats to that core value, while the core value itself remains elusive (known only through its corruption).

Crucially, the task of securing the welfare rights of the individual in old age is seen to fall upon society as a whole. This is expressed, in no small part, in the funding of pensions. Those who pay into national insurance schemes do not do so in order to fund their own pensions, but rather to fund the pensions of those currently retired (Phillipson, 1999, p. 39). The early welfare state is thereby grounded in a sense of social solidarity.

The combination of a recognition of welfare rights and social solidarity may readily be cashed out in terms of a complex understanding of the dignity of the older person. On the one hand it presupposes the need to secure the material resources that make possible a person's autonomy. There are certain indignities that no human being should be allowed to endure. On the other hand, the protection of the older person by society as a whole gives that society what Nordenfelt would call dignity of moral status. The mass welfare state allows the realization of certain collective moral ideals, and in terms favored by the moral economy perspective institutionalizes norms of reciprocity between young and old. (Kohli, 1991)

The problem with this analysis is that it is still partial. On the one hand, it may be noted, in passing, that for some people, the notion of accepting monies from the welfare state infringed their understanding of dignity. Welfare "handouts" were equated with a dependence on charity, and so with a public declaration of a person's lack of autonomy and, consequently, dignity. While we will return to this problem below as something to which neo-liberalism responds, here it may serve to underline the problem of the cultural relativism of dignity noted above. Understandings of "dignity" are highly contested, and as such dependent upon the cultural and political contexts within which they are articulated, and through which social actors understand themselves as autonomous beings. The politician and bureaucrat, for all their good intentions, may simply have a different conception of "dignity" from that of the person they seek to assist.

On the other hand, it may be seen that the welfare state expresses a highly restricted and indeed impoverished understanding of what it is to be an older person. For all the securing of welfare rights for that person, ageing is nonetheless understood as a problem. More precisely, the older population are seen as a burden on society. Biggs cites Beveridge's 1942 report on *Social Insurance and Allied Services*: "It is dangerous to be in any way lavish to old age until adequate provision has been assured for all other vital needs, such as the prevention of disease and the adequate nutrition of the young." (Biggs, 1999, p. 142) It is assumed that older people are less productive workers, and so that they represent a burden upon the working population (albeit one that can be sustained, given continued economic growth). In Nordenfelt's terms, dignity of merit, secured by active economic involvement, appears to be primary (if only for instrumental reasons, due to its relationship to economic productivity), and older people necessarily relinquish such dignity.

This perspective may be given more substance through a consideration of the theory of disengagement. While disengagement theory was developed as a description of the ageing process, based originally on a sample of 275 individuals between fifty and ninety years old in Kansas City in the 1950s, it readily acquires normative implications. As Elaine Cumming summarizes the theory, it proposes that:

> normal ageing is a mutual withdrawal or 'disengagement' between the ageing person and others in the social system to which he belongs .... When disengagement is complete, the equilibrium that existed in middle life between the individual and society has given way to a new equili-

brium characterized by greater distance, and a changed basis for solidarity." (Cumming, 2000, p. 25)

Positively, disengagement projects a clear goal for dignified ageing—one of "ego transcendence." (Moody, 1998, pp. 75, 404) Here something of Nordenfelt's dignity of identity comes to be articulated, in the sense of an understanding of what it means to age. Cumming sees in old age the possibility of freedom. (Cumming, 2000, p. 29) This is echoed in the work of Carl Jung. Jung argues for a fundamental shift in psychology between a person's early and later years. Middle life and beyond is a period of detachment and reflection, during which the person can seek deeper cultural and spiritual meaning than was available to him or her previously. In old age "it is a duty and a necessity to devote serious attention to [yourself]," and so turn away from youthful preoccupations with making money, bringing up a family, and being useful to others. (Jung, 1998, p. 454)

Such accounts would, nonetheless, seem to depend upon and reinforce the assumption that older people have little or nothing to offer to the modern economy or public life, or at best that the pace of economic and technological change leaves them behind. Again, the inevitable loss of any grounds for dignity of merit for the older person is emphasized. An alternative sense of dignity is therefore being sought. Dignity lies precisely in the acceptance of the natural and unavoidable process of ageing. This is to pick up on a sense of dignity passed over by Nordenfelt. Dignity may lie in the way in which one deports oneself. (Meyer, 1989, p. 522) It is undignified for the older person to rail against the inevitability of ageing. Such indignity is, in effect, a variation on being mutton dressed as lamb. Yet Nordenfelt is right to exclude this sense of dignity, for it tends to stereotype the behavior expected of an older person, thereby compromising autonomy and heavily restricting the sense of identity or meaning that the older person can find in his or her life. Here Kathleen Woodward's reflections on the problem of older people expressing anger, and not thereby being labeled as peevish and cantankerous, are pertinent. (Woodward, 2003, p. 59) The stereotype of dignity that is implicit in the theory of disengagement (and is perhaps echoed in the idea that there is a specific way of deporting oneself with dignity) tends to conceal the contestation of dignity. Dignity may as powerfully be expressed in Dylan Thomas's exhortation not to "go gentle into that good night," or Jenny Joseph's "Warning": "When I am an old woman I shall wear purple/With a red hat which doesn't go and doesn't suit me."

In summary, the post-war welfare state both protects older people and confines them, promising dignity (not least as freedom from fear of poverty and unmedicated illness), but in a context radically separated from public life. The naturalistic assumptions that inform disengagement theory, and that are present in the welfare state in the assumption of the natural progression of the older person into retirement and dependency, lead to policies that protect older people and give them space for a form of autonomy (and consequently dignity). Yet, as Biggs notes, this space is highly restricted (Biggs, 2001, p. 307). The older person can exercise autonomy only within the cultural and institutional framework of retirement. Put otherwise, the only language available to make sense of old age is the language of retirement. The notion of "dignity," and the space for personal development and understanding that makes this dignity possible, is radically compromised.

5. Neo-Liberal Policy

The criticism of a dependency culture that lies at the heart of much neo-liberal thinking can be construed as a response to the compromising of dignity under the mass welfare state. While neo-liberalism overtly presented its argument against an extensive welfare state in economic terms, such that dependency upon the welfare state led to economic inefficiencies and the stifling of an "enterprise culture," the neo-liberal position also has strong moral connotations. A dependence on the welfare state is seen to undermine the autonomy of the individual, in so far as it removes any motivation to provide for oneself, and perhaps more significantly in so far as it dictates a single course of action and a single source of help or support for the dependent person. (Marsland, 1996) It may equally well be seen to echo something of the conception that a dependency on the welfare state amounts to an undignified reliance on charity. The free market is seen as the space within which human autonomy can most effectively be realized. Risks within the life-course arc therefore not to be shared through collective contributions to a centrally organized welfare state, but instead taken on as individual responsibilities. Risks can be insured against, be these risks of illness, unemployment, or old age. The solutions made available to deal with these risks will be diverse, reflecting the aggregate demands of consumers exercising their individual free choice on the market. Neo-liberal policies led to a reduction in welfare state provision for older people in the UK (Phillipson, 1998, p. 118) and an attendant rise in the significance of private pension schemes.

For the neo-liberal, the individual is to be freed from the restraints of the welfare state, and so allowed to exercise autonomy in choosing (and purchasing) the old age he or she desires. In doing so, he or she must balance the utility of a comfortable and secure old age against that of current consumption, and so the life-style chosen while still young and employable. The market thereby allows an exercise of autonomy, not merely over old age, but over the shape of your entire life course. At the core of this may lie an attempt to defend a Kantian notion of rational autonomy (as the consumer makes informed decisions about his or her own life and goods). (Nozick, 1974, pp. 30–33) Yet, as an attempt to realize *Menschenwürde*, which is to say, that which is intrinsically valuable in human being, this vision remains fatally compromised. If "dignity" is understood as a trouser word, and if neo-liberal policy is understood as an expression of dignity, then it may fairly be understood as a reaction to the perceived indignity of dependency upon the state. In this, it may indeed have captured something of the shift in popular culture. In an increasingly affluent consumer society, those dependent on welfare may face the indignity of being "inadequate consumers." (Bauman, 1998, p. 38) Yet, in stripping away dependency on uniform state provision, neo-liberal policy frees only those affluent enough to be able to realize their choices on the market. Put otherwise, dignity of merit, grounded in a person's economic and public position and now the dignity of the consumer rather than that of the office-holder *per se*, is the only positive content left within the neo-liberal moral vision. Only those whose economic status is sufficient to allow them to continue to make (economic) choices into retirement and old age have dignity. The remainder are left to the indignity of increasing social exclusion (and so a restriction far more all-encompassing than that experienced under the old welfare state).

In addition, neo-liberalism marks a problematization of the moral economy. It may be suggested that popular understanding of pension provision ceases to be predominantly one of the employed supporting the currently retired. (Gilleard and Higgs, 2000, p. 109) Instead, national insurance payments (as well as payments into private and employed pension schemes) come to be understood as investments for the payee's own future retirement. (Phillipson, 1998, p. 71) The solidarity characteristic of the original welfare state is transformed into a culture of personal responsibility, and so any sense of dignity of moral status atrophies to the mere provision for yourself or your family. The obligation of unconditional provision for the stranger, characteristic of the old welfare state, is lost. This occurs in tandem with an intensification of the perception of older people as a burden upon the young and employed. In the face of the economic crisis of the 1970s and beyond, the expectation of the continuing economic growth securing the provisions of pensions is thrown into question.

In addition, with rising unemployment and lower mortality rates, the proportion of the population out of employment increases. Government concern over the situation intensifies throughout the 1970s and 1980s. Walker cites, as typical, the OECD report *Reforming Public Pensions*, from 1988. It states explicitly that public pension schemes are "likely to put a heavy and increasing burden on the working population in coming decades." (Walker, 1999, p. 372) Put differently, it may be suggested that the emphasis on economic efficiency, and so the instrumental value of human life, undermines the very possibility of finding a language through which the older, non-working person can be valued. *Menschenwürde* as intrinsic value is rendered largely meaningless. With the decline of the old moral economy, ageism increases under neo-liberalism, not least in areas of employment. (Walker, 1999, p. 371) As such, what Nordenfelt understands as the dignity of identity of the older person is undermined. Increasingly, the only language available to describe the experience of the older person is perhaps one of redundancy (as opposed to retirement), and therefore of uselessness. The very possibility of achieving a positive articulation of yourself or people like you, as an older person, is threatened.

6. The Third Way

The notion of a social democratic "Third Way" accepts that there is some validity in the neo-liberal criticism of the mass welfare state. The shift to an increasingly individualistic and consumerist society makes centralized mass provision of welfare inappropriate. Significantly, Anthony Giddens suggests that "[o]ld age is a new-style risk masquerading as an old-style one .... Becoming older presents at least as many opportunities as problems, both for individuals and for the wider social community." (Giddens, 1998, 119) This is to say that old age is not to be treated as an irresistible process of decline, assailing the passive victim (as earlier naturalistic approaches to ageing assumed), nor is ageing to be perceived any longer as a burden on society or the individual. (Department of Health, 2001, p. 2) Instead, individuals are required to take increasing responsibility for ageing, creating their older selves. However, consumerism and reliance on the market are to be mitigated. In early policy initiatives from the first "New Labour" administration, the role of the state becomes that of providing conditions for active ageing, and so for the older person to maintain quality of life and an active engagement in work and public life for longer. (Biggs, 2001, p. 310) The social exclusion and atomization of society that the pursuit of radical free market solutions might produce is to be checked by the repair and renewal of the moral economy. At a crucial level, social policy seeks to challenge the implicit and explicit ageism that had become institutionalized during earlier periods of welfare provision. This is done, not least, by breaking the association between age and retirement, and the prejudice that the older worker is unable to contribute to the modern economy (for example, by encouraging economic involvement by people beyond the official retirement age, and by making discrimination by age illegal). In addition, the government would seek, increasingly, to give older people an active voice in policy development, so reintegrating them into the polity. They cease to be the passive "beneficiaries" of policies developed by others. (Department of Health, 2000, p. 95; Department of Work and Pensions, 2005, pp. 90–94; Department for Communities and Local Government, 2007) Economically, culturally, and politically the older person is to be reintegrated into society, and thereby offered the cultural and material resources necessary for successful ageing.

Within the UK the concept of "dignity" has been used explicitly, and with increasing care, to articulate the goals of social democratic policy. Two distinct foci for the use of "dignity" may be identified. On one hand, social exclusion and ageism are articulated in terms of dignity. The Department of Work and Pensions' consultation document, *Opportunity Age*, presents both discrimination in employment and social exclusion as issues of dignity. Dignity in the context of discrimination is partially glossed in terms of the defense of human rights (Department of Work and Pensions, 2005, pp. 32–33), while dignity and social exclusion are linked as follows:

> all older people are entitled to dignity and respect at all stages of their lives. We will organize services to work for the most excluded, ensuring that they are respectful, flexible, and culturally appropriate. (Department of Work and Pensions, 2005, p. 46)

On the other hand, it is in the context of the provision of healthcare that the concept of "dignity" is most fully articulated. While *The New NHS Plan* (Department of Health, 2000) acknowledged the need to respect the dignity of older patients, the concept receives only a minimal gloss, as the identification of individual needs (Department of Health, 2000, p. 4), and through its association with respecting autonomy and privacy. (Department of Health, 2000, p. 124) Later documentation begins to use the term more reflectively. *The National Services Framework of Older People* appeals to dignity in the first of its four themes. (Department of Health, 2001, p. 12) The framework is presented as having been motivated by a recognition of the infringement of dignity and unfair discrimination against older patients. The conceptualization of "dignity" continues to focus on privacy, autonomy, and recognition of individual need. An addition is the recognition of the special place of dignity at the end of life, with a fuller discussion of what that might entail. (Department of Health, 2001, p. 26) Subsequent stages of the implementation of the National Services Framework led to the "Dignity in Care" initiative (Department of Health, 2006, pp. 4–6), and a more sustained reflection on what dignity entails, which is developed under the auspices of the Social Care Institute for Excellence. (SCIE, 2006) A working definition of "dignity" is offered:

> a state, quality, or manner worthy of esteem or respect; and (by extension) self-respect. Dignity in care, therefore, means the kind of care, in any setting, which supports and promotes, and does not undermine, a person's self-respect regardless of any difference. (SCIE, 2006)

From this definition, and its attendant commentary, SCIE derives practical guidance as to how to protect dignity (including benchmarks from *Essence of Care* (NHS Modernisation Agency, 2003)), and in a move that reflects the status of "dignity" as a trouser word, what should be recognized as threats to dignity (focusing on ageism, inequality, and abuse). Crucially, the problems and limitations of defining "dignity" are recognized, and the definition is supported by practical guidelines and examples of best practice. Dignity comes to be institutionalized in the management of the care of older people (for example, through the initiation of "dignity guardians," a coalition of non-governmental organizations and consumer groups monitoring performance within the NHS).

The two foci of "dignity" within social democratic policy may be summarized as follows. In focusing on discrimination, "dignity" addresses positive ageing and does so at what might be termed the macro-level of barriers to economic involvement; in focusing on healthcare, "dignity" addresses the vulnerability of ageing, and does so at the micro-level of interpersonal contact within the care setting. While the intentions behind the social democratic use of "dignity" are to be admired, problems may still be identified. In these two foci, the language of dignity at once embraces both the opportunities and threats of postmodern ageing. Yet by keeping the foci distinct, the policy constructs and negotiates a partial understanding of both the nature of ageing and the challenge that dignity poses.

While the use of "dignity" at the macro-level is less extensive and less well articulated, it may usefully be addressed first. If we treat "dignity" as a trouser word, the first question that might be asked concerns the threats that appeals to dignity are designed to highlight, and from which the older person must be protected. Discrimination and ageism serve to exclude the older person from continued economic activity and public participation. In terms of the experience of the victim of discrimination, the loss of dignity is recognized through humiliation and a loss of any sense of worth. In terms of Nordenfelt's varieties of dignity, what is at stake here are the dignities of merit and of identity. Dignity of merit is most clearly addressed. Social democratic policy presupposes that, if barriers to continued employment are removed, then the loss of social status or merit caused by compulsory unemployment is remedied. Further, if ageism in general is tackled, and negative evaluations of older people are removed from the ambient moral economy, then the language available to the older person to articulate his or her sense of self, and so his or her self-respect, will be a positive and constructive one. Combined with the freedom given through continued economic involvement, and so continued power as a consumer, this also allows for many different aspects of the older self to flourish. Taking on something of the influence that cultural studies has had on social gerontology, social democratic policy strives to open a space in which the older person becomes a consumer, constructing his or her own identity from the cultural resources available. The single meaning of old age offered by the mass welfare state is replaced by a plurality of possible meanings, and the "third age" of positive ageing thereby becomes "a potential crown of life" to which all might aspire. (Gilleard and Higgs, 2000, p. 23)

An exclusive focus on the culture of positive ageing, especially within the narrow framework of a consumer culture, is highly problematic, as Biggs and Larry Polivka and Charles Longino note. Biggs suggests that the conception of positive ageing is, in practice, restrictive. It requires the older person to continue in economic or quasi-economic activity (such as voluntary work). In Biggs's terms, the "social value" of the older person is therefore to be derived, seemingly exclusively, from "work or near-work situations." (Biggs, 2001, p. 311) Alternative models of positive ageing, including those such as Lars Tornstam's (Tornstam,1997), that might promote spiritual development or personal reflection are marginalized. The dominant valuation of older persons, and therefore the dominant source of their sense of dignity and self-respect, appears to be instrumental (in contrast to the intrinsic value of *Menschenwürde*), and so as contributors to the economy or wider society. It is not then immediately clear how social democracy moves beyond the market orientation of neo-liberal policy, other than by opening up opportunities for employment for older people. (Polivka and Longino, 2002, p. 290)

Moreover, the postmodernist experience, as is shown in its analysis by Giddens (Giddens, 1994), can become one that is potentially stressful and burdensome to the older person (and indeed to everyone else). The freedom of positive ageing that is championed by cultural theory is made possible through the breakdown of traditional patterns of behavior. The member of such a postmodern society may have the freedom to choose from a multitude of diverse cultural fragments, but equally he or she has no point of security and certainty. Tradition is replaced by "ephemeral fads and fashions." (Polivka and Longino, 2002, p. 288) In other words, postmodernism entails the radical undermining of the old moral economy that informed the mass welfare state. While social democratic policy may recognize this loss, and try to remedy it, it is not at all clear that it is possible to provide a remedy; and yet—and this is crucial—it is not clear that a dignified old age beyond the limits of neo-liberal consumerism can be secured without it.

There are two problems here. On the one hand, the restoration of a moral economy, promised by the early policy documents of New Labour, is not obviously within the control of a government. It presupposes that the administrative activities of a government can manufacture moral meaning, restoring the solidarity that grounded the mass welfare state. (Habermas, 1976, p. 70) A shared moral economy, however desirable (Green, 1996), cannot be imposed upon a postmodern capitalism characterized by the breakdown of tradition and communal ties, not least due to increased consumer opportunities and greater social and geographical mobility. Anti-discrimination law can act as a lever upon key areas of social life, such as the economy. The challenge to ageism in the wider culture is less easily enforced; and indeed, a need for enforcement would hardly represent the spontaneous embracing of a genuine moral economy. The limitations of policy and legislation therefore inevitably lead to a promotion of the dignity of merit, precisely because it is open to legal protection, albeit at the expense of other varieties of dignity.

On the other hand, an emphasis upon the cultural factors that inhibit positive ageing may entail a neglect of its material preconditions. The cultural approach to policy and social gerontology is in danger of neglecting the continuing economic inequalities that serve to exclude some older people from positive ageing. Inequalities within the older population and between that population and the rest of society remain highly significant, as a report from Help the Aged has indicated in the case of the UK. (Help the Aged, 2007) The issue here is not simply one of economic deprivation, although 11% of older people live in severe poverty and 21% in poverty (Help the Aged, 2007, p. 34), and 57% of the current working population are not contributing to a non-state pension. (Help the Aged, 2007, p. 35) Isolation remains significant. 13% of people aged over sixty-five report being always or often lonely. The inhibitions to a more active life include poor pavements, poor transport, concerns over crime, and a lack of public toilets. (Help the Aged, 2007, p. 11) These results are complemented by indicators of low and falling quality of life amongst many people over the age of sixty-five. (Help the Aged, 2007, p. 15) Only 8% of people aged between sixty-five and seventy-four are participating in lifelong learning. 82% of people aged over sixty-five have never used the Internet. (Help the Aged, 2007, p. 11)

Such figures suggest that a significant proportion of older people are being denied (or actively refuse) access to the opportunities of positive ageing and continue to be excluded from public life. The image of an economically active and political engaged older population propagated by policy documents is at best a highly partial image. This suggests that the threats to dignity that the mass welfare state sought to conquer remain, to an unacceptable degree, unchecked. The conceptualization of "dignity" within current policies on ageism and discrimination may actually serve to conceal this, and so conceal the continuing problem of material inequality as a threat to self-respect and dignity.

If the macro-level focus of "dignity" is flawed, so too is the micro-level, and for complementary reasons. The language of dignity is most readily associated with the care of older people. It is, we might suggest, the language of negative ageing. It is significant that we would not obviously think of demanding dignity for middle-aged patients or even for children. This is not accidental. "Dignity" here implies that older patients are unable to assert their own claim to be treated with dignity (unlike the middle-aged) and perhaps have no one to make that assertion for them (unlike children). Further, and this may be crucial, if dignity is grounded in a claim about the worth of the person, then the vulnerable older patient has no obvious instrumental worth. Unlike the middle-aged patient who will return to work or the family, or the child who will grow up to participate in social life, the vulnerable older person has, by implication, already entered a fourth age, beyond the instrumentally useful engagement of positive ageing and the third age. The demand that the vulnerable older person be treated with dignity is therefore a demand that must be grounded in their intrinsic value as a human being. It is, in effect, an assertion of *Menschenwürde*. So, dignity at the micro-level of interpersonal care is of a quite distinct variety from dignity within the macro-level of the economy and public life.

While the acknowledgment of *Menschenwürde* is to be applauded, the complex restrictions upon its use are problematic. Dignity in care is, it has been argued, separated from dignity in the work place and public life. The very focus on interpersonal care suggests that the world of persons in their fourth age has seemingly shrunk to that of everyday face-to-face interactions. Their exclusion from the wider world of public and economic life ceases to be of importance (or is perhaps beyond remedy). Further, dignity in the care setting is associated, almost exclusively, with older people and, more precisely, with the older patient. Because of the association of dignity with older patients, that patient is immediately presumed to be vulnerable. In effect, the appeal to dignity underlines the frailty of the older person. So, first, the vulnerability of the young patient is, as suggested above, at best construed as being of a different order or at worst ignored. Second, and perhaps more importantly, the vulnerability of the older person (and so "negative ageing") is confined to the healthcare setting. The older person is rendered vulnerable by illness, and not by economic or social inequality. Ironically, there is a vestigial trace of the notion of ageing as a purely biomedical phenomenon left within this use of "dignity."

In summary, the Third Way of social democratic policy attempts to engage with both positive ageing and the threats of old age. However, while the language of dignity plays a key part in articulating this policy, it also currently serves to give an impression of managing tensions that are perhaps in fact irreconcilable. The separate foci of "dignity" serve to constrict the use of the term, not least in separating uses that are amenable to instrumental definition from issues of intrinsic value. If intrinsic value were to be brought to the centre of the macro-level, then possibly broader forms of positive ageing could be explicitly recognized. Conversely, if instrumental conceptions of "dignity" were to be introduced into the language of care, the exclusion of the older patient from society could be more readily addressed. Crucial to both moves is the recognition of the continuing construction of the experience of ageing, and so of dignity and self-respect, through material inequalities. Unless the language of dignity is extended, so that it can embrace questions of material inequality, talk of dignity may continue to conceal the failure to address this problem. This failure is compounded by a constriction of the moral economy that serves to render "dignity" (as a term that appeals to a sense of social solidarity) almost meaningless in the context of the discussion of just allocation of material resources.

7. Conclusion

This chapter has sought to explore the changing conceptions of dignity that have informed post-war social policy. It has suggested that what a person experiences as a dignified or undignified life will shift as the moral and cultural concerns of his or her society shift. However, against this seeming relativism, social policy may be understood as a series of moral experiments, through which the meaning of "dignity" is tested and refined. The failures of previous policy initiatives, marked by the continuing or newly constituted experiences of indignity, humiliation, and exclusion, demand imaginative and reasoned responses. While the explicit and considered use of the language of dignity within social policy is to be welcomed, that language will remain problematic. The impasse of current social policy is indicative of the continuing need to reinvent dignity, not least in articulating anew a sense of intrinsic value, of *Menschenwürde*, that will challenge the instrumental reason that is dominant in capitalist economic activity, and yet which will not lose sight of the recognition that a person's dignity depends as much upon his or her access to material resources as it does upon cultural resources.

WORKS CITED

Austin, J. L. (1962). *Sense and Sensibilia.* Oxford: Oxford University Press.

Bauman, Z. (1998). *Work, Consumerism, and the New Poor*. Buckingham: Open University Press.

Bengston, V. L. and Warner Schaie, K. (1999). *Handbook of Theories of Aging.* New York: Springer.

Biggs, S. (1999). *The Mature Imagination: Dynamics of Identity in Midlife and Beyond.* Buckingham: Open University Press.

——— (2001). "Toward Critical Narrativity: Stories of Ageing in Contemporary Social Policy," *Journal of Aging Studies*, 15:4 (December), pp. 303–316.

Cole, T. R. (1992). *The Journey of Life: A Cultural History of Aging in America.* Cambridge: Cambridge University Press.

Cumming, E. (2000). "Further Thoughts on the Theory of Disengagement." In *Aging and Everyday Life*, eds. J. F. Gubrium and J. A. Holstein. Oxford: Blackwell, pp. 25–39.

Department for Communities and Local Government. (2007). *A Framework for Fairness: Proposals for a Single Equality Bill for Great Britain.* London: Stationery Office.

Department of Health. (2000). *The New NHS.* London: Department of Health.

——— (2001). *The National Services Framework of Older People.* London: Department of Health.

——— (2006). *A New Ambition for Old Age—Next Steps in Implementing the National Service Framework for Older People.* London: Department of Health.

Department of Work and Pensions. (2005). *Opportunity Age: Meeting the Challenges of Ageing in the 21st century*. London: Department of Work and Pensions.

Dickstein, M. (1998). *The Revival of Pragmatism: New Essays on Social Thought, Law, and Culture*. Durham, NC: Duke University Press.

Edgar, A. (2004). "A Response to Nordenfelt's 'The Varieties of Dignity'," *Healthcare Analysis*, 12:2 (June), pp. 83–89.

Estes, C. (1979). *The Ageing Enterprise*. San Francisco: Jossey-Bass.

Estes, C and Binney, E. (1989). "The Biomedicalization of Ageing: Dangers and Dilemmas," *The Gerontologist*, 29:5 (October), pp. 587–98.

Giddens, A. (1994). *Beyond Left and Right.* Cambridge: Polity Press.

——— (1998). *The Third Way: The Renewal of Social Democracy*. Cambridge: Polity Press.

Gilleard, C. and Higgs, P. (2000). *Cultures of Ageing: Self, Citizen, and the Body*. Harlow: Prentice Hall.

Green, D. G. (1996). *Community without Politics: A Market Approach to Welfare Reform*. London: Institute of Economic Affairs.

Gubrium, J.F. and Holstein, J.A., eds. (2000). *Aging and Everyday Life*. Oxford: Blackwell.

Habermas, J. (1973). *Legitimation Crisis*. London: Heinemann.

Health Advisory Service. (2000). *Not Because They are Old. An Independent Inquiry into the Care of Older People on Acute Wards in General Hospital*. London: Health Advisory Service.

Jung, C. (1998). "The Stages of Life." In *Ageing: Concepts and Controversies*, ed. H. Moody. Thousand Oaks, CA: Pine Forge Press.

Kant, I. (2005). *Groundwork for the Metaphysics of Morals*, ed. Lara Denis. Ontario: Broadview.

Kohli, M. (1991). "Retirement and the Moral Economy: An Historical Interpretation of the German Case." In *Critical Perspectives on Aging: The Political and Moral Economy of Growing Old*, eds. M. Minkler and C. l. Estes. Amityville, NY: Baywood, pp. 274–276.

Marsland, D. (1996). *Welfare or Welfare State?* Basingstoke: Macmillan.

Meyer, M. J. (1989). "Dignity, Rights, and Self-Control," *Ethics*, 99:3 (April), pp. 520–534.

Minkler, M. and Cole, T. R. (1991). "Political and Moral Economy: Not Such Strange Bedfellows." In *Critical Perspectives on Aging: The Political and Moral Economy of Growing Old*, eds. M. Minkler and C. l. Estes. Amityville, NY: Baywood, pp. 37–49.

Moody, H. (1998). *Ageing: Concepts and Controversies*. Thousand Oaks, CA: Pine Forge Press.

Myles, J. (1984). *Old Age in the Welfare State: The Political Economy of Public Pensions*. Lawrence, KS: University Press of Kansas.

NHS Modernisation Agency. (2003). *Essence of Care: Patient-Focused Benchmarks for Clinical Governance*. London: NHS.

Nordenfelt, L. (2004). "The Varieties of Dignity," *Healthcare Analysis*, 12:2 (June), pp. 69–81.

Nozick, R. (1974). *Anarchy, State, and Utopia*. Oxford: Blackwell.

Phillipson, C. (1982). *Capitalism and the Construction of Old Age*. London: Macmillan.

——— (1998). *Reconstructing Old Age.* London: Sage.

Polivka, L. and Longino, C. F. (2002). "Commentary: Aging Politics and Policy in Postmodern Society," *Journal of Aging and Identity*, 7:4 (November), pp. 287–292.

Putnam, R. A. (1998). "The Moral Impulse." In *The Revival of Pragmatism: New Essays on Social Thought, Law, and Culture*, ed. M. Dickstein. Durham, NC: Duke University Press, pp. 62–71.

Social Care Institute for Excellence. (2006). *Practice Guide 09: Dignity in Care.* http://www.scie.org.uk/publications/practiceguides/practiceguide09/index.asp

Tornstam, L. (1997). "Gerotranscendence: The Contemplative Dimensions of Aging," *Journal of Aging Studies*, 11:2 (Summer), pp. 143–154.

Townsend, P. (1981). "The Structured Dependency of the Elderly," *Ageing and Society*, 1:1 (Jan), pp. 5–28.

Walker, A. (1981). "Towards a Political Economy of Old Age," *Ageing and Society*, 1:1 (Jan), pp. 73–94.

——— (1999). "Public Policy and Theories of Ageing: Constructing and Reconstructing Old Age." In *Handbook of Theories of Aging*, eds. V. L. Bengtson and K. Warner Schaie. New York: Springer, pp. 361–378.

Woodward, K. (2003). "Against Wisdom: The Social Politics of Anger and Aging," *Journal of Aging Studies*, 17:1 (February), pp. 55–67.

Three

DANGERS AND DILEMMAS SURROUNDING THE CONSUMPTION OF ANTI-AGEING MEDICINE

Beatriz Cardona

1. Introduction

The dismantling of public provision for health, education, and welfare services and its replacement by services financed by flexible forms of capital accumulation is one of the main contexts in which the necessity of individuals looking after themselves has been increasingly advanced. (Moss, 1998) Consumers are faced with a "pluralism of authorities" and required to make choices, to become entrepreneurs in all spheres and to accept responsibility for the management of risk. (Beck, 1992) In the health sector, the United Kingdom, Canada, the United States, and to a lesser extent New Zealand and Australia, have seen cuts in public health programs, the introduction sometimes of compulsory private health insurance programs, and an increase in private healthcare for those who can pay for it. (McGregor, 2001) Anti-ageing medicine has emerged, particularly in the United States, as a tool for maintaining the "care of the self," a type of care which is morally laden, because "failure" to remain healthy is increasingly being perceived as due to a lack of moral responsibility.

The anti-ageing medicine movement is both a program of education and an industry, borrowing ideas and practices from established gerontology and science to promote specific ways of understanding old age and managing the anxieties of growing older in Western societies. It is supported by a culture of science which includes the belief that scientific knowledge can achieve ultimate control over nature, a "culture of hope and hype" brought about by the intersection of science, capital, and social discourses regarding the value of ageing populations in modern western societies. The main theme promoted by anti-ageing medicine—that ageing is an "illness," a pathological condition of great impact for the economic, social, and personal welfare of the individual and the state—is followed by other questionable claims. Among these are the claims that methods of biotechnological intervention already exist to ameliorate and even possibly "cure" ageing, through, for example, hormone treatment, genetic engineering, calorie restricted diets, early diagnosis, proper risk assessment, dietary supplements, anti-oxidants, and stem cell therapies.

Scientific research conducted in these areas, particularly in genetic and stem cell therapies, has produced promising areas of regenerative medicine and anti-ageing interventions. But scientists have so far been cautious in extrapolating positive results conducted on animals to humans. This caution, however, is less exercised by media, popular television, and corporate biotechnological companies and anti-ageing industries, quick to associate these developments with popular legends of the Fountain of Youth, the Holy Grail, and immortality which have been in existence since early civilizations.

The anti-ageing medicine movement also marks a "crisis of control" in both the theory and practice of biogerontology. Current debates over whether ageing is a disease or a "natural" biological process are an example, involving both theory and practice. The disputes between established gerontology and biogerontology over the way to conduct research on longevity and the way to use anti-ageing interventions are also a struggle for control over how in general ageing is to be understood and managed. It resembles other "wars" being fought by many establishments against the incursion of private capital and of consumer culture ideologies. In the last quarter of the twentieth century, there was strong pressure to roll back state regulation, and to transform non-market and social spheres such as public health and education services into arenas of commercial activity. This transition entailed the reconfiguration of the goods and services in question so that they could be priced and sold, the inducing of people to want to buy them, the transformation of the workforce from one working for collective aims with a service ethic to one working to produce profits for owners of capital and subject to market discipline, and the underwriting of the risks to capital by the state. (Smith, 2002, p. 2)

An important question to ask at this point is what sort of stories about the self, and in particular about the ageing self, are transmitted by social policies informed by this "neoliberal" political theory, and how they influence collective and individual understanding of the self in later life through the experiences of health and illness. What existing biases in the shared assumptions of the medical and gerontological establishments are exposed and contested by these theories and programs, and what new ones are created?

A good place to start attempting to answer these questions is with the current social policy campaigns affecting the life of the elderly community in the name of health. Terms such as "health promotion," "healthy living," and "healthy ageing" highlight the supposed moral requirement that the elderly should pay attention to and work toward attaining and maintaining health.

The notion of healthy ageing came partly from the New Gerontology movement, and built on the concept of successful ageing, in terms of personal responsibility for the maintenance of health and active participation in life. *Successful Aging* (Rowe and Kahn 1998), which has been widely adopted within the fields of geriatrics and gerontology in western countries, argues that there are three necessary preconditions for successful ageing: (1) the avoidance of disease and disability; (2) the maintenance of high physical and cognitive functional capacity; and (3) active engagement in life. (Holstein and Minkler, 2003) They further suggested that these three components are hierarchically ordered, the first being the most important. The maintenance of health is then the main condition for the achievement of successful ageing.

Despite its many merits and its wide publicity, the successful ageing model is problematic. Criticism has come from gerontologists such as Meredith Minkler and Carroll L. Estes (Minkler and Estes, 1999), Stephen Katz (Katz, 2002), Jason Powell (Powell, 2001), and Martha B. Holstein and Minkler (Holstein and Minkler, 2003). Such criticism has particularly been in relation to the model's medicalization of the ageing experience and its failure to consider how socio-economic factors and experiences of exclusion based on color, ethnicity, gender, or class impact on health choices and outcomes in later life. The model also ignores other ways of "successfully" ageing, which involve the acceptance of disability or illness. Also, such an approach to ageing absolves social and political institutions of their responsibility for the health and well-being of their aged populations (Holstein and Minkler, 2003) by advocating a prevention model dependent upon individual consumption choices and behavior, so that it can be claimed that social intervention in health provision can be dispensed with, because "the prudent don't need it while the imprudent don't deserve it." This ignores the fact that it is only the resource-rich who can afford this investment in self-care. (Powell, 2001)

2. Biomedical Models of "Successful" and "Healthy" Ageing

This increasing tendency to define notions of "successful," "healthy," and "productive" ageing using a biomedical model illustrates the influence of biomedicine in social policy. Biomedicine has penetrated a great deal of mass culture. It has become both a culture and an industry, both serving and being supported by the powerful commercial interests of the pharmaceutical and biotechnological companies. The biological model promotes a medical reductionist perspective on ageing and supports both technological determinism and the necessity for consumption . A good example of this technological determinism is in the medicalization of the way women see their ageing bodies, which is brought about through marketing strategies that create and capitalize on women's fear of ageing. The biochemistry of women of reproductive age is taken as the standard measure for what is normal and healthy, and ageing women's bodies are understood in terms of "endocrine deficiency disorder," a hormone deficiency disease that is to be treated with estrogen supplements. Although passage through the life cycle is both a social and biological process, the focus of attention in medicine has been increasingly confined to biological processes, such as "failing ovaries." (Kazanjian *et al.*, 1998, p. 3) Other examples of this medicalization of women's bodies include Bone Mineral Density tests, which, as Arminée Kazanjian, Carolyn J. Green, Ken Bassett, and Fern Brunger point out, have more to do with the marketing of fear, the fear of osteoporosis, the latest disease of ageing, redefined in 1993 by the World Health Organization strictly in terms of bone mineral density (BMD) threshold. These thresholds are based on reference populations of healthy young women. Unless women maintain bone mass at peak levels throughout their life span they will be labeled as "at risk" or "diseased." Using the WHO standards, 22% of all women over age fifty will be defined as having osteoporosis and 52% as having osteopenia. There is no epidemiological basis to support the cut-offs used by the WHO study group; therefore the resulting "epidemic" observed in the last few years is more apparent than real. (Kazanjian *et al.*, 1998, p. 4)

This cooperation between biomedicine and capital can necessitate a reframing of the notions of "natural" and "pathological." These notions are laden with supposed ontological certainties regarding the unchangeable character of nature and as such do not sit comfortably with technologies which alter what is supposed to be the "natural." Given recent changes, including genetic medicine and stem cell therapies, that center on biological life itself, the "natural" and "pathological" frame of reference has been replaced by a model based on notions of "functionality" and "dysfunctionality." (Katz and Marshall, 2004)

A good example of this transition can be seen in the expansion of the pharmacological culture in which bioscientific intervention produces social and cultural effects, so that we can no longer speak simply of "natural," "biological," and "cultural," but need terms such as "biosociality," "vital politics," "posthuman culture," and cybernatural life." (Katz and Marshall, 2004) Products such as Prozac exemplify this expansion of the pharmacological culture, with those who market them claiming that the drug can return the brain to "normal" or—to use the biosocial term—"functional." Other examples are Viagra, marketed as a drug for sexual "dysfunction," and Ritalin, for combating the supposed "epidemic" of Attention Deficit Disorder. This shift, Kaushik Sunder Rajan points out, is the result of the commercial logic of moving therapeutic interventions to earlier and earlier stages of disease manifestation, to the point that new "diseases" often get created. (Rajan, 2006) This is presented as a logical consequence of advocating self-governance and a "responsible self," and thereby shifting notions of when it is desirable to care for the self through diagnostic testing and therapeutic interventions. But in truth, "selves" are being governed by strategic actors in the pharmaceutical and biotechnological industry. (Rajan, 2006)

The functional/dysfunctional model comprises various elements, including measurability and standardization. Quantitative models can be applied to measure functionality while standardization is linked to bio-cultural standards of enablement. As pointed out by Stephen Katz and Barbara Marshall, these standards are connected to prevailing neo-liberal social requirements of individualism, active and mobile lifestyles, and responsible self-care. (Katz and

Marshall, 2004) Therefore the traditional concept of normality which focuses on being is replaced by a functional state of doing. These functional states are susceptible to interventions, mainly pharmaceutical, and geared toward "enablement" instead of cure.

Identifying risk factors and using products and services to minimize risk, argue Katz and Marshall, become areas of individual responsibility and lead to new classificatory terms, such as "patients without symptoms" or the "worried well." (Katz and Marshall, 2004) Once the fear of becoming diseased or "dysfunctional" has been created, ageing individuals are made to feel personally accountable for managing their risk of disease or "dysfunctionality" and for future illness, and are encouraged to take appropriate measures to prevent such disease. Afflictions such as obesity and even high blood pressure become "moral disorders," reflecting an individual's lack of skillfulness in learning how to stay healthy and acting on this knowledge by consuming the right products and pursuing the right lifestyles. (Katz and Marshall, 2004)

This assessing of people's bio-identities by lifestyle and health status, using quantified states of functionality, makes the avoidance of physical disorders part of the neo-liberal requirements of activity, enablement, responsibility, self-care, and independence, in which the individual is expected to be an active participant, striving toward functionality rather than normality. (Katz and Marshall, 2004) Anti-ageing medicine, as argued later in this chapter, creates bio-identities of ageless individuals striving to remain functional, productive, and independent at the expense of "normality" (or what might be reasonably expected at this stage of life), because this loses its relevance in an era of technological intervention.

3. The "Responsible Self" as a Neo-Liberal Requirement

In many industrialized countries the "successful ageing" model emphasizing physical ability and functionality has been adopted in social policy strategies such as "healthy ageing" programs. This is partly, I argue, because they fit well with neo-liberal governance models, emphasizing enterprise as an individual and corporate strategy concerned with inculcating a new set of values oriented toward incorporating older people as both players and partners in a market system. Older people are exhorted, indeed expected, to become entrepreneurs in all spheres and to accept responsibility for the management of risk. (Beck, 1986) Opportunities to diagnose the risk of possible future diseases, using evidence from such things as genetics and lifestyle, encourage the use of technologies as an insurance. The use of technologies to treat risks in its turn encourages a reconfiguration of subject categories away from normality and pathology and toward variability of risk, thereby placing every individual within a probability calculus as a potential target for therapeutic intervention. (Rajan, 2006, p. 167)

The rhetoric of responsibility and self-governance in the management of risk has become prominent in contemporary political agendas. (Moss, 1998) The dismantling of public provision of health, education, and welfare services, and the transition into flexible forms of capital accumulation, as Jeremy Moss points out, is one of the main contexts in which the idea and necessity of individuals looking after themselves has been increasingly advanced. Instead of a singular authoritative source of guidance, agents increasingly encounter a "pluralism of authorities" and in turn are required to make choices for "self-constitution."

New positive images of ageing in the media, advertising, and public consciousness depict ageing as a period of activity, autonomy, mobility, choice, and well-being, in defiance "of traditionally gloomy stereotypes of decline, decrepitude and dependency," and gloss over the negative realities of poverty and inequality in old age. (Katz, p. 1) Images of "healthy" and successful ageing have, however, been used by the marketing industry to promote anti-ageing cultures based on notions of timeless living and growing older unburdened by the signs of ageing. (Katz, 2001) Anti-ageing ideologies and practices include the belief that through the consumption of products and making of appropriate lifestyle choices individuals can delay or even halt the ageing process and the risks associated with it. The virtues of timeless, successful ageing take on an ethical dimension also through governments' attempts to transfer responsibility for caring duties to individuals who use self-management and self-control to avoid dependency and illness. More importantly, they provide a moral framework by which an individual's life can be measured—with physical decay, ageing, disability, and limited functionality being regarded as personal failures. (Katz and Marshall, 2003)

4. Anti-Ageing Medicine

The anti-ageing medicine movement emerged as a new specialty in the early 1990s, echoing on one hand biomedical discoveries and predictions about longevity, regenerative, and preventive medicine; and on the other, global demographic concerns with an ageing population, gerontophobic values of the anti-ageing popular media and consumer cultures, "new gerontology's" discourses on "healthy" and "successful" ageing, and a neo-liberal governmental concern with individual responsibility. For example, the anti-ageing medicine movement instigated and sustained mainly through the American Association of Anti-Ageing Medicine (A4M) presents itself as a pioneering medical specialty capable of addressing all of the above socio-economic, demographic, and health concerns through medical and therapeutic interventions aimed at halting, reversing, and even eliminating "ageing."

5. What is Anti-Ageing Medicine?

One of the difficulties when dealing with a topic such as "anti-ageing medicine" is that it is an ambiguous term, because it is associated both with the cosmetic industry and with longevity research. It includes hormone therapies (usually HGH or DHEA), antioxidants, vitamins, lifestyle changes, preventive medicine, repair of memory loss, and DNA repair (stem cell therapy). The anti-ageing industry often depicts anti-ageing medicine as transformative and capable of restoring older people to what is considered an ideal middle age. Such visual propositions could be seen as self-parody by A4M about its own practice, using a version of the popular myth of the "Fountain of Youth," in which instead of immersing the body in miraculous waters, we subject it to a list of therapies and interventions aimed at averting ageing and restoring youth.

Beneath this visual allusion to the miraculous and the mythical, the image, instead of portraying the aspirations of the older person to become younger, plays on the aspirations of younger people to avert old age for as long as possible. Ageing, particularly in America, is "so downright un-American" (Scannell, 2006, p. 3), because it creates an irreconcilable disjuncture with fierce American narratives about individual freedom, self-sufficiency, and independence. Images and narratives proposing the possibility that through consumption of anti-ageing medicine individuals would be able to remain competitive, independent, and productive, reflect values cherished by society and encouraged by social policy and economic institutions.

Nikolas Rose has described how the political aspects of our biological existence—biopolitics—have taken on a new dimension under the heading of "risk." (Rose, 2001) The handling of risks includes strategies based on identification of, and preventive interventions for, individuals at risk. The allocation of ageing to the risk category produces a call for middle-aged and older individuals to act "responsibly" to reduce these risks by subjecting themselves to the appropriate technology. The ethical obligation to exercise responsibility to minimize risks becomes a requirement of citizenship and part of our moral duty to the community, creating an alliance between political and personal aspirations for health in which the body is a key site for work on self-improvement. (Rose, 2001, p. 18) Anti-ageing discourse plays upon this notion of "citizenship" by highlighting the cost to the community of failing to take preventive action to limit the risks of ageing.

The "ethos of responsibility" for healthcare in later life enforced by neoliberal political theory, when combined with a biological model that reduces ageing people to their bodies and emphasizes the risks of bodily decline, illness, and disability, creates among the middle-aged a pervasive fear of the ageing process that drives them to pursue biotechnological and anti-ageing interventions (Polivka, 2000), and thereby encourage their proliferation.

This choice to consume anti-ageing medicine also needs to be understood as being informed by personal values, dispositions, and experiences, and by conditions such as social class and power structures. The transition taking place in most OECD countries from collective to individual responsibility for later life capitalizes on and perpetuates structural inequalities. (Kemp and Denton, 2003) Despite the increase in consumer choices regarding the management of later life, including anti-ageing medicine, these choices come at a financial and psychological cost for the consumer. Lack of resources to purchase a strategy, whatever this may be, is often blamed on the individual, and the individuals blame themselves for their lack of resources or failure to plan and be responsible. (Kemp and Denton, 2003) Moreover, because being dependent and a "burden" on others is "un-American," (Scannell, 2006) individuals in the United States in particular are further pressurized to purchase an alternative to these morally reproachable conditions, so fuelling the anti-ageing market still more.

The choice of anti-ageing medicine as a strategy to address the above issues raises many concerns. These include the health risks and financial risks associated with some of its products (GAO Report, 2002), the ageist way in which the products are marketed, and the values underpinning its practice. As a strategy for the management of later life, it was perceived by consumers in this study to facilitate the acquisition of attributes necessary to operate effectively as an ageing self (an ageless self) in our current social, political, and cultural environment. This care of the self which centers completely around the self's relation to itself might be expected to bring about the erosion of its connection to political life. (Pignatelli, 1993) However, Michel Foucault supplies evidence that ethical and political concerns are still central for us today. (Simons, 1995) Social relations are still involved in the process of subjectification; and attempts to resist modes of subjectification, in this case, associated with narratives of ageing as decline and illness, can have political significance. Resistance to treating ageing as illness, decay, or loss can impact on social relations and provide new spaces for ageing individuals to develop other narratives. I think this type of resistance can resonate in many important ways. It can however raise problems: it ignores the socio-economic, gender, and race issues affecting the capacity of individuals to invest in this type of "care of the self," the relationship between class, health, and lifestyle (Williams 1995), the dangers in exonerating the state from its responsibility to provide healthcare, and the possibility of successful ageing within narratives of illness and disability.

Another difficulty that arises here is that, as illustrated in this chapter, anti-ageing medicine is not about health in old age but more about ageless selves. Challenging not the possibilities of ageing but ageing itself—ageing as the "problem"—instead of the cultures (including the culture of science under which it is constructed) reinforces, instead of transcends, the limits of biomedical and anti-ageing models of ageing. The effectiveness of such "contestations" of normative narratives of decline seems to be dependent on material and cultural resources—especially considering the expensive character of most anti-ageing treatments—and the capacity of biotechnology to intervene successfully in the biology of ageing. As to the ethical implications of adopting such strategies for the "care of the self," important questions need to be asked, questions which resonate with the "bigger war," between neo-liberalism and those opposed to it, and the increasing global hegemony of market rationality in all spheres of life.

A significant body of literature has emerged in the last fifteen years contesting the social, economic, and cultural implications of holding economic markets up as the ideal model on which to structure society. (McGregor, 2000; Smith, 2002; Bourdieu, 1998) Significant evidence has emerged from these studies regarding the insidious implications of transferring state responsibility for the provision of public goods such as education, health, and social security to the individual, under the rubric of "personal responsibility" and "empowerment." These include exacerbation of inequalities, proliferation of unregulated markets in healthcare and "self-health practices," and the stigma attached to individuals who lack the "positions and human disposition" to be participants in the "project of modernity." The "ethics of responsibility" has therefore been brought into disrepute. What remains yet to be decided, as pointed out by Frank Pignatelli, is what forms of resistance can be best brought into practice to reanimate a "care of the self" congruent with ethico-political choices that refuse to restrict themselves to the dictates of scientifically regulated norms and market rationality, and encourage instead the courage and skill required to labor patiently and continuously to shape creative and liberating alternatives. (Pignatelli, 1993)

Important examples of challenges to the biomedical model of ageing and decay and the anti-ageing model of "successful ageing" as optimal physical and mental health are emerging through strategies such as life-narrative models, which give individuals an opportunity to reflect on and provide a personal account of what matters to them in life. A recent project conducted in Australia called the "Tenant by Tenant Project," co-ordinated by the national arts organization Big hART, is an excellent example of narrative models being used to challenge stereotypes of individuals living in government-funded housing estates. Many of the participants in this project were ageing residents and their narratives, including views about what matters in life, reflect a richer and much more complex view of the ageing experience than is available through mainstream advertising and anti-ageing markets.

Developing opportunities for a greater variety of images and narratives of ageing to circulate in media outlets and public discourses can shape creative and liberating alternative conceptions of what ageing really is—a complex human experience. They can also shift ideas that link notions of "responsibility" with medical benchmarks and agelessness toward a more multifaceted reflection on important life experiences and achievements based on individual life courses.

WORKS CITED

Beck, U. (1992). *Risk Society: Toward a New Modernity*. London: Sage Publications.
Bourdieu, P. (1998). "The Essence of Neoliberalism," *Le Monde Diplomatique*, http://mondediplo.com/1998/12/08bourdieu
Bytheway, B., Keil, T., and Allat, P., eds. (1989). *Becoming and Being Old*. London: Sage.
Council on the Ageing (2004). "Healthy Ageing: The Big Picture," *Fifty Plus News*, http:// www.fiftyplusnews.com/cota/march00.shtml

Featherstone, M. and Hepworth, M. (1989). "Ageing and Old Age: Reflections on the Post-Modern Life Course." In *Becoming and Being Old*, eds. B. Bytheway, T. Keil, P. Allat, and A. Bryman. London: Sage, pp. 143–157.
Foucault, M. (1984). "What is Enlightenment?" In *The Foucault Reader*, ed. P. Rabinow. New York, NY: Pantheon Books, pp. 32–50.
Giddens, A. (1991). *Modernity and Self-Identity*. Oxford: Polity Press.
Gilleard, C. and Higgs, P. (1998). "Ageing and the Limiting Conditions of the Body," *Sociological Research Online*, 3:4. http://www.socresonline.org.uk/3/4/4.html
Heinrich, J. (2001). *Health Products for Seniors: Potential Harm From "Anti-Aging" Products*. Wahington, DC: United States General Accounting Office. Available for download at http://www.gao.gov/new.items/d011139t.pdf
Holstein, M. and Minkler, M. (2003). "Self, Society, and the 'New Gerontology,'" *The Gerontologist*, 43:6 (December), pp. 787–796.
Katz, S. and Marshall, B. (2003). "New Sex for Old: Lifestyle, Consumerism, and the Ethics of Aging Well," *Journal of Aging Studies*, 17:1 (2003), pp. 3–16.
Katz, S. (2001). "Growing Older Without Aging? Positive Aging, Anti-Ageism, and Anti-Aging," *Generations*, 25:4 (January), pp. 27–32.
Kazanjian, A., Green, C., Bassett, K, and Brunger, F. (1998). "Bone Mineral Density Testing in Social Context," *International Journal of Technology Assessment in Health Care*, 15:4 (October), pp. 679–685.
Kemp, C. and Denton, M. (2003). "The Allocation of Responsibility for Later Life: Canadian Reflections on the Roles of Individuals, Government, Employers and Families," *Ageing & Society*, 23:6 (November), pp. 737–760.
Minkler, M. and Estes, C. L. (1999). *Critical Gerontology: Perspectives from Political and Moral Economy*. Amityville, NY: Baywood.
Morgan, C., (2006). "From the Darkness Humanity Emerged," *Sydney Morning Herald*, 24 November.
Moss, J. (1998). *The Later Foucault*. London: Sage.
McGregor, S. (2001). "Neoliberalism and Health Care," *International Journal of Consumer Studies*, 25:2 (June), pp. 82–89.
Phillipson, C. (1998). *Reconstructing Old Age*. London: Sage.

Pignatelli, F. (1993). "Dangers, Possibilities: Ethico-Political Choices in the Work of Michel Foucault," http://www.ed.uiuc.edu/eps/PES-Yearbook/93_docs/pignatel.htm

Polivka, L. (2000). "Postmodern Aging and the Loss of Meaning," *Journal of Aging and Identity*, 5:4 (December), pp. 225–235.

Powell, J. L. (2001). "Theorizing Gerontology: The Case of Old Age, Professional Power, and Social Policy in the United Kingdom," *Journal of Aging and Identity*, 6:3 (September), pp. 117–135.

Rabinow, P. (1984). *The Foucault Reader*. New York, NY: Pantheon Books.

Rajan, K. (2006). Biocapital: The Constitution of Postgenomic Life. London: Duke University Press.

Rose, N. (2001). "The Politics of Life Itself," *Theory, Culture, and Society*, 18:6 December), pp. 1–30.

Rowe, J.W. and Kahn R.L. (1999). *Successful Aging*. New York, NY: Dell.

Scannell, K. (2006). "An Aging Un-American" , *New England Journal of Medicine*, 355:14 (October), pp. 1415–1407.

Simons, J. (1995). *Foucault and the Political*. London and New York, NY: Routledge.

Smith, M. K. (2002). "Globalization and the Incorporation of Education." http://www.infed.
org/biblio/globalization.htm

Vincent, J. (2003). "What is at Stake in the 'War on Anti-Ageing Medicine?'" *Ageing and Society*, 23:5 (September), pp. 675–684.

Williams, S. (1995). "Theorising Class, Health, and Lifestyles: Can Bourdieu Help Us?" *Sociology of Health and Illness*, 17:5 (November), pp. 577–604.

Four

LONELINESS IN OLDER PATIENTS

Harry Lesser

A general tendency of illness is in some degree to isolate the sufferer from other people, both physically and mentally. This is by no means invariable, and may happen to any degree, from the very mild to the intense, but it is the tendency. Physically, the person may have to give up shared activities, go to bed for a time, or go to hospital and be separated from their family. Mentally, even being ill, except very mildly, makes a person a little different from others. Once they are categorized as "ill," or put on a "sick list," or become a patient, the difference increases, and they enter a special ethical condition, in which they are in some ways privileged, because they may be excused certain duties and have a claim to sympathy, but in other ways are taken less seriously and expected to be properly grateful to their carers. If in addition, they are experiencing any or all of pain and discomfort, disability, fear of future pain and disability, and fear of death, and feel that no other person can really understand what they are experiencing, the mental isolation increases still more, even if physically they are seldom alone.

It is therefore worth noting that in the loneliness of the unwell there are three different elements, not always all present. There is the physical isolation, sometimes for much of the time from anyone, sometimes simply from the people with whom one usually associates, sometimes limited to activity, when one still sees family and friends constantly but cannot join in the usual activities with them. There is the sense of being a special kind of person, privileged in some ways, but for the time being not to be seriously listened to. Finally, there is the sense that other people, however well-meaning, cannot understand your situation and your feelings.

For many reasons the loneliness of older patients is more often, though not always, in this high category. The illness is often more serious; friends and relations who live near are often fewer in number; death seems, and often is, nearer. The aim of this paper is to consider a bit more carefully the nature of loneliness, and to suggest one small way in which it can be relieved. In a sense, I am trying to analyze the concept of loneliness, not as a pure academic exercise, but because, as often, understanding the concept helps us to see how to relieve the condition itself.

I have already indicated that loneliness is both physical and mental. A person may be said to be lonely in the sense that they are largely alone or in the sense that they miss company or feel to some extent isolated. These do not necessarily go together. Physical solitude does not always produce mental loneliness: some people positively welcome it, at least for limited periods. A few people, such as hermits, remain very much part of a community while being physically isolated; some people retain very strongly the sense of being part of their family even while being often separated from them. On the other hand, the mere presence of other people, even in large numbers, does not always dispel mental loneliness, and indeed, as is well known, may increase it.

What this shows is, first, that it is essentially mental loneliness, rather than solitude, which causes suffering, and second, that making sure that a person is not physically alone is not enough to relieve loneliness. This is hardly news, but its consequences have not always been faced. To begin with, this means, with regard to hospital, that being in a ward will not necessarily save a patient from loneliness. It certainly may do so: friendly conversations between patients, and even the general bantering of a group, may achieve much. But there is no guarantee: it can also happen that people remain isolated, each in their own suffering. And this is particularly likely with older patients, for whom it is often less easy to move around and chat, less easy to make friends, less easy to explain how they feel, since the younger people may not understand, and so on.

Nor does the mere presence of the staff, or of visiting relatives, automatically help. I know of an occasion when a member of staff in an institution for older people was cleaning the room of one of the residents. To make conversation, she asked the resident if she was all right. "No," said the resident, a strong-minded lady, as she had always been, "I am not all right. I am always alone." " Well, I'm here." "Yes, you are here. But when you are here you are always elsewhere." Indeed, one may say that not only is presence not enough: interaction is not enough, if it is automatic, or if it is of the wrong sort—for example consisting of "jollying along."

One may contrast this with the following, also a true incident. The patient was a man in his eighties, and very much a thinking man, though often keeping his ideas to himself. He was having an operation under local anesthetic; and the nurse, as nurses do, addressed him as "sweetheart." His feeling, as he explained afterwards, was that this was, for the moment, meant—not, one might say, mere scattering of endearments, but showing how for a short time he was the person of most importance to her. The example is particularly instructive, in that the word itself is used both in meaningless and "jollying along" contexts and in serious expressions of support and appreciation of a person's situation.

This is perhaps the nub of the matter. If the hardest part of loneliness is the sense of mental isolation, and if it is often the case that much of the suffering of those who are ill, especially in old age, comes from this sense of isolation, then part of what carers, whether in hospital or at home, have to do, is to try to relieve it. And merely being there and performing the physical tasks, however vital these are, will not do it; nor will interaction which is experienced as being meaningless. On the other hand, exhibiting sympathy and empathy for long periods is not necessary. What seems to be required is that at least for short periods the patient is given really full attention and treated as being for that period really important. This is perhaps both easier and harder than one might think. It is easier in that the periods need not be very long, except under special circumstances, and no deep emotional feeling or commitment is required. It is harder in that it requires real paying of attention and granting of respect, and this, as the stories show, cannot be feigned or faked. To put it another way, it requires brief periods of real quality time, of proper listening and talking.

It is said that in the days when there were Foundling Hospitals, there were some hospitals where women came each day simply to cuddle the orphaned babies for a short time, and that in these hospitals the death rate was lower. The elderly do not need this except from their closest family, but they do need attention and respect. Moreover, although this requires human compassion, if it is to be carried out successfully, it is not, to use the jargon, a "work of supererogation." It is something they are entitled to by virtue of being human, a need whose satisfaction is a matter of justice, not of pure charity. For it seems reasonable to maintain that the right to respect is one that cannot be forfeited. As a thought experiment, one may consider a criminal, whose crime has involved violation of the rights of others. There are good grounds for thinking that he or she should be punished severely, but no grounds for maintaining that the punishment may be of a degrading or insulting nature, even if the crime was degrading or insulting. Similarly, the elderly are entitled to respect, even if they have failed in their own lives to grant this respect to others.

So, we may conclude as follows. The suffering of those who are seriously ill is often made worse by a sense of loneliness and isolation, and this is often particularly hard for the elderly. This sense of loneliness has a number of different elements (not always all present), and a number of causes. But the mental causes are more powerful, on the whole, than the physical ones. This means that the problem can be relieved, if at all, only by a willingness to show genuine respect and to pay, at least for short periods, genuine attention to the patients or clients and to what they say. If this is done, then, as the example shows, there can be some real relief of some of their suffering. Moreover, this paying of attention, though it has to be done with compassion, is not charity but an obligation. The patient or client has an actual right to it, and a right that cannot be forfeited by their own shortcomings.

Five

THE EFFECT OF AGEING ON AUTONOMY

Caroline Dunn

1. Defining Autonomy

The issues raised by the question of the relationship between ageing and autonomy are considerable, but this chapter will be limited to considering the fundamental issue of the effect of ageing on autonomy. In order to do this, of course, it is first necessary to have a definition of autonomy, and this is not as straightforward as might be imagined. Although autonomy is a central issue in the Western conception of a person and features prominently in ethical theories of post-Enlightenment Western culture, it is an ill-defined notion, equated or associated with liberty, self-rule, dignity, integrity, individuality, independence, freedom of will, responsibility, freedom from obligation, and the absence of external constraints, among other things; it therefore simultaneously encompasses political, moral, and social ideals. Gerald Dworkin has concluded that:

> About the only features held constant from one author to another are that autonomy is a feature of persons and that it is a desirable quality to have. (Dworkin, 1998, p. 6)

The essence of autonomy would appear to be that a person is autonomous if and only if he or she is self-governing. Dworkin's own definition of autonomy defines it as:

> ... a second-order capacity to reflect critically upon one's first-order preferences and desires, and the ability either to identify with these or to change them in the light of higher-order preferences and values. By exercising such a capacity we define our nature, give meaning and coherence to our lives, and take responsibility for the kind of person we are. (Dworkin, 1998, p. 108)

The relationship between the definition of a person and the ascription of autonomy is a somewhat circular one. To be a person is a necessary, though not sufficient, condition for the ascription of autonomy; no-one seriously suggests that animals possess autonomy. But equally, the non-autonomous are likely to be regarded as to some degree less than fully human, for if autonomy is perceived as a fundamental feature of persons, someone's humanity is likely to be perceived as diminished to some extent if autonomy is diminished.

The equation of autonomy with personhood and self-identity raises problems, however. Babies and young children are not autonomous; neither are patients in a comatose state nor those under an anesthetic; nor indeed is a sleeping person. Yet none of these groups would be considered to be less than fully human—Joe does not cease to be Joe to those who know and love or hate him simply because he is comatose or asleep or undergoing an anesthetic while his appendix is being removed. In the case of the comatose patient, it might be argued that, after a certain period of time, when all hope of recovery has been abandoned and brain death has been established, his or her essential humanity exists no longer; this is the justification for switching off life support systems. But someone does not necessarily lose his or her humanity simply by virtue of being in a coma, for many coma patients recover consciousness and their autonomy.

It follows from this that autonomy must be recognized as a matter of degree, not an absolute, for an individual's autonomy may—and does—alter in degree and over time. And it also follows that although autonomy may be restricted in many ways and to varying degrees, there are essentially only two basic ways in which it may be restricted; these are by external constraints—the actions of others; or internal constraints—what might be called limitations in oneself. The process of ageing affects both these constraints upon autonomy.

If autonomy is a feature of persons, then autonomy is intimately connected with notions of what it is to be human, and, by extension, what constitutes human needs. Certain needs are fundamental to human beings, the needs for food and shelter being the obvious ones; for if these needs are not met the question of autonomy becomes largely irrelevant, since the individual will die. But needs on this basic level are no more than the needs that any animal, human or otherwise, possesses. These needs must be met if the animal is to survive, but if only these needs are met for the human animal, it very soon ceases to be fully human, for the essence of what it is to be human lies in the more complex needs that the species has, and these needs are intimately related to values. All the concepts associated with the definition of autonomy have value judgments embedded in them.

Meeting the basic human needs of food and shelter can be done in many ways. In contemporary Britain, it is left to what remains of the welfare state to meet these very basic needs for those unable to do so for themselves. Similarly, the law enshrines basic rights which govern the relationship between individual rights and needs and the requirements of the community, in an attempt to ensure that all are treated equally.

The human animal also has other, very important, needs which differentiate it from the rest of the animal kingdom and define it as a human being.

These needs are for things such as love, respect, and dignity, which are every bit as important as the basic needs for food and shelter. These needs cannot be met by the welfare state or enshrined as rights because their provision depends upon the compassion and respect for others that can only come from the feeling of one person for another. In other words, the needs which define us as human can only be met by other humans, and meeting these needs depends upon an acknowledgement of a shared, common humanity between individuals, a feature of which is respect for the autonomy of others. Respecting the autonomy of others not only entails acknowledging their right to be self-governing. It also involves treating their views and wishes with respect, accepting them as individuals and being aware that their needs are not limited to the bare necessities required for survival. But acknowledging a shared humanity and respecting the autonomy of others does not mean demanding identical values from other individuals. Autonomy also means having your individual differences respected, having a voice which is listened to and taken seriously. Having these uniquely human needs met makes the difference between surviving as little more than an animal and thriving as a human being.

In these respects the elderly are no different from any other persons. Ageing need not be detrimental to autonomy; indeed, at some stages in life, it is a prerequisite for it. The law prohibits an individual gaining full legal autonomy until the age of eighteen; young children are not considered to be fully autonomous precisely because their immaturity renders them incapable of making fully rational or fully informed decisions. But in the context of the consideration of ageing and autonomy, it is taken as read that we are dealing with old age, and that old age carries with it certain factors that may affect autonomy. In Western culture, it is almost invariably taken for granted that the effects of old age on autonomy must be detrimental. Given the attitudes to ageing that are current in contemporary Western society, this is hardly surprising.

Ageing is not simply a matter of chronology: there is an element of social construction involved in the concept. One may be considered old at forty in the job market, but a man of fifty who is Head of State of a powerful nation may be considered to be young. The socially constructed aspects of ageing may be reflected in the meanings attributed to old age, which in contemporary Western culture are often pejorative.

Certainly the physiological deterioration that generally accompanies ageing in various degrees is very real, and may result in the elderly becoming less able to care for themselves and consequently more dependent on others. But family structures in the West no longer assume a responsibility to care for elderly members. This, coupled with medical advances that have resulted in greater numbers of elderly or very elderly people, means that the old are increasingly the responsibility of the state, with the concomitant financial burdens this places on a population seemingly ever-more reluctant to pay taxes for the provision of social services. The elderly may therefore be seen to be consuming continually increasing resources, in terms of pensions, medical services, and social services, and contributing nothing to their provision. Another consequence of medical technology is that not only are far more people enabled to live for much longer, but conditions which were regarded as an unpleasant but inevitable consequence of old age may now be alleviated, giving a much better quality of life, but making yet more demands on scarce resources. As a result, the old are increasingly seen as a problem at best and a nuisance at worst, rather than being valued for their wisdom and experience.

The meanings ascribed to old age may affect the treatment of the elderly, both in the specific sense of therapeutic treatment and the general sense of the way society reacts to the old. The illnesses that particularly affect old age are often assumed to have degrading effects. They are seen as demeaning, and as either producing or giving evidence of decay, loss of control, loss of reason, and dependency. The old consequently may suffer both from the negative perception of old age that permeates our culture and from the assumptions made about illnesses related to old age.

Such attitudes to old age diminish the autonomy of the elderly, since they often result in a perception of the elderly as somehow less than fully human, and to be regarded as less than fully human means that you will be denied a voice, or that your voice will not be listened to or taken seriously. In this respect, the elderly may experience a similar diminution of their autonomy to that experienced by the mentally ill. They may be ignored, regarded with contempt, be perceived as worthless and in extreme cases may suffer neglect, abuse, and even death.

Such gross denial of autonomy, resulting in this appalling treatment of the elderly, may be extremely rare (though that is arguable), but the granting or withholding of autonomy is always partly dependent upon the socially constructed meanings that individuals attribute to ageing. No matter what rights may be enshrined in legislation, they cannot guarantee that the autonomy of the elderly will be respected. Laws may protect people from physical maltreatment, but cannot protect them from contempt—it is quite possible to carry out the letter of a law while disregarding its spirit.

Another aspect of old age has significant repercussions. In a society obsessed with youth and beauty, the manifestations of old age may be feared and found repulsive, as they remind every young, beautiful person that this will be their lot too one day. In Franz Kafka's *Metamorphosis*, Gregor Samsa's transformation into a giant beetle is used as a metaphor for disease and its hidden meaning, but it might equally be a metaphor for some of the meanings that Western society attributes to ageing and the elderly. Gregor's transformation renders him repulsive, frightening, and shameful to his family; it strips him of his humanity and denies him the moral consideration which we take to be a right. Gregor retains his human feelings but his metamorphosis leads his family to begin a slow process of dehumanizing him, and they ultimately reject him entirely, feeling only relief when he is dead. This sometimes happens to the old: they may be characterized as smelly, useless, senile wrecks, with a disregarded past and no future.

This may seem to be exaggerating the case, and it is certainly an extreme, but can we really deny that such attitudes exist and are far from uncommon? So the meaning of old age goes far beyond that of a person who has lived for a specified number of years. It has a subtext, frequently hidden and denied, but one that is very real nonetheless, and if the social construction of old age is such that old age is perceived to be a problem, associated with negative conditions such as loss of control and dependency, the elderly may undergo a form of metamorphosis similar to that experienced by Gregor, which renders them less than fully human in the eyes of the rest of society.

All the above may be regarded as the malign consequences of diminished autonomy which result from the hidden meanings of old age being pejorative. But the autonomy of the elderly may also be unwarrantedly diminished as a result of the best of intentions—the result of benign but misplaced paternalism. The right of the elderly to be cared for may be given freely and with great compassion, but if the elderly are nonetheless characterized by illness and dependence they may be seen as childlike and helpless, deserving of care and consideration but largely non-autonomous. They may then experience the "Does he take sugar?" syndrome, which is often the lot of the disabled. Decisions may be made for them, or their wishes ignored, on the grounds that they are not competent to decide for themselves. Or they may be seen simply as members of a group—the elderly—without individuality. Calling old people "granny" or "granddad" is a classic example of this, denying them the dignity of being an individual, Mrs X or Mr Y.

It must surely be obvious that the pejorative meanings of old age must be challenged and replaced with an attitude that sees the old as persons just as much as any other members of the human race. If this were done, then the moral imperative that requires us to respect the autonomy of persons would require us to treat the elderly as self-governing agents, and the elderly would be as free as any other autonomous beings to do whatever they choose insofar as the exercise of their autonomy does not infringe the autonomy of others. This would include things that might be considered to be dangerous or stupid, just as the autonomy of younger people is respected when they choose to do dangerous or stupid things, such as motor racing or steeplechasing. Equally, the elderly would be subject to the same considerations regarding conflicts between the respect for autonomy and other values that apply to anyone else. So, for example, age alone would not be sufficient justification for preserving one individual's autonomy at the expense of another's. In all issues relating to autonomy, age as such would be irrelevant.

There is another aspect of ageing and autonomy that must also be considered: the apparently inexorable growth of consumerism in Western society (this may finally be about to change, as a result of economic recession, but it is too early to say). I have argued that autonomy is not absolute, but a matter of degree, and increasingly autonomy seems to be related to a person's power as a consumer—a case of "to those who can consume shall be given." In this respect, we are increasingly being made aware of "gray power"—those elderly people who by virtue of their increased numbers and their spending power are set to become a force to be reckoned with in the years ahead. Of course, the wealthy have always been able to enjoy more autonomy than the poor, for wealth brings with it power. Since autonomy necessarily requires the juggling of individual autonomy with the needs of the social group, which must result in compromises being made, and generally speaking the powerful are more likely to juggle things to their advantage, there is nothing surprising about this. But increasingly things such as autonomy, dignity, respect, and the provision of basic social and medical services, which should be taken as a right in a civilized society, appear to be becoming the prerogative of those with money—or, to use the term that is becoming increasingly popular, with consumer power.

So the elderly poor are increasingly seen as a problem. They are not just relatively worse off, but may well lack decent living conditions and an adequate income to enable them to eat well and keep warm enough. They may have to wait for a very long time for medical treatments, such as hip replacements, that will greatly improve the quality of their lives. Their social life may be limited or non-existent as a result of poverty and lack of mobility. Those fortunate enough to possess "gray power," however, are portrayed as having choices—the choice of living in specially designed retirement apartments, for example, where any degree of dependency can be catered for with dignity and designer decor; or the choice to enter a private hospital to have quality-of-life-improving medical treatment. The elderly poor are increasingly condemned to a life of being grateful for seemingly reluctantly given charity, while the elderly wealthy have the right to have their needs met by virtue of their consumer spending power. They are not portrayed as a problem, a drain on resources, but instead as important members of the economic community. Autonomy may be in the process of being redefined as a function of consumer spending power—what price then human needs and the autonomy of the elderly poor?

If it is accepted that respect for autonomy should be considered to be one of the primary values of a civilized society, it should nevertheless not be assumed that this value overrides all others in any circumstances. There will always be cases where an individual cannot be regarded as autonomous, by virtue of some form of incapacity. Dworkin's definition of autonomy as being the "second-order capacity to reflect critically upon one's first order preferences and desires, and the ability to either identify with these or to change them in the light of higher-order preferences and values" requires as a necessary condition that you be free from internal constraints—what can be called limitations in yourself. Ageing may certainly result in limitations in yourself, for physiological performance declines with age. The physical manifestations of ageing may leave the elderly with little choice in some areas. You may have to relinquish your hopes of exercising your autonomy to become an Olympic athlete (not a situation exclusively related to ageing). More significant in relation to autonomy, however, are the results of ageing which affect mental functioning and cause its deterioration. For such deterioration results sometimes in partial irrationality, and rationality must be considered to be a necessary, though not invariably sufficient, condition for autonomy, because it is a necessary condition for critical reflection.

2. Ageing and Rationality

> Rationality is the fundamental premise by virtue of which we understand ourselves as human beings; that is, as creatures capable of adjusting their actions as reasonably efficient means to intelligible ends (Moore, 1980, p. 60).

Loss of rationality can also affect the autonomy of the elderly externally, and sometimes unjustifiably, by rendering them semi-human in the eyes of some, with the result that they are denied autonomy. But irrationality can genuinely diminish an individual's autonomy by limiting his or her competence to make informed decisions. Although perception of the elderly as necessarily irrational is both morally wrong and empirically unjustifiable, serious irrationality has profound consequences for autonomy.

There are several conditions which affect the elderly and may result in irrationality and consequent incompetence. Such incompetence may be total or limited, chronic or intermittent, and may result from degenerative neurological disorders (for example, Alzheimer's Disease or Parkinson's Disease), cerebrovascular accidents, or mental disorders that impair cognitive function. In addition, certain drugs may impair mental functions which may in turn impair the recipient's competence.

As a result of incompetence, decisions may have to be made on behalf of the incompetent person which affect not only medical treatment but issues of a broader nature, such as whether or not she needs to be cared for in an institution and who should manage her finances if she has any money. None of these issues relates solely to the elderly, as incompetence may be suffered by anyone as a result of injury or disease. But it is also true to say that the elderly are more susceptible because of the incidence of chronic illness being higher amongst the elderly, since in the later stages of chronic illness many people become incompetent, particularly nowadays, where the very success of medicine has resulted in many more elderly people surviving for a considerable time after their cognitive functions have declined.

Making decisions for someone considered to be incompetent raises the problem of the conflicting values of autonomy, freedom, paternalism, and protection. The problems are exacerbated by the fact that there is no clear test to establish competence; and the fundamental question of how incompetence is determined, and by whom, must also be addressed. Taking the latter question first, we will consider the hypothetical case of Mrs X, a lady in her late seventies who is in reasonably good health. She is fortunate enough to have savings, and decides that she will use some of this money to explore Australia, something she has always wanted to do, but never had the opportunity to do before. Her relatives are horrified, feeling that at her age this is a totally irrational decision and must therefore be evidence of senile dementia, and are arguing that she should be prevented from going. But consider the situation from Mrs X's perspective. She knows that it is highly likely that she will die in the next ten to fifteen years, and possibly much sooner than this. She also knows that her money will be of no use whatsoever to her when she is dead. It seems entirely rational to her to decide to realize a lifelong ambition now, while she still has the chance. The very worst that can happen to her is that she might die while on her travels—but she is old, she might die anyway, so why not risk dying while she is enjoying herself? And she probably will not die—she is not proposing to walk to Australia—so why not enjoy her last years? By whose criteria shall we judge her rationality? I do not think that there is any contest here. We should all be wishing Mrs X "G'day and happy travelling." And indeed, were she forty years younger that would probably not be disputed.

But what if Mrs X were proposing to canoe down the Amazon, rather than taking a jumbo jet to Australia? This must be a much riskier undertaking. But why should Mrs X's age be the deciding factor? People do life-threatening things which others consider utterly ridiculous and irrational—consider the climbers who scale vertical rock faces with no ropes or other equipment to help them. If Mrs X were to die exploring the Amazon it could be argued that she had nothing to lose, having lived most of her life, whereas a "twenty-something" climber has the rest of her life before her, but nobody argues that she is irrational to pursue her sport.

I have used this example to illustrate the problems of deciding whether an elderly person's rationality is impaired. What may seem to be a rational course of action from one person's perspective may not be so from another's. And these examples also illustrate the importance of examining who is making the claim when an elderly person is declared to be acting irrationally. In the examples given, could it be relatives, more concerned that Mrs X will be spending all the money that they hoped would have been left to them in the next few years? Or perhaps it is simply a case of a loving but overprotective child who has succumbed to the notion that the elderly by definition must be significantly diminished in terms of mental and physical functioning.

The concept of competence always relates to a particular action. I am not competent to direct a NASA space mission, ride in the Grand National, or perform a Mozart piano concerto. I am perfectly competent, however, to direct a motorist from Manchester to London, ride a horse, or play a reasonably simple cello continuo part. And, as these examples illustrate, competence is also a matter of degree. If I say I am competent enough to ride a horse it does not follow that I am competent to ride a horse in the Grand National, nor does my level of musical ability mean that I can claim to be a competent musician. I am competent, however, to make the decision that, having weighed up the risks and the costs and the benefits, I wish to try and gain the expertise to enable me to ride in the Grand National or justly claim to be a competent musician. The point is that in all these situations, competence is related to a specific task; it is not a global facility. So in deciding whether an elderly person is competent, it is always necessary to be aware of the question, "Competent to do what?"

It is also necessary to be aware that the notion of competence has values embedded in it. To return to the case of Mrs X, why should anyone bother to claim that she is incompetent to explore Australia or canoe down the Amazon? Would they bother whether she was competent to express a preference for tea or coffee? Of course not. The difference relates to the underlying values involved. Preferring tea or coffee does not generally involve serious value judgments (though not bothering to ascertain which is preferred is a diminution of respect for another's autonomy). But in the other examples, the claim that Mrs X was incompetent to decide to set off round the world is justified by virtue of the underlying values that relate to the issue. If an individual is to make a competent decision about the choices open to him or her, then he or she must necessarily have some conception of what is good or bad—both in a personal sense and in a wider sense.

So my decision not to drink and drive may be based on the belief that it is wrong to risk the safety of others, and that such an action would therefore be bad. It might be a more selfish decision, based on the knowledge that if I am caught, I might lose my license, which would be bad for me, or that I might injure or kill myself, which would be very bad for me. In the case of Mrs X, her relatives might genuinely believe that it will be bad for her well-being to canoe down the Amazon; her decision that it will greatly enhance her well-being may conflict so greatly with their values that they simply cannot accept it as rational. Or, to be cynical, they may believe that it will be bad for their bank balance if she spends her money this way rather than leaving it to them, although it is likely that they would claim the first reason rather than admit to the second. All in all, then, competence is a tricky thing to decide, and it is hardly surprising that there are no definitive measures of it. Indeed, it can be equally difficult to decide what constitutes anyone's well-being. Moral philosophy encompasses a number of theories concerning what constitutes individual well-being, which it is beyond the scope of this chapter to consider. However, each allows that a considerable degree of subjectivity is involved in the definition of well-being, and also that an individual may be mistaken as to what course of action will genuinely promote his or her well-being.

This is an important consideration. Notwithstanding the problems associated with competence and incompetence—where the threshold is to be set, who decides, and who should make decisions for those judged incompetent—it is the case that some elderly people are indeed incompetent to make decisions that will enhance their well-being. I suggested earlier that autonomy is only one value, albeit an extremely important one, among others, and cannot necessarily override all other values. As such there will be occasions where autonomy may conflict with other values, one of which is beneficence, which can broadly be considered to be a responsibility to care for the welfare of others. There are a number of issues surrounding the notion of beneficence, such as whether it can rightly be considered to be a duty or merely a moral ideal, which I shall not consider here. In the context of ageing and autonomy the most important issue that beneficence raises is that of paternalism. If we take the position that autonomy is one of the prime values and should therefore be preserved and promoted whenever possible, then it is inevitable that paternalism will conflict to some degree with it, because paternalism involves substituting another's judgment of what is good for an individual instead of their own, and overriding their wishes in order to promote their well-being or to prevent harm to them.

3. Ageing and Paternalism

Can paternalistic intervention ever be justified in overriding the wishes of the elderly in order to promote their well-being or prevent harm to them? In general terms, the answer must be yes. Consider the situation with young children. No-one would seriously argue that respect for their autonomy must always be the paramount value. Indeed, below a certain age, young children may be argued to have very little, if any, autonomy, by virtue of immaturity. But because young children are generally valued, we consider it justified to protect them from themselves where necessary. If we are to value the elderly and respect them as individuals, which we are morally bound to do, then we cannot simply ignore those situations in which they may be as incompetent to make rational judgments as young children, on the spurious grounds that their autonomy is all important, even if the exercise of it may lead to great harm. Such an argument is spurious because in such situations one cannot be considered to be fully autonomous, by virtue of limitations in oneself.

Paternalistic intervention must be acknowledged to be the lesser of two evils in some cases. I suggest that the conditions for justifying it are met if the benefits of paternalism outweigh the harm that might result from loss of autonomy in cases where an individual cannot be considered fully autonomous by virtue of his or her condition—the limitations in oneself that by definition restrict autonomy. Let us translate these concerns into an all too familiar scenario that affects many of the elderly. Mrs Y is eighty years old and lives on her own. She is frail and becoming increasingly confused. Her home is getting very dirty because she is unable to clean it adequately, but she refuses any help on the grounds that "they" will only use it as an excuse to put her in a home, a course of action she adamantly refuses. She is not eating adequately and is at risk of hypothermia in the winter because her home is so cold. It is very obvious to all who have dealings with Mrs Y that she is no longer competent to care for herself, and that to meet her needs for adequate care would require that she be considerably dependent on others. If her autonomy is respected, she will in all probability die of hypothermia during the next spell of cold weather, if not sooner, as a result of injuring herself. In any case, the quality of her life is rapidly diminishing. On the other hand, to deny her autonomy and remove her into care against her will might also precipitate her death, and result in her being deeply unhappy in the interim, thereby diminishing the quality of her life. Which is the lesser of the two evils?

I think there is a more fundamental problem here. Given the shift in the demographic profile of the Western world, with increasing numbers of people expected to live to a very old age, we must surely start to acknowledge that dependency in adult life is going to become much more a fact of life than it has been for previous generations. If we are to respect the elderly as human beings, and this will include respecting their autonomy, we can no longer go on asking questions of the "which is the lesser of two evils" type—respect for autonomy and possible consequent suffering or denial of autonomy and possible consequent suffering. It is time to acknowledge that although there will always be cases where there is no possibility of a happy outcome, there is every possibility of reducing their occurrence if we have the will to alter things. In a society where even a cursory glance down the aisles of any supermarket shows a bewildering choice of such mundane articles as washing powder, lavatory paper, and pet food, it surely is not beyond our power to construct a society where there are feasible and valid choices for the dependent. Such a society would need to be organized to enhance the capabilities of the elderly and promote autonomy in the areas where it will not produce undue harm. In situations where autonomy cannot be fully respected because to do so would result in harm, the alternatives offered should be sensitive and tailored to the needs of the individual, not bureaucratically motivated.

In our culture dependency, except in the case of young children, is seen as somehow shameful. It has connotations of having to be grateful for whatever one is given, and is seen to be virtually concomitant with loss of autonomy. Yet this need not be the case. We are above all else social animals, and as such interdependent. The principle of respect for individual autonomy is a vital one, but in the process of respecting it we seem to be taking autonomy out of the context of what human beings need to thrive rather than merely survive. Perhaps it is not the state of dependency as such that is so abhorrent but rather the way it is interpreted that causes so much misery to the elderly dependent. Being dependent should not mean that we lose our autonomy, dignity, and respect.

4. Conclusion

Respecting the autonomy of the elderly must mean that age as such is an irrelevant factor. The only relevant consideration is that the elderly are human beings, and the same respect for autonomy that is due to any human being is due to the elderly. Like that of anyone else, an elderly person's autonomy may be restricted in certain situations, because in any society there must always be compromises made between the sometimes conflicting interests of individual members.

If the old are to be granted the same right to autonomy as anyone else, it must also follow that old age by itself cannot be used as an excuse for behavior that would not be acceptable in younger people. Old age does not necessarily transform our personalities for the better—many people are just as bloody-minded and unpleasant in old age as they were in their youth, and old age must not therefore be seen as an excuse for intolerable behavior. Irrational behavior, which is likely to affect considerable numbers of elderly people by virtue of their age, may well manifest itself in behavior that is unpleasant for others, but such behavior must be regarded in a different light because it can be argued to be the result of illness and therefore non-volitional. The same considerations that apply to anyone in this situation apply to elderly irrational people. It is not the age factor that is important, but the fact of irrationality.

Old age may diminish our faculties, both mental and physical, but it does not and should not diminish our essential humanity. Many elderly people are hale and hearty, and have the right to defy old age in the sense of rejecting restrictions imposed upon their autonomy by virtue of their age alone. They have the same right to autonomy as any other human beings. Such autonomy is not immutable and eternally fixed, any more than anyone else's, but fluctuates according to circumstances and is necessarily influenced by the interactions of the many individuals who together make up any society composed of moral agents.

For some, old age may indeed bring with it a diminution of those faculties which are a necessary condition for autonomy, and this may necessitate a justified paternalism on their behalf in order to promote their well-being to the greatest extent possible. If we were to shift our moral emphasis, no longer put so much emphasis on autonomy as the prime value that even unavoidable dependency is seen as somehow diminishing a person, and acknowledge our mutual dependency, we might be able to afford the respect to the dependent elderly that any human being deserves, irrespective of age.

WORKS CITED

Dworkin, G. (1988). *The Theory and Practice of Autonomy*. Cambridge: Cambridge University Press.

Kafka, F. (1961). *Metamorphosis and Other Stories*. Harmondsworth: Penguin.

Moore, M. (1980). "Legal Conceptions of Mental Illness." In *Mental Illness: Law and Public Policy*, eds. B. Brody and H.T. Englehardt. Boston, MA: Reidel Publishing.

Six

AUTONOMY FOR OLDER PATIENTS IN BEDSIDE MEDICINE: OBSERVATIONS FROM A DEVELOPING NATION

Ashish Goel, Wilma Wilson, and AB Dey

1. The Importance of Maintaining the Autonomy of Older Patients

The word "autonomy" is derived from the Greek "autos" ("self") and "nomos" ("law"), and consequently means self-rule or self-determination. Human beings have the power to make normative or value judgments about how their lives should go. The question is: when should they be allowed to act on these judgments? Some have argued that only those who meet some standard of rationality should be granted autonomy. Others, with whom the authors agree, have challenged this, and argued for the right to make decisions about our own lives.[1] This becomes increasingly important in the case of the mentally unstable older patient, who should not be denied this right of making his or her own decisions because he or she fails to meet some standard of rationality, itself an abstract and little understood concept, which is perhaps conceived differently by each individual. J. Tsevat *et. al.* have shown that even very old patients are able to assess their own health values and arrive at considered decisions about their own lives, and have concluded that the health values even of the very old should be elicited directly from the patients whenever possible.[2] The assumption should be that every patient is capable of autonomous decision making unless there is good evidence to the contrary.

But autonomy does not merely involve being allowed to make decisions. It also involves refusing to be a passive object of social influence, or to show automatic conformity, compliance, or obedience to social norms. According to M. Deutsch and H.B. Gerard,[3] most people conform to the norms of their groups because of a desire to be liked or accepted by others, or a desire to be correctly informed. The former is called normative social influence and involves altering our behavior to meet others' expectations, while the latter is called informational social influence, and is based on our tendency to depend on others as a source of information about many aspects of the social world,. Both of these are applicable to older persons living in the family or in long-stay institutions.

Increasing longevity has been hailed as a triumph of medicine in recent years. With increasing life expectancy, ageing has been seen to outpace social and economic development. Declining mortality rates and total fertility rates result in a relative increase in the proportion of older individuals. It has been estimated that by the year 2050 over 80% of the older world population will be living in the developing world. Despite a higher life expectancy in developing nations, there has also been an escalation in the risk of having chronic ailments during the increased years; a result of life-long accumulation of risk factors.[4]

In India, the proportion of seniors in the total population increased from 6.1% in 1988 to 6.8% in 2004, and the old age dependency ratio rose from eighty-nine to 119 per 1000 of the "productive" population in the same period.[5] About 10% of older persons living alone get hospitalized in any given year. In the face of poorly established long term institutional care, overstretched acute care facilities and a permanent struggle to maintain critical care, it is not surprising to find these patients frequently passed from one ward to another, or even one hospital to another in "patient-unfriendly" tertiary care centers scattered across the country. The same is true in many developing nations. Frailty and disability make the situation still worse for many of these ailing seniors, who become dependent for essential healthcare not only on the system but also on relatives and friends for mere access to the system. Consequently, an assumption that one is helpless, leading to the giving of automatic consent to any medical treatment that is offered, often by reluctant caregivers, becomes the norm rather than the exception, and is not seen as an aberration.

With this increasing burden of care, it becomes important to understand that respect for autonomy helps not only the individual patient but also the patient community at large. The ability to understand her medical condition and take her own decisions creates in the client or patient a sense of confidence in the healthcare provider, thereby establishing a stronger bond between the patient and the doctor. Not only would this bring down the rising rates of conflict seen in recent times but respect for another individual's autonomy also helps to produce an open, kind-hearted, and progressive society.

Any illness is accompanied by fear, pain, stress, and tension, and the effect of the disease is sometimes compounded by the treatment itself. The condition may diminish a patient's ability to understand and make apt decisions. Hospitalization itself clouds free judgment, and restricts autonomy and the ability to exercise preferences. Along with restrictions on activities of daily living (ADL), the atmosphere of hospital wards and the attitudes of hospital staff compound a patient's misery, especially in institutions not patient-friendly in design and organization. In such instances, lack of knowledge about your illness increases uncertainty. It is important to enable older patients to maintain autonomy despite continued healthcare requirements.

2. The Doctor-Patient Relationship

To understand the factors that control patient autonomy and influence decision making, it is essential to analyze the doctor-patient relationship in some detail. Several models of patient care operate under different conditions, in different cultural, regional, religious, and clinical settings. In the *paternalistic*, also called parental or priestly, model, the physician acts as a guardian and determines the best intervention to ensure the patient's health and well-being. At the same time, the physician has the obligation to place the patient's interest above his or her own and solicit the views of colleagues when lacking adequate knowledge.

In the *informative*, also called the scientific, engineering or consumer, model, the physician provides the patient with all relevant information to select a medical intervention and then carries out the selected intervention. In this informative model, the physician is a source of technical expertise, and bears a moral obligation to provide truthful information and to consult others when her knowledge or skills are falling short. Here the patient has control over medical decision making.

The *interpretive* model requires the physician and patient to make explicit the patient's intrinsic values and views, and the physician to help the patient select the available medical interventions that promote, or at least do not work against, these values. Contrasting with the informative model, which provides the patient only with information on the nature, risks, and benefits of possible interventions, the interpretive model requires the physician to act as a guide, helping to elucidate values and suggesting appropriate medical interventions. The physician's obligations include engaging the patient in a joint course of action. The conception of patient autonomy is one based on self-understanding, as the patient evaluates who he or she is and how the various medical options bear on his or her identity. In the *deliberative* model the physician is expected to go still further, and act as a teacher or friend, engaging the patient in dialogue on what course of action would be most suitable. Not only does the physician indicate what the patient could do, but, knowing the patient and wishing what is best for them, the physician indicates what the patient should do, what decision regarding medical therapy would be best. But the decision is not forced on the patient, who still makes the final choice.

Under different clinical, regional, or cultural circumstances different models may be appropriate. Moreover, different models may be applicable to the same patient at different times. Therefore, no ideal physician-patient relationship has been conclusively identified, and it is not possible to present any one model of the relationship as being absolutely utopian. Nevertheless, the interpretive and deliberative models, when they are practicable and when the physician does not try to convert the patients to values they do not share, may be considered as normally the best for maintaining autonomy.

3. Factors Affecting Autonomy

Having outlined the models of patient care, we must now discuss the factors that influence patient autonomy and what can be done to reduce those working against it. Ireen M. Proot *et. al.* studied hospitalized patients with stroke in the Netherlands and identified three dimensions of autonomy: self-determination, independence, and self-care. The authors pointed out that the patients' clinical condition and their strategies for dealing with it inevitably inhibited autonomous decision making, but health professionals could facilitate autonomy by giving therapy, support, information, attentiveness, and respect, especially when working with the patient as a team and when the institution provides a hopeful and encouraging environment.[6] But a great many factors remain, as this table shows.

Internal patient dependent factors		External factors		
Individual	Social	Healthcare professional	Healthcare organizations	Caregivers
General understanding. Ability to plan, control and pursue personal goals. Communication skills. Knowledge. Competence. Previous functional status and social role.	Religious beliefs. Social customs. Regional patterns. Language barriers.	Respect. Knowledge. Competence. Confidence. Ethical considerations. Law of the land.	Institutional structures. Residents' and users' committees. Professional organizations.	Caregiver stress. Individual health values. Individual preferences Relationship with patient

Table 1: Examples of factors influencing patient autonomy

However, despite all these factors and no doubt others, the pattern of patient autonomy is governed first and foremost by the physician-patient relationship and the clinical setting in which the interaction is occurring. The opportunity to exercise autonomy is different in an inpatient care setting, an acute care setting, and an intensive or emergency care setting. In life-threatening situations, even though the options available are always limited, the patient is virtually never in a position to exercise whatever limited choice is available, unless advance planning has been done to handle such situations in the way he or she would wish. Situations with no such planning are common, and the decisions are as a result taken mostly by the doctor, or sometimes the caregivers present at the scene.

Our society supports the right of its members to make decisions based on their personal values and beliefs. However, in instances where the patient lacks the capacity to make decisions on their own, the role of the surrogate decision maker comes into play. The concept of "surrogate consent" assumes greater importance in the care of older persons who often present with memory disturbances and mental instability. Several factors distinct from self consent come into play in cases of surrogate consent, including the health values of the surrogate, and his or her relation with the patient. When older patients are unable to respond adequately and with informed consent, advance directives could maintain the medical empowerment of the elderly, as they themselves would have opted out of their own decision making, at a time when they could still make decisions. Empowerment refers to the process of increasing power or creating autonomy in a social system to help people take charge of their affairs. It should promote the ability to act both individually and collectively to solve problems, influence important issues, and contribute to the achievement of people's main objectives.[7]

The competence of an individual depends on the possession of a set of values and goals necessary for evaluating different options, the ability to communicate and understand the information provided, and the ability to reason and to deliberate about your choices.[8] Assessment of competence plays a pivotal role in determining when a decision needs to be taken on behalf of an individual. The vulnerability of the patients may act as a major obstacle to determining their competency in decision making.[9] Accurate and reliable screening instruments should be developed to attain accuracy in the clinical decision-making process. One such piece of software developed is the Functional Autonomy Measurement System (SMAF), a twenty-nine-item scale measuring functional ability in five different areas in older individuals. It has been recommended for use for home care, for developing care plans in institutional settings, and for epidemiological and evaluative studies.[10]

A physician's skill to judge the competency of an older patient is tested to the hilt at a time when the patient refuses a life-saving treatment.[11] This judgment is based on the information perceived by the doctor assessing the capacity of the patient to comprehend facts and make independent decisions. A physician at such a time should instigate discussions, keeping in mind the patient's level of understanding, and the socio-economic situation of the patient and his or her family, and with the aim of ensuring that the patient fully understands the implications of accepting or refusing treatment. The final decision may be determined by the law of the land,[12] but in any case it should if possible be an autonomous decision by the patient, unless there is clear evidence that he or she is no longer competent.

But different clinical conditions need to be handled differently. Also, medical research requires a different perspective on patient autonomy from that used in clinical bedside practice. Here, unless proper standards to regulate the conduct of research are made mandatory, including more stringent protection of autonomy than is needed in clinical practice, there is a great danger of patient autonomy being severely compromised if not positively violated. To try to create a uniform code of conduct for maintaining patient autonomy in all the many kinds of clinical conditions and in both clinical and research situations would be a very misguided exercise.

Not only does medical practice differ according to clinical situations, it also may have to be modified because of prevailing religious or cultural practices. For example, in traditional patriarchal Indian society, the oldest male member has been the head of the family and decision making powers have rested on his shoulders. As a result of demographic and economic social trends of westernization, migration, and improved life expectancy, the traditional support systems of extended families have reappeared within nuclear families. If the head of the family becomes ill, the eldest working member of the family takes over as the head of the family and takes decisions for the family, especially in cases where intergenerational transfer of wealth takes place. This has led to socio-economic dependency and vulnerability among the family's older members. To help these older members to maintain their sense of worth and their autonomy may require much awareness of their situation and much sensitivity.

A cross-cultural study, conducted to present quantitative comparisons between groups of patients and physicians in Japan and the United States with regard to the ethics of medical decision making, similarly revealed that culture is crucial in shaping the relationship between the physician, the patient, and his or her family. While Japanese patients and physicians emphasized the role of family and physician in clinical decision making, American subjects stressed patient preferences as against the preferences of the family.[13] One thing that is crucial here is to recognize that autonomy and individualism are not the same thing, and that although both the American and the Japanese patients can, admittedly, be simply following social convention, both can also be autonomously acting in accordance with their values, although the values themselves are different.

4. Formal Ways of Improving Patient Autonomy

So far, we have identified four ways in which a physician can encourage patient autonomy: by choosing the model of the patient-physician relationship best adapted to the situation; by encouraging hospitals and care homes and centers to create a patient-friendly environment; by using the most thorough and accurate methods available for determining patient competence; and by being sensitive to the patient's cultural, religious, and socio-economic background. Patient autonomy can also be improved in more formal ways by introducing and establishing (1) the process of informed consent; (2) an ethical, culturally acceptable consultation procedure within the existing legal framework; and (3) advance care directives (we have mentioned these already). Of these, the basic element in maintaining patient autonomy is the process of informed consent. It involves patient rights and professional responsibilities, and the giving of proper information to patients about the nature of his or her condition, the proposed treatment, the benefits and risks involved, and the available alternatives.

The universal ethical principles of beneficence, non-malevolence, distributive justice, and social equity have been the basic tenets under which the medical system is supposed to function. Patient autonomy is now being recognized as another important principle that should govern medical practice. Informed consent is a measure developed to safeguard this autonomy and thereby allow medical practice to develop under the basic ethical framework acceptable to a society. Informed consent has the aims of making intervention to improve health lawful and of preserving the ability of an individual seeking healthcare to make their own decisions. Although informed consent is believed to be a relatively new concept, there is evidence to show that the doctor's intervention has always needed to be approved by the patient in some form prior to implementation. There is evidence, for example in Book One of Plato's *Laws*, that even defensive medicine—the pressure on the doctor to conform to the patient's expectations by always taking some action, even if he knew it would do no good—existed already in the ancient world, at least if the patient was wealthy. But this often applied only to the initial decision of the patients to put themselves in the hands of the doctor. Subsequently the physician exercised professional responsibility based on moral and ethical principles, taking decisions in the best interest of the patient, with no further consent involved (this, of course, would nowadays be legally unsound in many, perhaps most, jurisdictions).

The conviction that the physician would act in the best interests of the patient was passed on through the generations, giving doctors moral responsibility and often legal indemnity.[14] But with recent changes in social structure there has been a shift in the position of doctors in society, and they have much less legal protection, unless they secure informed consent. Born in the early twentieth century, the modern concept of informed consent includes the retention throughout the treatment of the fundamental autonomy of the patient to decide (something which stems from his or her personal rights), and it makes crucial the transfer of information. It may be argued that patients are not competent to understand medical matters properly, and that to avoid unnecessary panic it is better not to divulge the entire information to them, but it has been shown that patients are more contented if they are adequately involved in decision making about their health.[15] Nevertheless, although it is in most countries legally mandatory for a doctor to obtain informed consent before administering treatment, this condition is still all too often flouted, and all too rarely carried out in the spirit in which it was instituted.

A. Akkad *et al.* found that many current consent procedures are inadequate as a means of obtaining informed autonomous choice, and their ethical standing and legal credibility should be readdressed.[16] In recent times doctors have become liable to malpractice charges, often relating to the absence of informed consent, yet in developing nations and traditional Indian societies, obtaining consent is still considered to be merely a customary ritual and is treated as such. This is primarily because of an incorrect belief that patients are unable to understand the complexities and tend to forget the facts sooner or later. A study on 100 consecutive patients admitted for gastrointestinal surgery found that a majority (70%) of the patients recalled data relating to details of the surgical procedure explained to them during the informed consent taken prior to surgery.[17] The older patients fared worse in recollecting the details but remembered that such detail had been explained to them, and appreciated the disclosure prior to surgery because it reduced their anxiety.

Written consent, unless the patient cannot write or objects to putting anything in writing, is preferable to oral consent, especially in cases where the older patient is suffering from amnesiac states, cognitive dysfunction, or mood disorders.[18] Appropriately worded handouts, or leaflets containing the consent form, maximize recall in such cases.

Doctors may sometimes be faced with clinical situations where it is difficult or impossible to obtain informed consent, either because the patient is unable to provide consent or because there is an urgent need to intervene in a life-threatening situation. In the case of some older patients, it could also be argued that there is no measure of the extent to which the patient has an understanding of the information provided.[19]

A professional approach to these problems involves the use of advanced care planning (ACP), wherein patients and physicians together explore the possibilities of care in the context of current illness states, discuss treatment options if there are future complications or developments, and analyze the patients' preferences for care, thereby reinforcing patient autonomy.[20] Advanced care planning has been practiced in more developed nations but needs to be established in developing nations, where decision making usually involves the patients' own wishes being either unexpressed or ignored.

In conclusion, dignity at the twilight of life should be maintained at all levels. Developing systematic guidelines and multidisciplinary courses of action regarding the approach to patient autonomy from admission onwards is recommended for the multidisciplinary care of older patients. Physicians should be like advocates, who assist in making, not in enforcing, decisions. The relationship between a patient and a doctor, however, cannot be simply that between a provider and a client. The physician needs to provide correct information to patients and assist them to arrive at decisions that they feel are best for them. Patient autonomy and physician beneficence should not be viewed as conflicting values, but dealt with intelligently as tools for effective and humane patient care.

NOTES

1. Eric Matthews, "Autonomy and the Psychiatric Patient," *Journal of Applied Philosophy*, 17:1 (2000), pp. 59–70.

2. J. Tsevat, N.V. Dawson, A.W. Wu, J. Lynn, J.R. Soukup, E.F. Cook, H. Vidaillet, and R.S. Phillips, "Health Values of Hospitalized Patients 80 Years or Older," *Journal of the American Medical Association*, 279:5 (February 1998), pp. 371-5.

3. M. Deutsch and H.B. Gerard, "A Study of Normative and Informational Influences upon Individual Judgement," *Journal of Abnormal Psychology*, 51:3 (1955), pp. 629–636.

4. C.J.L. Murray and A.D. Lopez, "Global Burden of Disease and Risk Factors," www.dcp2.org/pubs/GBD.

5. K.V. Rao, Morbidity, Healthcare, and the Condition of the Aged (National Sample Survey Organisation, Ministry of Statistics and Programme Implementation, Government of India, 2006).

6. Ireen M. Proot, Harry F.J.M. Crebolder, Huda Huijer Abu-Saad, Ton H.G.M. Macor, and Ruud H.J. Ter Meulen, "Facilitating and Constraining Factors on Autonomy: The Views of Stroke Patients on Admission into Nursing Homes," *Clinical Nursing Research*, 9:4 (2000), pp. 460–478.

7. Julian Rappaport, Carolyn Swift, and Robert Hess, *Studies in Empowerment: Steps Toward Understanding and Action* (New York, NY: Haworth Press, 1984).

8. Edward Etchells, Peteris Darzins, Michael Silberfield, Peter A. Singer, Julia McKenny, Gary Naglie, Mark Katz, Gordon H. Guyatt, D. William Molloy, and David Strang, "Assessment of Patient Capacity to Consent to Treatment," *Journal of General Internal Medicine*, 14:1 (January 1999), pp. 27–34.

9. A.J. Rosin and Y. Van Dijk, "Subtle Ethical Dilemmas in Geriatric Management and Clinical Research," *Journal of Medical Ethics*, 31:6 (June 2005), pp. 355–359.

10. Patrick Boissy, Simon Brière, Michel Tousignant, and Eric Rousseau, The eSMAF: A Software for the Assessment and Follow-Up of Functional Autonomy in Geriatrics," BMC Geriatrics, 7:2 (February 2007).

11. S.M. Gallagher, "Competency in Informed Consent," *Ostomy Wound Damage*, 45:12 (December 1999), pp. 8–9.

12. C. Frank, D.K. Heyland, B. Chen, D. Farquhar, K. Myers, and K. Iwaasa, "Determining Resuscitation Preferences of Elderly Inpatients: A Review of the Literature," *Canadian Medical Association Journal*, 169:8 (October 2003), pp. 795–799; M. Gordon, "Ethical Challenges in End-of-Life Therapies in the Elderly," *Drugs and Aging*, 19:5, pp. 321–329.

13. G.W. Ruhnke, S.R. Wilson, T. Akamatsu, T. Kinoue, Y. Takashima, M.K. Goldstein, B.A. Koenig, J.C. Hornberger, and T.A. Raffin, "Ethical Decision Making and Patient Autonomy: A Comparison of Physicians and Patients in Japan and the United States," *Chest*, 118:4 (October 2000), pp. 1172–82.

14. V. Mallardi, "The Origin of Informed Consent," *Acta Otorhinolaryngologica Italica*, 25:5 (October 2005), pp. 312–327.

15. Raanan Gillon, "Consent," *British Medical Journal*, 291:6510 (December 14, 1985), pp. 1700–1701.

16. A. Akkad, C. Jackson, S. Kenyon, M. Dixon-Woods, N. Taub, and M. Habiba, "Patients' Perceptions of Written Consent: Questionnaire Study," *British Medical Journal*, 333:7567 (September 9, 2006), p. 528.

17. A.K. Sanwal, S. Kumar, P. Sahni, and S. Nundy, "Informed Consent in Indian Patients," *Journal of the Royal Society of Medicine*, 89:4 (April 1996), pp. 196–198.

18. C. Lavelle-Jones, D.J. Byrne, P. Rice, and A. Cuschieri, "Factors Affecting Quality of Informed Consent," *British Medical Journal*, 306:6887 (April 3, 1993), pp. 885–890.

19. D.J. Byrne, A, Napier, and A. Cuschieri, "How Informed is Signed Consent?" *British Medical Journal*, 296:6625 (March 19, 1988), pp. 839–840.

20. R.S. Morrison and D.E. Meier, "High Rates of Advance Care Planning in New Your City's Elderly Population," *Archives of Internal Medicine*, 164:22 (December 13–27, 2004), pp. 2421–2426.

Seven

INTERVENTION WITHOUT PATIENT CONSENT

Harry Lesser

A common moral dilemma in clinical practice, not only in dealing with elderly patients and clients, but, like loneliness, more likely to occur when the patient or client is elderly, is the problem of when it is right to intervene and apply treatment without the consent of the patient, or even against their expressed wishes. In this chapter, I would like to discuss this issue by considering two cases, both from the decade of the 1990s and both, as it happens, described by the medical practitioner involved in the course of a class in medical ethics.

The first case was described to me some years ago by a dentist in Manchester, who treated, among his other patients, the residents of a home for the elderly. One lady, of the generation with a deep fear of dental treatment, had a mouth full of ulcers, which were giving her much discomfort. When asked to open her mouth for inspection, leading perhaps to treatment, she would say "Yes," and give signs of understanding the request, but would not actually open her mouth, so that no inspection could be made or treatment offered. In the end the lady was put under heavy sedation, and the ulcers in her mouth were removed. She was much more comfortable, but the dentist still wondered whether he had the right do this for her by force.

The second case was described by a General Practitioner. One of his patients was an elderly widower, whose main wish was to join his wife in death, in her grave "under the apple tree." He did not wish to commit suicide, nor was he in a state of depression. Instead, he considered that the appropriate thing for him to do was, so to speak, to allow himself to rot, or to sink into death: he expressed this intention to the doctor very clearly, in somewhat poetic terms, and saw it as the correct and reasonable way to end his life. But the result was that he did not clean himself or his house, and simply allowed the uneaten food and ordure to pile up. The neighbors demanded with increasing violence that the doctor do something about the smell and the health hazard, whether by persuading the old man to clean himself and his house or by having him sectioned and taken compulsorily into hospital. The neighbors, it would seem, were convinced both that the man was acting irrationally and that this was a sufficient reason, given that other people were suffering because of his irrationality, for him to be declared legally incompetent and removed to hospital. The General Practitioner was by no means convinced on either point, but eventually, though with misgivings, he yielded to pressure and obtained an order to have the man taken compulsorily into hospital on the grounds of incompetence. The doctor visited him in the hospital that evening and his patient said to him "I've got a bone to pick with you: why didn't you bring me here sooner?" The next morning he was dead. The doctor does not know whether the comment was made because the patient was that much more comfortable or because he knew that, as often happens, as a result of the removal to hospital he was going to die very soon, and he welcomed the prospect.

In both of these cases the intervention was against the expressed wishes of the patient, but they were glad of it afterwards. In both, also, the patient was being to some degree irrational. The lady was suffering entirely needlessly; with the gentleman, though his aim of sinking gently into death was, given his situation, entirely reasonable, his way of achieving it was needlessly objectionable to his neighbors and perhaps to himself. The question is whether this is enough to make the intervention right. In the case of children, no one doubts that this is enough to justify overriding their current wishes. Indeed, if this were not done, they could as adults legitimately complain, "Why didn't you make me?" In the case of adults in full possession of their faculties, it is not enough, unless they are harming others. In the case of adults who may not be in full possession of their faculties, as with some (though a minority) of the elderly, there is uncertainty. Moreover, in many jurisdictions this uncertainty regarding the elderly shows itself in the law—not in the framing of the law, but in the way it is interpreted. A young or middle-aged adult can refuse treatment "irrationally" without this being taken as evidence of incompetence and grounds for treatment without consent. An elderly person may well find that they are differently treated, as did the two people whose cases are described here.

One may put the problem this way. The clearest case for intervention without patient consent occurs when the patient is unconscious and needs treatment. To wait for consciousness to be recovered is clearly absurd—in some cases, if the patient were not urgently treated they would never regain consciousness—and someone has to make the decision on their behalf. But, as even as fervent a libertarian as Thomas Szasz has admitted, it is possible for a person to be conscious and yet no more capable of any decision making than an unconscious person. Szasz's example (given in a television interview with Jonathan Miller in 1983) is of a person with advanced dementia, for example someone with advanced Alzheimer's disease; and this might be the only one he would admit. Most people, however, would add to this a number of conditions in which, unlike the person with dementia, someone can make a very clear decision but is in a condition in which they cannot make a rational decision, and may do themselves or others great harm. This can arise, for example, in delirium, through the influence of drugs or alcohol, or through serious mental illness.

But what should be done when none of these is the case, and the person is simply being irrational? First, can "irrational" mean more than "making a decision with which the doctor disagrees?" I suggest that it can, that it can mean acting in a way that is causing appreciable suffering, or risk of suffering or injury, to themselves or others, which (1) could be relieved or avoided and (2) is not necessary for any other purpose. This is clearly the case with the lady. I think it is also the case with the gentleman, and that his slow descent toward death could have been achieved without so much uncleanliness and disorder. This restricts the notion of irrationality, or of the kind of irrationality that justifies intervention, to irrationality by a person's own criteria. So on this definition a person who refuses painkillers because they wish to remain mentally alert is not being irrational, nor is a person who refuses treatment because for them death is welcome, though in this case the person needs to be encouraged to consider carefully whether they really have come to the end of the road. But a person who cannot or will not take some simple steps to improve their condition, when they would lose nothing by doing so, is displaying irrationality.

This, though, is not the only consideration. It might well be argued that irrationality alone cannot justify compulsory treatment of the elderly, and there must also be a strong likelihood that after they have been compulsorily treated they will be glad that the intervention took place, so that in one sense their wishes have not in the end been thwarted or violated. This, indeed, is not always easy to determine. But it can sometimes be fairly clear: in these two examples, the gentleman actually said he was glad (though this perhaps could not have been predicted beforehand) and the lady was left much more comfortable. So there remains a problem presented by these two cases: a problem of which the medical men involved were very aware, even though both of them did decide to intervene. The problem may be stated as follows. If an elderly person is not mentally ill in any way, or under the influence of alcohol or drugs, but nevertheless is refusing treatment which is very likely to be beneficial, has no aims or purposes with which the treatment would interfere, and on all the available evidence would be glad to have received the treatment, is this enough to justify a compulsory and enforced intervention? To refuse to intervene respects a person's wishes but savors of insensitivity to their comfort and well-being. To intervene is humane but paternalistic. Which should the conscientious doctor or nurse go for?

Eight

IS A GRAY WORLD DESIRABLE?

Simona Giordano

Indeed old age is believed to be miserable for four reasons: the first is the lack of activity; the second is the weakness of the body; the third is the absence of pleasures; the fourth is the fact that it is closer to death. Let us look, if you don't mind, at the strength of each of these reasons. Old age causes inactivity—but what activities does it prevent? [...] Are there no activities for the elderly, in which, in spite of a weaker body, the older can participate with the mind? The opinion of those who assert that elderly people are excluded from active life is groundless. It is like saying that the pilot does nothing because he sits and directs, whereas others [...] run here and there on the ship [...]. It is not with strength, agility or speed that great enterprises are realised, but with wisdom, authority and teaching. And of these, old age is not devoid, but, indeed, richer. [...] They say that memory becomes weaker. Of course, but only if it is not exercised, or if by nature one is not bright. Themistocles knew all his fellow citizens by name, and I know not only all my living fellow citizens, but also their fathers and grandfathers [...] Sophocles composed tragedies till he was very old, and because this occupation seemed to lead him to neglect his family interests, he was brought before the tribunal, and they were asked that he be declared unfit to manage the family's properties, as if he had become imbecile. The story is that he performed his last tragedy to the judges [...] and asked them if they thought that to be the produce of an imbecile; and the judges found in his favour. [...] It is not white hair or wrinkles that give us authority: it is a life conducted honourably. You will object that old people are extravagant, disquieted, tense, irascible, or even stingy, but these are defects of character, and not of age [...] and besides, these defects might be somehow not justified, but understandable. Old people fear being neglected, disvalued, ridiculed: to a frail body, every little blow is painful.

Cicero, *De Senectute* (On Old Age)

This passage contains an account of some of the worries about old age which concerned people in Cicero's time. The same worries concern people today, more than 2,000 years on. Cicero understood that many of these worries are exaggerated and misplaced, and that they are the product either of misrepresentation of old age and poor recognition of the value of the elderly or of a culture that tends to devalue and marginalize the elderly. This understandably causes fears and anxieties in the older person. Like Cicero, many throughout human history have written about and discussed old age, often trying to highlight the good that this season carries. However, old age continues to worry us, to remind us of our finitude, our ineluctable descent toward death. Old age worries not only individuals, but also our collective psychology, our concern about what is going to happen to our planet, given that the elderly are becoming the largest section of society.

1. Introduction

The growing presence of elderly people in societies is the result of one of the greatest triumphs of humankind.[1] The human species has always fought to postpone death, as seen in the myths of the philosopher's stone and the elixirs of long life and immortality. Science has had a crucial role in this. Not only do a much larger percentage of the human species reach the "natural span" of seventy or eighty than used to be the case, but stem cell science is now offering the hope that we can correct the effects of ageing, replacing dead or damaged tissues and even organs with younger versions. In this way, people in the next generation could live beyond 120, the current maximum life expectancy, to perhaps 150 or beyond. Further into the future, more radical prolongation of life is possible. However, we are unlikely to obliterate ageing entirely, but are more likely to postpone the effects of biological ageing and thus increase the proportion of older people in the population.

Indeed, an unprecedented rapid increase in the proportion of older persons is being observed. According to World Health Organization (WHO) estimates, the population aged sixty and over is growing faster than any other age group. It is expected that by 2025 there will be a growth in older persons of some 694,000,000, so passing from 605,000,000 people aged sixty or more in 2000 to 1,200,000,000 in 2025. By 2050 a population of 2,000,000,000 people over sixty years old is expected. Population ageing is linked both to a decline in the proportion of children and young people and to an increase in the proportion of people aged sixty or over. In turn, this is due on the one hand to a decline in fertility rates and on the other to an increase in longevity. The largest proportion of people aged sixty or over is in Europe.[2]

The prolongation of human life raises profound issues about intergenerational justice and what we owe future generations, and about whether such long lives would be meaningful to the persons who live them. Will the labor force be able to assist the ever growing proportion of older people? Will the healthcare systems be able to cope with the demands posed by the elderly? And is a "gray world" desirable, overall?

I will show that these worries are exaggerated and misplaced. The value added by the elderly to society is often underestimated; and, in addition to this, there are strategies to be implemented to ensure that the elderly do not become a burden and are not perceived as such. There are many different ways in which old age could be made more desirable, but I propose that we should start off with simple and practicable steps: prevention of diseases (including promotion of physical activity), intergenerational dialog, and promotion of research with significant import for affecting the ageing process.

2. The Burden of Care

Old age is sometimes considered as a season of illness, disability, poor quality of life, unproductiveness, and dependency, and elderly people are often perceived and feared as a burden falling disproportionately on the working population.[3] Until 2000, the European Union did not express particular concern over who should care for the elderly in a graying world. In the OECD document *The Welfare State in Crisis* the issue of long-term care was given only marginal coverage.[4]

Where long-term care is part of the state's responsibility, this represents a significant public expenditure. For example in Sweden (where local authorities are responsible for the care of the elderly), in 1997 long-term care represented as much as 27% of the municipalities' total expenses. Care for the older person, in many European countries, has been traditionally an integral part of family responsibilities. However, factors such as the increase in life expectancy, the growing participation of women in the labor market, the greater incidence of divorce, increased geographical mobility, and the changes in moral values in family life have reduced the family's capacity to provide long-term care, and the community (institutions, organizations, and paid care) is called in to help. One consequence of this is that public long-term expenditure may well have to increase.

Although it is indisputable that if the responsibility of the dependent elderly is placed on the state and if the number of frail older people increases, then public long-term expenditure increases, it is a mistake to deduce from this that if people live longer this will cause more public long-term care and higher public expenditure. Not all older people are frail, dependent, and in need of assistance, and there is every hope that the proportion who are will decrease if the right steps are taken.

At present many older people continue to work in either the formal or informal labor sectors.[5] The elderly often take responsibility for household management and childcare, which allows younger adults to work outside the home. In this way, the elderly actively contribute to the labor market and to the flourishing of our society. Older people often offer the skills and experience accumulated during their working life in the voluntary sector, acting as volunteers in schools, communities, religious institutions, business, and health and political organizations. Many elderly people, then, far from being a "burden" for society, provide an important contribution to the development of the community, and ultimately benefit the overall economy.

3. The Burden of Healthcare

The growing numbers of older people in industrialized and developing countries is producing changes in disease patterns and consequently in the demands for healthcare services. Non-communicable diseases (NCDs) have become the leading causes of death in industrialized countries.[6] NCDs are often chronic conditions, and it has been observed that it has become notably less common for people to die immediately from their diseases, so that they live with them sometimes for long periods.[7] The main NCDs affecting the elderly are listed in Box 1.

BOX 1: NCDS[8]
Cardiovascular diseases
Hypertension
Stroke
Diabetes
Cancer
Chronic obstructive pulmonary disease
Musculoskeletal conditions (such as arthritis and osteoporosis)
Mental health conditions (mostly dementia and depression)
Blindness and visual impairment

NCDs may be significant and costly causes of disability and reduced quality of life.[9] They can be expensive to treat, and long-lasting.[10]

It is a fact that NCDs affect older people more than they do younger people. However, old age in itself does not automatically bring increased illness and healthcare costs. What is costly is not "old age," but disability and poor health. Disability and poor health are often linked to old age, but they are not a function of chronological age. NCDs are to a large extent preventable, and consequently medical spending may not increase as rapidly as is sometimes thought in a graying world.[11] In a number of countries, indeed, falls in the level of disability among the elderly have been registered.[12] This decline is thought to result from preventive measures,[13] improved medical technology,[14] better control of hypertension, and medical innovations, both technological, such as open heart surgery, and institutional, such as special coronary care units in hospitals.[15]

The WHO argues that:

> Research in countries with aged populations has shown that ageing *per se* is not likely to lead to healthcare costs that are spiralling out of control, for two reasons.
>
> First, according to OECD data, the major causes of escalating healthcare costs are related to circumstances that are unrelated to the demographic ageing of a given population .... There appears to be considerable scope for policy makers to ... improve the effectiveness of healthcare. Second, the costs of long-term care can be managed if policies and programmes address prevention and the role of informal care. Policies and health promotion programmes that prevent chronic diseases and lessen the degree of disability among older citizens enable them to live independently longer.[16]

The view that a graying world might represent an unbearable burden is therefore based on false assumptions. But there are also active measures that could be taken by society (state, regions, and communities), to ensure that older people both do not become, and are not treated as, a burden.[17] The main steps, as mentioned above, are:

- Prevention of diseases and disability
- Promotion of intergenerational dialog
- Openness toward scientific research

4. Step 1: Prevention of Disease and Disability

NCDs are largely preventable. According to an OECD report, a number of countries have included the implementation of a prevention-oriented paradigm among the key policies of public health. This paradigm includes improving health education, changing health behavior, expanding access to healthcare, expanding primary care services, and addressing risks to health (for example, by an anti-smoking campaign or a campaign encouraging a healthy lifestyle).[18]

Sam Shapiro points out that:

> prevention of disease and relief from distress due to adverse health conditions have been major objectives of public health. Primary prevention that seeks to eliminate specific diseases and other departures from good health is central to goals in the field of public health. Immunisation against childhood diseases, anti-smoking campaigns and reduction of environmental pollutants are examples of long-standing activities in which the practitioners of public health have exerted great influence.[19]

Healthy ageing begins at birth, and is not the result of a set of interventions aimed specifically at "the third age." The factors that are responsible for the onset of NCDs and that are controllable are in part behavioral, in part psychological, in part sociological, and in part environmental. Tobacco smoking, for example, increases the risk of stroke and lung cancer, accelerates the decline of bone density, muscular strength, and respiratory capacity, and so may lead to important losses of functional capacity. Excessive alcohol consumption and a diet high in saturated fats and salt and low in vitamins and fiber are also associated with higher risk of NCDs. From a psychological and sociological point of view, both decline in cognitive capacity and the sense of loneliness are often related, in the elderly, to the loss of relatives and close friends. In their turn, lack of participation in activities and social isolation are related to a higher risk of disability, both physical and mental. These factors can be modified, and they do not automatically "come with age."

The environment is also at times a cause of NCDs, rather than chronological age. Musculoskeletal conditions, one of the major afflictions for the elderly, often result from accidents such as falls, fires, and traffic collisions. An unsafe environment increases the chance of injury. A safe environment should include safe housing, and the provision of essential services and means of transport, which may make it possible for the older person to be independent as much as possible and for as long as possible, and to prevent isolation. The *Brasilia Declaration on Ageing* recommends that:

> [a]ll actions must … take into account the bio-physical, social, psychological, economic, and environmental determinants of health. Policies across sectors [of local government and its employees] must be coordinated and harmonized.[20]

For example, information about active ageing should be incorporated into training programs for all health and social workers, as well as city planners and architects.[21]

It will be objected that many NCDs are to a large extent genetic conditions. While this is true, whether or not a genetic predisposition will actually result in the appearance of the disease often depends on environmental factors and lifestyle (and luck of course). The National Service Framework, in England, has recommended a number of policies and key actions aimed at preventing the onset of NCDs, of which the most relevant are:

- Improving the standards of care in care homes (a Commission has been appointed, to control the improvement of care in nursing homes);

- Extending access to services (for example, free sight tests for those aged sixty and over, improved access to cataract services, extension of breast-screening programs to women aged up to seventy);
- Ensuring free nursing care for people in nursing homes;
- Providing free influenza immunization for people aged sixty-five and over;
- Promoting oral health (for example, with specific campaigns);
- Developing services which support independence.

Improving the older person's ability to function independently appears to "reduce the need for emergency hospital admission and decrease the need for premature admission to a residential care setting."[22] It consequently decreases public long-term expenditure. Physical activity is also one of the major ways in which NCDs can be prevented.

A. Physical Activity

Whereas we all know that keeping fit is good, the importance of physical activity both for the individual and for society is often underestimated in ethics literature. Physical activity has a direct positive impact on the older person's quality of life, and on public spending.

Physical inactivity costs the national health services as much as smoking. It has been shown that physically active people incur fewer direct medical costs than inactive people (the difference was estimated at $330 per person, based on 1987 dollars). If all inactive Americans became physically active, this could produce a saving of some 76,600,000,000 dollars (at the 2000 valuation of the dollar).[23] Physically active people have fewer periods in hospital, go to the doctor less frequently, and use less medication than inactive people. The most remarkable difference is among women aged fifty-five and over. How does physical activity prevent the onset of NCDs?

B. Physical Activity and NCDs

i. Musculoskeletal Injuries

Falls are one of the major causes of disability and the leading cause of mortality due to injury in people aged over seventy-five. In England, 400,000 older people attend Accident and Emergency wards because of an accident and up to 14,000 people die every year following an osteoporotic hip fracture. It is estimated that one in three women and one in twelve men over fifty suffer from osteoporosis, and that 50% of women experience an osteoporotic fracture by the age of seventy. The fear of falling may also affect the quality of life, providing a significant limitation of daily activities.[24]

The effects of falls depend to an important extent on loss of bone mineral density.[25] Bone mineral density decreases to some extent physiologically with age. Proportionally, the risk of bone fractures increases.[26] Loss of bone mineral density, also known as osteoporosis, begins at around age forty, and mainly afflicts women, due to particular hormonal changes that affect them especially after their forties. Weight-bearing exercise is a standard treatment for this condition. But exercise has also a major role in prevention of falls.[27] In fact, bone mineral loss can be slowed down significantly with exercise. Moreover, muscular strength, neuromuscular coordination and postural stability, which also contribute to the prevention of falls,[28] can all be improved with regular physical activity.[29]

Bone mineral density also depends on muscle mass. After the age of thirty, the size and number of muscle cells decreases. This decline contributes to an increased risk of falls and consequent fractures. Activities such as walking, climbing stairs, and overall mobility rely on leg muscular strength, and when this is poor, the person clearly becomes more dependent and increasingly frail. The elderly person's quality of life is thus to an important extent dependent on leg muscular strength. Loss of strength, and the ill health that results from this, is not an inevitable outcome of age, and older people can do effective strength training programs to recover leg muscular mass and regain independence. Research shows that after only six months' strength training, muscular strength increases by 9% (lower body) and 18% (upper body) in people aged seventy to seventy-nine.[30]

ii. Reduced Mobility

Loss of mobility may mean dependency. Mobility clearly has a direct influence on a person's functional capacity and quality of life. The first age- related changes that affect mobility are anthropometric changes. They are related to both stature and the joint range of motion. People between sixty-five and seventy-four years old are approximately 3% shorter than people between eighteen and twenty-four years old. This is likely to depend on the shortening of intervertebral disc spaces and resulting kyphosis. The range of motion of the joints also declines physiologically. In addition, decrements in the sensory-motor system produce a decline in postural balance. Poor balance, posture, and physical coordination may clearly also increase the risk of injuries or falls due to wrong movements.[31]

Deterioration of the musculoskeletal system is, however, preventable with gymnastic and physical activity. There are specifically designed physical activities to improve the range of motion, balance, co-ordination, and skeletal flexibility. It is therefore mistaken to assume that these deteriorations are the irremediable consequences of age, and an inevitable part of what it means to be older.

iii. Metabolic Diseases

The steady decline in metabolic rates observed as a person gets older is now believed to depend upon a decrease in muscle mass, which is generally the result of both the physiological response to ageing and of the person's becoming less active. Maintaining good metabolic fitness is important in order to prevent obesity, which is often associated with greater risk of coronary heart diseases and diabetes (type II). Energy metabolism can be improved significantly with exercise, and so again reduction of metabolic rates can be delayed, prevented, and contained.

Among the metabolic changes that affect us all, as we age, those relating to glucose metabolism are particularly worrisome. Poor glucose tolerance may lead to diabetes (Type II, which generally occurs after age forty), which is characterized by variable degrees of insulin resistance and relative insulin deficiency. In its later stages, diabetes is associated with a number of serious disorders that have a great impact upon a person's quality of life (for example, blindness, kidney diseases, heart diseases, stroke, and peripheral vascular diseases severe enough to result in the amputation of the leg or the foot). Physical inactivity increases the risk. Exercise improves the glucose metabolism, and so not only can prevent metabolic diseases, but can also assist in the treatment of those who have contracted them.

iv. Cardiovascular Diseases

Epidemiological studies show that physical activity reduces the risk of death from cardiac disease by twenty to twenty-five per cent among people with established heart diseases.[32] Positive changes are manifested in cardiovascular efficiency, blood lipids, blood pressure, and thrombotic tendency.[33] Physical activity may have a direct effect on the heart, as it may increase oxygen supply and improve myocardial contraction and electrical stability. Moreover, physical activity increases the diameter of the coronary arteries and this also contributes to reduction of blood pressure at rest (both systolic and diastolic). Blood lipid profile is also positively affected.

What is more, regular exercise prevents occurrence of cardiovascular diseases in those predisposed to them. This is one of the clear cases in which genetics and biology can be, to an important extent, controlled with behavior. A person initially "at risk," because of her family history, can turn out to be a "fitter than average" person.

In short, illnesses of the cardiovascular system, which, it is worth remembering, are the leading cause of death in industrialized countries, are to an important extent preventable. Therefore, it is simply a mistake to believe that they are the inevitable consequence of age.

v. Mental Illnesses

Dementia and depression are two major afflictions of the older person. They go often unnoticed, as what is a preventable and curable disease is mistaken for an inevitable consequence of ageing.[34]

Whereas there are extensive studies on the connection between physical activity and mental health in young and middle-aged people, not so extensive is the research on the connection between physical activity and mental health in older people. From studies in gerontology, it may be inferred that regular physical activity helps to maintain and improve functional ability, health, and mental well-being of the older person.[35] It has also been noticed that people who practice regular aerobic exercise tend to suffer from depression less than inactive people, although it has been impossible to establish what the causal connection is between the two. Some studies suggest that exercise may make elderly people able to cope independently, and may thereby enhance their self-esteem and confidence, which, in turn, may help to prevent or reduce depression.[36] Physical exercise is also considered as a treatment for anxiety. It is associated with improved general satisfaction and well-being.[37] Moreover, physical activity is associated with better social adjustment and cognitive functioning. It may enrich the social life of the elderly, as it may be a way of meeting with other people. Social participation affects greatly the quality of our life, and isolation is associated with higher mortality among elderly people.[38] Finally, physical activity has significant financial benefits.

C. Physical Activity and Savings

Better ageing has a positive impact on medical spending. Older people (and people of all ages) participating regularly in physical activities would mean:

- Fewer premature deaths (people dying at the highly productive stages of their lives);
- Fewer chronic disabilities at later stages of life;
- Improvements in the quality of life of ageing people;
- More people actively participating in social, cultural, economic, and political life;
- More people actively contributing to the labor market (either informal or formal);
- Lower costs related to medical treatment and care services;[39]
- Fewer emergency admissions to hospital and premature admissions to long-term residential care settings.[40]

D. Key Actions

Physical activity can be promoted by relatively simple key actions:

- Provision of safe areas for walking;
- Provision of well-lit streets;
- Provision of adequate sidewalks (together with pedestrian traffic lights that have sufficient duration for the elderly);
- Support for community activities that encourage physical activity;
- Provision of recreational services that offer elderly people exercise programs that help them to maintain their mobility;
- Inclusion of information and education about ageing in the training programs of healthcarers, social carers, recreational workers, city planners, and architects;[41]
- Improvement of the location and appearance of stairwells to encourage walking when at work instead of using lifts;
- Provision of sidewalks and cycle tracks close to residential areas, to encourage walking or cycling as a part of daily activity;
- Easy access to information and education about the benefits of physical activity.[42]

A process of prevention of diseases commonly related to old age should be seen as an integral part of respect for the older person's dignity. Universal ethical principles supposedly shared by EU countries with regard to the care of the older person (dignity, life, and integrity) remain only abstract and empty concepts, mere unfulfilled ideals, unless a policy directed at improving people's lives is implemented. When a policy involves relatively minor costs and high benefits for all (older and younger), it is clearly morally irresponsible not to endorse it.

The next step to prevent the older person from being perceived as a burden or from becoming a burden is the promotion of intergenerational dialog.

5. Step 2: Intergenerational Dialog

The WHO has recognized the importance of intergenerational dialog in order to promote the older person's quality of life.[43] When, as in many Asian countries, extended families live in multigenerational households, intergenerational dialog is simply part of daily life. In many European countries, where the nuclear family has replaced the extended family, intergenerational dialog has to be a conscious choice.[44]

The WHO has advised that schools and communities provide intergenerational activities such as training in new technologies for the older person and opportunities for lifelong learning.[45] This would allow the older person to have some interests in common with younger generations, to have richer communication with younger generations, to exercise his or her skills (memory, learning, and cognitive capacities) and to continue to contribute to the changing labor market.

Intergenerational solidarity could also be enhanced by "supporting traditional societies and community groups run by older people, voluntarism, neighbourhood helping, peer monitoring and visiting, family caregivers, intergenerational programmes and outreach services".[46] Intergenerational dialog promotes the transmission of values between different age groups and a more positive and realistic attitude of the younger toward the older.

It is important to note that giving fair value and place to the elderly benefits all generations, and not only the older generation. Negative discrimination against the elderly differs from other forms of discrimination in an important way. Discrimination against people of a different color, for example, is made by those who will never have the color of the discriminated group. Discrimination against children is operated by adults, who will never become children again. Discrimination against women is operated by men, and so on. In the case of the older generation, a culture of disvalue disadvantages both the discriminated and the discriminating group. Today's young or middle-aged adult will be "the elderly" of tomorrow. No age group benefits from a culture which devalues old age. It has also been noted that old people have a growing electoral power,[47] and it is consequently important that a balance of values is recognized reciprocally, in order for all members of the human family to have an equally pleasant place in society.

6. Step 3: Openness to Genetic and Cellular Research

Step three might seem unrelated to the discourse of this paper, as genetic and cellular research has generated all sorts of debates in ethics and public policy: whether it can be right to manipulate the human being, whether it can be right to use embryos, whether these scientific developments will have long-term disastrous effects on humankind, and so on. However, whether and how genetic and cellular research develops will have a strong impact on how people age.

The twentieth century saw a marked improvement in the health of the population. But the extension of life expectancy has caused an upsurge in the occurrence of chronic conditions such as heart disease, stroke, cancer, diabetes, Alzheimer's, and arthritis. If genetic and cellular research realized the hopes set out below, this would mean that many NCDs would be reversed, many elderly people would be freed from the illnesses that affect them, and many people would live longer and not be dependent on others. This would impact upon debates on resource allocation and the role of age in the distribution of healthcare resources. But, more importantly, it would mean that many afflictions that affect mainly the elderly would be improved or controlled. According to the UK Department of Health, these are the treatments that stem cell therapy might offer:[48]

CELL TYPE	TARGET DISEASE
Neural (nerve cells)	Stroke, Parkinson's Disease, Alzheimer's Disease, Spinal cord injury, Multiple Sclerosis
Heart muscle cells	Heart attack, Congestive heart failure
Insulin producing cells	Diabetes
Cartilage cells	Osteoarthritis
Blood cells	Cancer, Immunodeficiencies, Inherited blood diseases, Leukemia
Liver cells	Hepatitis, Cirrhosis
Skin cells	Burns, Wound healing
Bone cells	Osteoporosis
Retinal (eye) cells	Macular degeneration
Skeletal muscle cells	Muscular dystrophy

On the basis of the animal research and limited research on human cells undertaken to date, most of these targets are considered realistic prospects. Examples of application of stem cell therapies to age-related conditions are the use of stem cells to repair nerve cells lost in Parkinson's disease and Alzheimer's disease. Another example is the use of stem cells to replace insulin-producing cells in diabetes, or to replace lost heart muscle cells in cases of congestive heart failure, or bone cells in osteoporosis.

Unfortunately some countries have banned, or put in place serious obstacles to, the development of this field of research. Two procedures raise particular concerns: the use (and creation) of human embryos for research, and the development of Cell Nuclear Replacement techniques (CNR).

Legislation on embryonic stem cell research and CNR varies across Europe and worldwide, and this seems consistent with the fact that there are differing and opposing sentiments, attitudes, and moral beliefs around the moral status of the embryo and, more generally, around genetic and cellular research. New regulations may have legal implications, as they may require a revision of current national legislation on fertilization, embryology, and abortion.

There has, however, been one issue over which consensus has (at least apparently) been reached almost immediately. As soon as the news of the birth of Dolly the sheep was released, in 1997, national and international organizations, such as UNESCO and the Council of Europe, lined up to ban the use of CNR for human reproduction.

> Practices which are contrary to human dignity, such as reproductive cloning of human beings, shall not be permitted.[49]

> Any intervention seeking to create a human being genetically identical to another human being, whether living or dead, is prohibited.[50]

Of course CNR was also immediately recognized as a precious instrument for genetic and cellular research. If CNR techniques were perfected, it would be possible to create blastocysts from which stem cells could be harvested, without having to engage with the ethical, theological, and sometimes political issues relating to the use of an embryo for scientific purposes. Some, however, asked what the difference is between a blastocyst derived from a fertilized egg and one derived from CNR. Some were even worried that if CNR techniques were perfected, this, on a slippery slope, might lead unscrupulous scientists to use the technique for reproductive purposes. John Harris and I have explored the technical and ethical issues surrounding genetic and cellular research elsewhere.[51] We have discussed the potential of stem cell research and the technical problems that need to be surmounted before many of these can be applicable to humans. We also discussed the use of adult stem cells, which now appears to attract many scientists.[52] What matters here is that the diatribes against stem cell therapy, sometimes characterized by highly metaphysical or exquisitely theological arguments, and the worries of the general public, sometimes fuelled by the media, sometimes by fiction, have all contributed to a significant curtailment of freedom of scientific research in some countries. This has had a deleterious impact on science generally, on scientists, and ultimately on the people who could benefit from these therapies, especially the elderly.

Legislation meant to ban or obstruct scientific research bears the responsibility of preventing or ostracizing potentially life-saving or life-enhancing treatments, and so the responsibility for condemning to misery, pain, and death people that could be saved, when there is no proof beyond any reasonable doubt that this sacrifice is somehow ethically necessary. Instead, promoting a culture of openness toward genetic and cellular research would contribute to rendering old age a flourishing season of life.

7. Conclusion

Many people perceive the elderly to be a burden, especially a care burden and healthcare burden. Not only is the pressure that the elderly are perceived to present exaggerated, it can also be further reduced. There are of course other strategies by which being old could be made more desirable, but I have proposed that we should start off with simple and realistic steps: prevention of diseases (here including promotion of physical activity), dialog, and promotion of research with significant import for affecting the ageing process.[53]

As Cicero recognized over 2,000 years ago, the elderly are easily made the object of ridicule and contempt. Ageism describes the discrimination against the elderly. Ageism is not only an attack on the dignity and the worth of the elderly, it is also likely to diminish their own sense of value and their quality of life. But in addition, ageism brings no good to younger generations, because we all will, hopefully, be elderly one day, and so none of us should want to live in a society where the elderly are discriminated against, and regarded as a burden.

The growing proportion of elderly people is the sign of the achievements of humankind in extending life and improving life conditions. This growth means that all of us get a better chance to live longer. This is to be celebrated as one of our greatest accomplishments, and the contribution that the older people offer to society is to be appreciated, promoted, and defended.

NOTES

1. World Health Organization, *Active Ageing: A Policy Framework* (Geneva: World Health Organization, 2002), p. 6.

2. *Ibid.*; A. Kalache and I. Keller, "The Graying World: A Challenge for the Twenty-First Century," *Science Progress*, 83:1 (February 2000), pp. 33–54.

3. Anthea Tinker, *Older People in Modern Society* (London: Longman, 1997).

4. World Health Organization, *Home-Based and Long-Term Care: Report of a WHO Study Group*. Available at http://whqlibdoc.who.int/trs/WHO_TRS_898.pdf.

5. World Health Organization, *Active Ageing*, p. 9.

6. *Ibid.*, p. 14.

7. David W. Kalisch, Tetsuya Aman, Libbie A. Buchele, *Social and Health Policies in OECD Countries: A Survey of Current Programmes and Recent Developments* (Paris: OECD, 1998), § 7.1.

8. World Health Organization, *Life in the 21st Century: A Vision for All* (Geneva: World Health Organization, 1998).

9. World Health Organization, *Active Ageing*, p. 34.

10. World Health Organization, "Healthy Ageing is Vital for Development," WHO Press Release WHO/24, 9 April 2002.

11. World Health Organization, *Active Ageing*, p. 17.

12. Stephan Jacobzone and Howard Oxley, "Ageing and Healthcare Costs," *International Politics and Society*, 1 (January 2002). http://library.fes.de/pdf-files/ipg/ipg-2002-1/artjacobzone-oxley.pdf.

13. World Health Organization, *Active Ageing*, p. 35.

14. David M. Cutler, "Declining Disability Among the Elderly," *Health Affairs*, 20:6 (November/December 2001), pp. 11–27.

15. Victor R. Fuchs, "Though Much is Taken—Reflections on Aging, Health, and Medical Care," *Milbank Memorial Fund Quarterly*, 62:2 (June 1984), pp. 143–166.

16. World Health Organization, *Active Ageing*, p. 42.

17. Simona Giordano, "Healthcare Rationing: Demographic Revolution and Inescapable Consequences," *Cambridge Quarterly of Healthcare Ethics*, 14:1 (January 2005), pp. 83–92.

18. Kalisch *et al.*, *Social and Health Policies in OECD Countries*, pp. 337, 343, and 346.

19. Sam Shapiro, "Screening for Secondary Prevention of Disease," *Epidemiology and Health Services*, eds. Haroutune K. Armenian and Sam Shapiro (New York, NY: Oxford University Press, 1998), pp. 183–206.

20. World Health Organization, *Brasilia Declaration on Ageing* (Geneva: World Health Organization, 1996).

21. World Health Organization, *Active Ageing*, p. 39.

22. Department of Health, *National Service Framework for Older People* (London: Department of Health, 2001), pp. 8 and 10.

23. Michael Pratt, Caroline A. Macera, and Guijing Wang, "Higher Direct Medical Costs Associated with Physical Inactivity," *The Physician and Sportsmedicine*, 28:10 (October 2000), pp. 63–70; World Health Organization, http://www.who.int/dietphysicalactivity/publications/facts/pa/en/.

24. Department of Health, *National Service Framework for Older People*, p. 17.

25. World Health Organization, *Growing Older, Staying Well: Ageing and Physical Activity in Everyday Life* (Geneva: World Health Organization, 1998), pp. 6–7.

26. S. Cheng, H. Suominen, R. Sakari-Rantala, P. Laukkanen, V. Avikainen, and E. Heikkinen, "Calcaneal Bone Mineral Density Predicts Fracture Occurrence: A Five-Year Follow-Up Study in Elderly People," *Journal of Bone and Mineral Research*, 12:7 (July 1997), pp. 1075–1082.

27. World Health Organization, *Active Ageing*, p. 28.

28. P. Dargent-Molina, F. Favier, H. Grandjean, C.Baudoin, A. Schott. E. Hausherr, P. Meunier, and G. Bréart, "Fall-Related Factors and Risk of Hip Fracture: The EPIDOS Prospective Study," *The Lancet*, 348:9021 (20 July 1996), pp. 145–149.

29. World Health Organization, *Active Ageing*, p. 28.

30. World Health Organization, *Growing Older*, p. 5.

31. *Ibid.*, p. 5.

32. C. Noel Bairey Merz, Alan Rozanski, and James S. Forrester, "The Secondary Prevention of Coronary Artery Disease," *The American Journal of Medicine*, 102:6 (June 1997), pp. 572–581.

33. World Health Organization, *Growing Older*, p. 6.

34. Department of Health, *National Service Framework for Older People*, p. 19.

35. J.M. Ruuskanen and I. Ruopilla, "Physical Activity and Psychological Well-Being Among People Aged 65 to 84 Years," *Age and Ageing*, 24:4 (July 1995), pp. 292–296.

36. Patrick J. O'Connor, Louis E. Aenchbacher III, and Rod. K. Dishman, "Physical Activity and Depression in the Elderly," *Journal of Aging and Physical Activity*, 1:1 (October 1993), pp. 34–58.

37. World Health Organization, *Growing Older*, p. 9.

38. H. Sugisawa, J. Liang, and X. Liu, "Social Network, Social Support, and Mortality Among Older People in Japan," *Journal of Gerontology*, 49:1 (1994), pp. 3–13.

39. World Health Organization, *Active Ageing*, p. 16.

40. Department of Health, *National Service Framework for Older People*, p. 8.

41. World Health Organization, *Active Ageing*, pp. 23, 37, and 39.

42. *Ibid.*, p. 37.

43. World Health Organization, *Active Ageing*, pp. 29, 44, 46, 54, 52; World Health Organization, *Brasilia Declaration*; World Health Organization, "Healthy Ageing is Vital for Development."

44. World Health Organization, *Active Ageing*, p. 20.

45. *Ibid.*, p.52.

46. *Ibid.*, p. 28.

47. Fuchs, "Though Much is Taken," p. 144.

48. Department of Health, *Stem Cell Research: Medical Progress with Responsibility* (London: Department of Health, 2000).

49. UNESCO, *Universal Declaration on the Human Genome and Human Rights* (Paris: UNESCO, 1997), Article 11.

50. Council of Europe, *Additional Protocol to the Convention on Human Rights and Biomedicine on the Prohibition of Cloning Human Beings* (Paris: Council of Europe, 1998), Article 1.

51. Simona Giordano and John Harris, "On Cloning," *The New Routledge Encyclopaedia of Philosophy Online*, ed. Edward Craig.

52. "Skin Transformed into Stem Cells," BBC News Online, 20 November 2007, http://news.bbc.co.uk/1/hi/health/7101834.stm.

53. Nick Bostrom, "The Fable of the Dragon Tyrant," *Journal of Medical Ethics*, 31:5 (May 2005), pp. 273 277.

Nine

PERSONAL DEVELOPMENT IN OLD AGE

John Hostler

1. Introduction: Giving Objective Content to the Concept of Personal Development in Old Age

If you ask people—especially young people—how they picture old age, most of them will tell you that they see it as a time of enfeeblement and decline. Their image of an old person is of someone whose hearing and eyesight are beginning to fail and who is becoming tottery, forgetful, and easily confused. This image is not new, of course: you have only to think of Shakespeare's "seven ages of man" speech, with its portrait of the old person "*sans* teeth, *sans* eyes, *sans* taste, *sans* everything,"[1] to be reminded that it has a long history. What is more recent is the acknowledgment that it has a sound basis in fact. The discipline of gerontology has given impetus to scientific investigations of ageing, and there is now plenty of evidence to confirm that most old people suffer various forms of impaired functioning.[2] Decay in short-term memory and in auditory and visual acuity are well documented, as are lengthening reaction times and a tendency to mental confusion; and many studies have mapped the ways in which old age is often characterized by increasing helplessness and dependency. Indeed, some gerontologists use these indicators to define the ageing process: "old age is *defined* by an individual's diminished ability to cope with the ordinary affairs of everyday life … without help [italics added]."[3] By this definition, "old age" denotes not so much a chronological period (although many writers agree that its onset in our society is usually around the age of seventy) as a process of decline and deterioration in personal ability.

So it may seem almost a contradiction to assert that personal development can occur during old age. Can a period of life that is characterized by decay and decline also be a time of development and growth? Many people affirm that this is possible. Most of us are acquainted with elderly individuals who would claim that they are still developing, and some of my colleagues who are professionally concerned with old people (as educators, medical practitioners, or counselors) say that this is not uncommon. So the assertion is often made, at least informally, that personal development does occur in old age. The philosophical question I address in this paper is whether that statement has objective meaning. Is it just a way of expressing a feeling of approval about some of the changes that occur in old age, or does it convey significant information about the kind of changes they are? If we are told that a woman in her eighties is still "developing as a person," can we infer anything about the way she is changing? To answer that question I will consider some familiar concepts of personal development and will examine how they might be applied to old people.

2. Clarifying the Concept of Personal Development in Old Age

It will help to start by reflecting on some of the criteria for an adequate concept of personal development in old age. One of these, obviously, is that it must concern development of the person: it must be about the person himself or herself, not just about changes in their body. When we talk about "the person" in this sense, we usually have in mind the distinctive attitudes, values, and outlook that characterize someone, which we refer to loosely and informally as their "personality." Within the discipline of psychology this is a much debated term, and one that designates an important field of investigation.[4] Informally, however, it denotes those aspects or elements of a person's character that are thought to underlie and somehow to account for their behavior. We use it as a concept with explanatory force: we talk about someone's personality when we are trying to make sense of what they have done ("he stormed out of the meeting because he's short-tempered") or are hoping to predict how they will behave ("watch out for her, she's so jealous"). Although phrases like these can be just a way of referring to frequent patterns of behavior, they can designate distinct and identifiable aspects of the psyche. The short-tempered man may have learned to control his irascibility much of the time, and keep it well hidden, but occasionally it may break out unbidden and betray him; the woman may struggle against her tendency to jealousy and be miserable at the way it wrecks her relationships. In contexts like these, our informal concept of "personality" refers to emotional traits, aspects of character, attitudes, and values that are relatively difficult to change, and that shape, direct, and so help to explain daily behavior.

If personality (in this informal sense) comprises such diverse elements, how does it develop? When we say that someone is developing as a person, what kind of changes do we have in mind? Once again we use an informal concept, different from that used by professional psychologists, for whom some aspects of "personality development" can be quantified and measured by means of tests and questionnaires.[5] When we talk about a headache developing, or the onset of a storm, we mean that the item in question is becoming bigger or more intense. This simple, informal sense of "development" cannot be applied straightforwardly to a collection of different elements, such as personality. It may be, of course, that one aspect of someone's personality "becomes greater" in the course of their development, but that can occur without the personality developing as a whole. So when Susan Hooker remarks (about the process of ageing) that "there are usually changes in personality, but only in the sense that previous traits become more exaggerated,"[6] she is acknowledging that particular elements of personality may "become greater," but is also intending to deny that personal development (in the more inclusive sense discussed here) occurs. For that to happen, we look for some novelty in the whole, over and above any increase or enlargement of particular aspects. Contrary to Hooker's claim, there probably are occasions when new traits appear, but novelty consists more often in the fact that existing elements in the personality combine and interact in new ways. For example, tensions within the psyche may be resolved, leading to a growing sense of inner calm as the person ages, or traits which were somewhat restrained in the person's earlier life may come to dominate, giving a new complexion to their personality as a whole. As James E. Birren suggests, personality development can be thought of as a process of cumulative growth, in which different aspects of the psyche develop and interact in complex ways to produce a gradual but discernible change in the whole.[7]

But clearly more is needed for an adequate description, for what has been said so far could equally well describe a process of deterioration. Consider for example a woman who becomes increasingly crabby and cantankerous in old age. Her friends and family begin to avoid her, so she becomes lonely. So she comes to feel ill-used and aggrieved, and becomes somewhat of a recluse. This is a comprehensible (and perhaps not uncommon) sequence of changes, and it satisfies the description given above of a cumulative process leading to a discernible difference, but we would hesitate to offer it as an example of "personal development." The reason is that, as the phrase is commonly used, it connotes a *desirable* process. We associate personal development with growth in maturity, wisdom, self-knowledge—all of them "good" characteristics: someone who is "developing as a person" is to be admired and perhaps even envied.

So far this discussion has identified three general conditions that must be satisfied by an adequate concept of personal development in old age. It must be about the development of "personality" as that term is generally (and rather loosely) understood; it must conceptualize a process of cumulative change; and it must interpret the process as one of betterment or improvement. A final condition to be mentioned here is that there must also be reasonably definite criteria for its use: we must know when the concept applies, when we have a case of personal development and when we do not. Without such criteria for use the concept would be vacuous, for a concept that could apply to any and every case would be a mere cipher. We must therefore be able to cite specific features in the life history of an elderly person as evidence that theirs is (or is not) a story of personal development in old age. For that to be possible, of course, these features must be identifiable and thus (in a familiar sense) "objective." Which features will count as relevant evidence, however, will depend on the concept of personal development we employ, since different conceptions of the process have different criteria. By way of illustration, and to introduce some further general issues, I will consider three concepts or "models" of personal growth which are most often used in thinking about personal development in old age.

3. Personal Development as Progress

The first, which in some ways is the simplest and most general, is the model of progress or advance. This is often used when we think about human development: for instance, in learning a subject or a skill we speak of "making progress," and we talk of a child's growth (psychological as well as physical) as "progressing" toward adulthood. In the same way an elderly person may describe their personal development as a sense of movement or advance, a feeling that they have not yet "come to a stop." But does this metaphor have any significant content? Such language can be vacuous: talk of "life's journey," for example, may just be a picturesque way of speaking about change, and does not necessarily capture the principle that change must be both cumulative and desirable in order to count as personal development. One way in which the metaphor of progress can be made more meaningful is by reference—implicit or explicit—to a "normal" path of development, a sequence of changes or a series of states though which most individuals are expected to pass.

A familiar example is the well known series of "milestones" in the growth of infants. Such a pattern would certainly allow us to speak meaningfully of personal development in old age, did it exist, but all studies, together with our own experience, confirm that in the later years of life there is no such common path.[8] The pattern of personal development, insofar as there is one, appears to be one of increasing diversity. In early years most children pass through roughly the same sequence of stages, but as they grow up and mature into adulthood their life histories become increasingly different. But if that is so, how can one speak meaningfully about "progress" and "advance" in old age? Clearly, if not by reference to a norm, then only by appealing to criteria within the life history of an individual.

Two such criteria suggest themselves. Prospectively, people have personal goals and aspirations, and they may be thought to be making progress insofar as they appear to be getting nearer their desired state. For example, a man might want to become more serene and detached as he ages, trying consciously to be less disturbed by everyday events. Necessarily he sees his goal as desirable, and therefore progress toward it counts as "improvement" by his own standards at least. Without doubt some elderly people strive toward personal aims like this, but there is evidence to suggest that many do not. As they get older and become more aware of the likelihood of death, people tend to think less in terms of "futurity," as Birren calls it.[9] They commonly spend less time thinking (or fantasizing) about "what I am going to do or become," and invest less energy in planning for the future. Instead, many old people develop a retrospective outlook, sometimes becoming quite preoccupied with the past. This need not be (although it sometimes is) maudlin reminiscence: as Birren also explains, elderly people often undertake a "life review," actively trying "to integrate one's life as it has been lived in relation to how it might have been lived."[10] They recall their past choices and decisions, the events that happened to them and how they reacted, asking (in effect) "If I could live my life again, would I do it differently?" Clearly, through such a review genuine progress can be discovered. For example a woman might realize how much she has developed by seeing how different she is now from the person she used to be. She no longer makes the same mistakes in her relationships, perhaps, or she has overcome personality traits (such as shyness) that used to hinder her.

4. Personal Development as Learning

Personal development in old age can be thought of in individual terms as a form of progress, as a movement either toward future goals or away from our past self. A second, closely related way of conceiving it is as a form of learning. Particularly influential here is a model of learning as a process of problem solving, for this underlies the notion of "successful" ageing that is favored by many gerontologists. The core of this idea is that the process of growing old confronts the individual with a series of "learning tasks": these are generated by changing conditions of life to which the individual must try to adapt. For example (to borrow from Robert C. Peck's list[11]), retirement from work is a challenge for many people. As they get older and the opportunity for work (paid and unpaid) diminishes, they are less able to feel useful to others (for example as a trusted colleague or as someone with valuable expertise), and this creates an emotional need to find alternative sources of self-esteem. Another challenge is presented by physical deterioration and the bodily infirmities of old age. When people can no longer enjoy active pursuits requiring strength or vigor, the sense of purely physical capability and achievement is diminished, and a corresponding need arises to find alternative sources of satisfaction—through social relationships, perhaps, or in cultural and intellectual pursuits.

Peck also discerns a need for people to transcend their own selves as the focus of interest and concern. He argues that as the limitations of self become more evident (both temporally and in other respects), people feel a need to find sources of interest in abiding things, larger than themselves. Not all individuals are able to make these adjustments, of course: some cling to work (even to the pretence of it), for example, in order to "feel useful"; others act and think as if they were immortal, refusing to make a will, for instance. But these, presumably, are "failures" in ageing: the "successful" ones are those who manage to "solve" these problems and adjust to their new circumstances and conditions of life.

In elaborating this kind of account of personal development in old age it will clearly not be hard to identify potential "problems" in the ageing process. Philosophically the difficulty lies rather in specifying the criteria for "success" so as to do justice to the notion of "change for the better." In some accounts the emphasis is merely on adapting to changed circumstances, but there may be several ways of doing that, and not all of them will be equally desirable. When a woman retires from work, for example, we could say that she "adapts" to her new circumstances by sitting at home, and reminiscing fruitlessly and increasingly bitterly about her past career. Terms like "adaptation" and "adjustment" are not sufficiently evaluative by themselves. That is why Bromley finds it necessary to write about "*good* adjustment [italics added],"[12] and why Eric Pfeiffer recommends "making adaptation to ageing a positive success,"[13] as if success could somehow be negative. But if these adjectives are to be sufficiently meaningful there must be some criterion by which to distinguish the "right" kind of adaptation from other forms of adjustment. One that is offered by many writers is essentially hedonistic. It consists in the view that people who overcome the problems of ageing can be identified by the fact that they remain happy and content. So, Pfeiffer says that people who "age successfully" are those who "have a good time in later years … far from complaining ... [they] have prepared for this phase of the life cycle and now welcome it."[14]

Elaborated in that way, this model too gives a definite, objective meaning to the notion of personal development in old age. Indeed, we could argue that the meaning is *too* definite, in that hedonistic criteria exclude important forms of personal growth. Consider a man, in his youth somewhat self-centered and complacent, who comes to care increasingly about people and the world around him. As he gets older he becomes ever more conscious of all that is wrong with the world and in need of improvement, and of time running out; and in old age he "rages against the dying of the light," regretful at how little he has accomplished when so much remains to be done. Such a man would scarcely meet Bromley's criteria of "happiness, confidence, ... self esteem"[15] but he could well be a remarkable instance of personal development in old age. Nevertheless, hedonistic criteria do paint a clear picture, and that is an important feature of this model. For as we have seen, the idea of personal development as a form of progress is purely schematic: it does not define the changes that are to count as progress, but leaves them to be determined by criteria derived from an individual's life history. In contrast, the "success" model offers a fairly complete picture of successful ageing, which functions as an ideal (albeit a limited one, perhaps) of what an old person should be like.

5. Personal Development as Self-Realization

The third model is that of self-realization. In outline, it conceives personal development as a process in which a person's self, which is thought of as being partly latent or concealed, becomes manifest, actual, or "real." The image is one of blossoming or unfolding, and the language derives ultimately from Aristotle's analysis of growth in nature and his view that when development occurs, that which was already "potentially" present in the organism becomes part of its actual being. Taken literally, this is not a very helpful way to conceive the processes of human development, for in practice this model is nearly always employed *ex post facto,* which deprives it of literal significance. Suppose, for instance, that someone "develops as a person" through a new interest or hobby which extends their knowledge and outlook. On the basis of this model we can say that the potential for this development must have been latent within them, but that claim evidently explains nothing and adds nothing to our understanding of what has taken place. Such judgments only give us useful information when we can identify potential *before* it is realized, and indeed use it to predict future developments. But that kind of forecasting about human beings is notoriously difficult, and there are relatively few cases in which it can be done with well-founded confidence. The best-known instance is probably the use of IQ tests which (to a limited extent, and only in aggregate) can give some indication of children's later academic attainments.[16]

As a metaphor, however, the model of self-realization has more value, directing our attention to aspects of personal development that other models may incline us to overlook. For example it reminds us that the process of development may be judged best by the person who is developing and who is aware of it "from the inside." By contrast, the "success" model considered earlier implies that an external observer could monitor not only the challenges of ageing but also an individual's adjustment to them. That model supports a somewhat clinical understanding of personal development, which makes it useful in the context of scientific research, but it probably does insufficient justice to the felt experience. The "progress" model too can usefully be modified by the concept of self-realization. As we have seen, it tends to emphasize the change involved in personal development, stressing that the individual becomes somehow "a different person." In a sense she does, indeed; but still she remains crucially (and not only numerically) the same, the later self being linked to the earlier not only by temporal continuity but also by the continuing presence of personality characteristics and other traits which survive in a scarcely altered form. For only in that way can the later self be seen as a *development* of the earlier, a blossoming or fruition of potential that was always there.

The idea of self-realization also helps to underpin and to make sense of the evaluative dimension of personal development. We saw earlier that the notion of development entails that of betterment, and that personal growth in old age tends to be seen as excellent and admirable. For example, Brown cites "some magnificent examples of old people" (naming Albert Schweitzer, Bertrand Russell, and Winston Churchill) to illustrate her thesis that old age can be a time of growth and achievement.[17] But on the basis of the first two models discussed it is not wholly clear why these individuals should be seen as "magnificent." For instance, if they are envisaged as people who have continued to make progress (rather than coming to a stop) why not just call them "fortunate?" Or if they are seen as successful in overcoming the problems of old age, why not think of them as "enviable?" The thought that they are *admirable* surely derives from the notion that they somehow embody or are approaching an ideal, that in some respects they are how others ought to be.

Not everyone can be thought of like this, as an exemplar for others. In the present context at least, the notion of an "ideal" implies a model that *many* people can reasonably hope to emulate. It would be self-defeating to describe as "a magnificent example" someone who (because of rare talents, perhaps, or an uncommon quirk of personality) the rest of us could never imagine ourselves to resemble. Crucially, it implies also a model that we *ought* to emulate, an example that (in some particular respect at least) we should all seek to follow. The choice of model therefore cannot be arbitrary. We have to be able to envisage the possibility of there being many similar individuals, and to welcome that as a vision of a possible human society. If the prospect of many Schweitzer- or Churchill-like individuals were somehow self-contradictory, Brown's claim that those people are "magnificent examples" would be negated.

The concept of self realization can underpin this notion of an ideal in two ways. One is through a notion of stewardship that is deeply rooted in our culture: the idea that each of us has a certain potential which it is our duty to realize to the full. Parents and teachers urge us to "make the most of ourselves," and not just in the sense of achieving worldly success. Those who appear to accomplish this are therefore liable to be held up as examples for the rest of us to emulate. The other way is through the notion of something being "good of its kind." We generally accept that a more developed and mature specimen (of a plant, say, or an animal) is "better" than an immature one, in the sense that it is a better or more perfect example. It is in this way that cattle and produce are judged at agricultural shows, for example, where points are given for the shape, color, and so on characteristic of the variety or breed. The same sort of evaluation can be applied to human beings.

To use the model in this way we have to have in mind some characteristic features of human beings that constitute an implicit ideal of humanity, but given that, we will naturally think of those who embody these features to a high degree as "fine specimens" or (in Brown's phrase) "magnificent examples." This presupposes, of course, that everyone possesses these features to some extent. The features therefore have to be thought of as constituting a common "human nature," which exists potentially in all of us but which blossoms fully only in a few individuals. So Carl Jung writes that those who develop their personalities are "the flower and the fruit, the ever fertile seeds of the tree of humanity":[18] the significant aspect of his remark is that he sees humanity as a *single* tree and implicitly believes that everyone (despite the many obvious differences between us) shares a common nature. On this assumption, an elderly person who continues to develop can be thought of as realizing a potential which is latent in us all and as providing an example of what human beings can become.

6. Applying the Concept of Personal Development in Old Age

We have now considered three models of personal development and the criteria for applying them in old age. Each is still attended with considerable vagueness, of course, but that is probably inevitable in treating a subject such as this. It is nevertheless clear that each model can be applied definitely in some cases, and equally definitely not in others; and that is sufficient for us to conclude, despite the remaining uncertainties, that we can give objective meaning to the concept of personal development in old age. It is also evident, however, that clear and exact thinking is required in order to do so. It may help to conclude by outlining two further difficulties which attend the enterprise.

One, which has been hinted at already, is the fact that people are usually best placed to judge their own development for themselves. This is simply because they have the most information: by the time someone reaches an advanced age, it is difficult for anyone else to know as much about them and their life history as they do. In this matter, then, as in so many others in the field of psychology, the first-person perspective is privileged, and the judgment "I am developing as a person" has a claim to be listened to seriously by others. However there is obviously a danger that such judgments may be merely an expression of complacency or self-esteem. To avoid that, the speaker must be able to explain the judgment to others in such a way that they too can understand it and at least find it plausible. For example a man who becomes increasingly introverted and withdrawn in old age may appear, *prima facie,* not to be developing as a person, but if he can convince us that the changes we see in him are symptomatic of inner growth (such as spiritual preparation for the next life, like that of the Hindu *sannyasin*) we may revise our opinion.

This kind of explanation presupposes a number of conditions. For instance, the man in question will need to use a conceptual model like those already discussed, perhaps representing the changes that are taking place in him as a form of self-realization or progress. In addition we, the hearers, have to listen with sympathetic imagination: we have to be able to conceive what it is like to be him and to have his experiences. This is akin to the use of imagination in moral judgment emphasized by Hare, the ability to put ourselves "in someone else's shoes" and to see the world as it appears to them.[19] But there are real limits to the extent to which this is possible, and these result not merely from our limited powers of imagination. To the extent that someone's experience departs from that which is common and widely shared, it necessarily becomes more difficult for others to share it imaginatively. Therefore, we will be more ready to acknowledge a person's sense of inner change as an instance of personal development if it relates to psychological processes and traits that are part of our experience too.

For example, if a woman tells us how, in old age, she has overcome her fear of dying, we can easily recognize that as "success" since most of us share her original apprehensions, whereas if her account concerns something that few of us experience it will be less comprehensible to us as personal development. The point that emerges here can be expressed as a paradox: although personal development is felt by most people to be an individual, "personal" process, and is often best judged by individuals for themselves, it can only be conceived *as* personal development in relation to changes and realities which are common to us all. That is because it is fundamentally the notion of development as "a person," where that is understood to mean development as a human being, rather than an individual personality. Yet it cannot be fully understood without detailed reference to individuals, for if the concept of "a human being" is not to be a bloodless abstraction it must be derived from and illustrated by individual personal histories.

That conclusion is important in relation to the second problem, which arises from the fact that judgments about personal development are essentially interpretive. As we have seen, they depend on ways of looking at a person's life history. We cannot take the bald facts of a particular biography and just "read off" that it is or is not a story of personal development. The facts have to be interpreted and evaluated; they have to be seen in relation to each other and in the light of appropriate models of growth. Judgments of personal development therefore take place at a high level of synthesis and abstraction. They are second-order judgments. Given the raw, uninterpreted events and actions in a person's life, the first step is to understand these as forming what Malcolm Johnson calls "careers,"[20] or stories of how the person fulfilled particular roles (for example, was a parent) or behaved in recognizable situations (for example, helped a friend in difficulty).

When a person's life story is understood in such meaningful patterns we can then set about viewing a succession of these "careers" as illustrating personal growth. In such a complex process of interpretation intellectual models are indispensable, helping us to connect and to make sense of otherwise unrelated facts. The problem is that our models may themselves determine what facts we are able to see. There is no doubt that this kind of limiting determination takes place sometimes in science and psychology,[21] but does it also occur in our more informal judgments of personal development? My inclination is to say that it does. If people's horizons are bounded by the stereotype mentioned at the beginning of this chapter, which portrays old age as a time of decay and decline, that itself may inhibit them from developing as they become old. Conversely, if we have a clear and usable concept of personal development in old age, we can not only interpret other people's lives as examples of personal development, but are ourselves more likely to be open to a similar process of change. If that is so, developing and disseminating a clear and workable concept of personal growth in old age may itself be a means of helping elderly people to develop.

NOTES

1. William Shakespeare, *As You Like It*, Act 2, Scene 7.

2. Dennis B. Bromley, *The Psychology of Human Ageing* (Harmondsworth: Penguin Books, 1978), pp. 78 ff.

3. Bromley, *The Psychology of Human Ageing*, pp. 23–24.

4. David Peck and David Whitlow, *Approaches to Personality Theory* (London: Methuen, 1975), pp. 10ff.

5. R. B. Cattell and P Kline, *The Scientific Analysis of Personality and Motivation* (London, Academic Press, 1977).

6 Susan Hooker, *Caring for Elderly People: Understanding and Practical Help* (London: Routledge and Kegan Paul, 1981), p. 4.

7. James E. Birren, *The Psychology of Aging* (New Jersey: Prentice Hall, 1964), p. 8.

8. Bromley, *The Psychology of Human Ageing*, pp. 29–30.

9. Birren *The Psychology of Aging*, p.275.

10. *Ibid.*, p. 274.

11. Robert C. Peck, "Psychological Development in the Second Half of Life," *Middle Age and Aging: A Reader in Social Psychology*, ed. Bernice L. Neugarten (Chicago: University of Chicago Press, 1968), pp. 90–91.

12. Bromley, *The Psychology of Human Ageing*, p. 263.

13. Eric Pfeiffer, "Successful Ageing," *Quality of Life: The Later Years*, ed. Leo E. Brown and Effie O. Ellis (Acton, MS: Publishing Sciences Group, 1975), p. 13.

14. *Ibid.*, p. 14.

15. Bromley, *The Psychology of Human Ageing*, p. 263.

16. Brian Evans, *IQ and Mental Testing* (London: Macmillan, 1981), p. 137.

17. Pat Brown, *The Other Side of Growing Older* (London: Macmillan, 1982), p. 176.

18. Carl Gustav Jung, "The Development of Personality," *Jung: Selected Writings*, ed. Anthony Storr (London: Fontana Press, 1983), p. 198.

19. R. M. Hare, *Freedom and Reason* (Oxford: Oxford University Press, 1963), pp. 126–127.

20. Malcolm Johnson, "That Was Your Life …," *An Ageing Population: A Reader and Sourcebook*, ed. V. Carver and P. Liddiard (Sevenoaks: Hodder and Stoughton, 1978), pp. 108ff.

21. Marie Jahoda, "One Model of Man or Many?," *Models of Man*, ed. Antony J Chapman and Dylan M Jones (Leicester: British Psychological Society, 1980), p. 279.

Ten

THE GLOBAL DISTRIBUTION OF HEALTH-CARE RESOURCES IN THE TWENTY-FIRST CENTURY

Robin Attfield

1. Introduction

Speaking at the 2003 Labour Party Conference, Gordon Brown (then the United Kingdom's Chancellor of the Exchequer) conveyed the astonishingly small amount of money spent on global healthcare: "Today two million people round the world die each year from tuberculosis—a curable disease. One million die from malaria—a preventable disease. Three million die from AIDS—a treatable disease …Yet all the world's development aid amounts to just five pence a week for the health of each sick African child."

In response to an invitation to update my previous essay "The Global Distribution of Health Care Resources,"[1] I shall seek to comment below on relevant trends since that paper was written during the 1980s, and to apply the argument to these trends. However, the original problem of global maldistribution of healthcare resources has not gone away, and is in some respects more acute. Equally, the original survey of diverse kinds of ethical theory retains its relevance, and readers of the current essay are entitled to discover how the problem was introduced and theorized in the earlier essay and what that survey brought to light. I shall accordingly include some of the earlier characterization of global healthcare provision and of my concomitant appraisal of applicable ethical theories, as well as relating all this to the twenty-first century context of climate change, Millennium Development Goals, and the Earth Charter.

There has been a salutary increase in recent decades in the study of medical ethics, and many philosophers have been applying their skills to themes such as informed consent, *in vitro* fertilization, and choices between lives in matters such as the allocation of kidney machines. This study has probably been of assistance to individual physicians and health administrators, and even if it has seldom been of assistance to national governments, this has not been the fault of the philosophers.

Much less, however, has been heard about international priorities and international equity in healthcare, and this despite the well known disparities between facilities in the poorest countries and those in more developed ones.

There has, admittedly, been a slight increase in attention to these matters since the millennium began, with philosophers such as Julia Tao (Hong Kong) and Godfrey Tangwa (Cameroon) discussing the values implicit in their own traditions, whether about individual issues or international ones. Yet even the welcome heightened awareness of international aspects of medical ethics is largely ascribable to a new era and a new ethos in one country, South Africa, where concerned ethicists such as Solomon Benatar, Keymanthri Moodley, and Anton Van Niekerk have felt impelled to bring to international attention the problems of HIV and AIDS in Africa, and in southern Africa in particular. Others too (including Richard Ashcroft and Udo Schüklenk) have discussed the underlying issues, and it is to the credit of the *Journal of Medicine and Philosophy* that this debate has been held within its covers.

But in most respects, the attention of medical ethicists remains confined to issues of individual treatment and interpersonal relations, plus their cultural implications as discussed in the pages of the *Journal of Medical Humanities*. This could be because, besides the staff of the World Health Organization, there are few professionals liable to be influenced by such reflection. Or it could be because problems which are difficult enough at local and national levels become mind-boggling and intractable when writ large and considered in their international version. Thus the *Journal of Medical Ethics* in particular had carried little or nothing on international disparities of health and healthcare in the period when I was first writing on these themes, to judge from its own "Thematic Review of Past Issues,"[2] and (despite the publication of my earlier essay in its pages) recent numbers suggest that little has changed. Yet health and sickness know no boundaries, any more than morality and justice do, and it is high time for some of the global aspects of medical ethics to be explored and debated, as well as more circumscribed and familiar issues. Indeed the task of defending the tendency among medical ethicists to limit themselves to the problems of wealthier societies would be an unenviable one, were anyone bold enough to attempt it. (Internationalist journals such as *Medicine, Conflict, and Survival* do better, but make no claims to be doing medical ethics.)

In this essay I shall therefore be investigating the requirements of justice in healthcare at an inter-societal and international level. After reviewing some of the current imbalances in healthcare, I shall investigate what different accounts of justice involve, and what policies, in present circumstances, those agents and agencies capable of affecting healthcare provision might, accordingly, be expected to adopt. While little attention is paid directly to the distinctive needs of the elderly, the adoption of the conclusions derived would bring it about that many more people would have the opportunity to reach that stage in life; for plausibly one unacceptable aspect of life in much of the Third World is that far too many people die young, and that there simply are too few elderly people (although there will soon be many more in Asia and Latin America). But as little more than an exploratory excursion can be made into these subjects here, my principal aim remains that of stimulating others to develop these themes much more thoroughly and in much greater detail.

2. The Gravest Problem of Medical Ethics

When I first wrote on these themes in the late 1980s, life expectancy in most of Africa, at about fifty years, was considerably lower than in most of Northern Europe and North America, where it was already over seventy years. Since then, life expectancy in Africa has actually fallen. (In Botswana and Swaziland it has shrunk by twenty years since the 1970s.) As the life-prospects of individuals depend to no small extent on life-expectancy, these facts already constitute a serious and, on almost any account, an unacceptable imbalance. There again, this imbalance is accompanied by others: by imbalances, that is, in the infant mortality and infant morbidity rates of those regions (compared with others), in their immunization rates, and also in the ratios of doctors, of hospitals, and of dispensaries to potential patients. Further, many Asian and Latin American countries, while faring better than most of Africa, compare poorly with Northern Europe and North America with regard to these same rates and ratios. Granted also the prevalence of diseases like schistosomiasis and of the all-too-prevalent famine-related diseases in the poorer countries, the impression of radical inequalities in health and healthcare between most developed and most developing countries is readily confirmed.

These inequalities are, of course, related to more fundamental imbalances between levels of wealth and of development, which are attested further by differential rates of literacy, productivity, investment, and trade. This is sufficient warning against regarding the problems as relating to the distribution of medical resources and facilities alone. Yet these healthcare imbalances are considerable enough in themselves to constitute what must be considered by those with a sense of proportion as the gravest of the many problems of medical ethics.

For example, at least 150,000 people already die needlessly each year as a direct result of global warming, according to the World Health Organization, mostly in the poorer countries. While some of these deaths have occurred in Europe, some tropical locations such as Lima (Peru) have seen a 12% increase in diarrhoeal diseases for every one degree centigrade rise in temperature in cooler months, and a 4% increase in hotter months. Eighteen Pacific islands have undergone similar increases, which are intensified by high rainfall or drought, when water supplies often become contaminated. Diseases spread by vectors such as rats and insects are also more prevalent in warmer weather; for example, malaria, dengue fever, and Lyme disease have been increasing. The number of extra cases of malaria in 2000 has been estimated at 1,000,000. In

Africa, where malaria is most prevalent, mosquitoes that carry this disease are spreading into mountain areas which were previously too cool for them.[3]

Much disease has been prevented by vaccinations, and many countries have received financial support to improve their health infrastructure. More than 500,000 lives have been saved since 2000 because of support from the Global Alliance for Vaccines and the Vaccine Fund for children's vaccination. Yet 2,000,000 to 3,000,000 children a year continue to die who could be saved, and more than 30,000,000 of those born each year never receive any immunization at all, even though the cost of immunizing each of them with standard vaccines is no more than thirty dollars.[4] (These figures bear out the extract from a speech of Gordon Brown with which this article opened.) Unless the resources are found, this pattern will continue or become exacerbated, and the Millennium Development Goals relating to child mortality, to HIV/AIDS, and to malaria will have no chance of being attained by their target date of 2015.

As if this were not enough, climate change is expected to have large future impacts on human health in the poorest nations. The poorest nations are more vulnerable than developed countries to cardio-respiratory problems caused by the increased intensity and duration of heat waves. And it is the poorest nations that are most at risk from vector-borne infectious diseases, such as malaria, dengue, yellow fever, and viral encephalitis, resulting from extensions of the geographic range of vector organisms, and of the seasons when they are most active, again due to climate change. Most of the 50,000,000 to 80,000,000 expected additional malaria cases will be situated in the poorest nations, as well as new cases of other infectious diseases caused by global warming, such as salmonella and cholera. In addition, scarcities of freshwater supplies will be more frequent in the developing world, with predictable consequences.[5]

Yet modern medicine has saved many lives, and with the large exception of Africa, life expectancy has been increasing, and with it the demography of ageing in the developing as well as the developed countries. Within thirty years there are expected to be 1,000,000,000 additional elderly people in the less developed world.[6] But this prospect introduces another large problem for medical resources, for these people, like senior citizens elsewhere, will all need healthcare provision, although their prospects of receiving it are in many cases problematic. Asia in particular can expect massive challenges to satisfy the healthcare needs of the elderly of the twenty-first century.

Meanwhile, one in four new cases of HIV is occurring in Asia. There have been sharp increases in China, and in India 5,100,000 people are already infected (the second largest number in any single country, after South Africa). Yet methods of HIV prevention (education, access to condoms, and access to clean needles for those injecting drugs) are available to no more than one in five worldwide. As to treatment, only 440,000 of the 38,000,000 infected with HIV are receiving antiretroviral drugs, half of them in Brazil. Economic factors have until recently impeded their availability in Asia, and continue to make them unavailable in Africa to most of the 25,000,000 people affected there.[7] These extreme and growing inequalities in healthcare provision make them not only the gravest problem of medical ethics, but an intensifying one.

3. Justice: Rawls, Nozick, and Needs

The most influential theory of justice of recent years, that of John Rawls, as presented in *A Theory of Justice*,[8] has relatively little to say about a just international order. Rawls envisaged a contract being made between self-interested but rational individuals who, from behind a veil of ignorance about their own life-prospects, choose rules for their shared life in society. But these individuals were assumed to be potential members of the same geographic community, rather than potential members of international society. Rawls occasionally recognized that the principles which the contracting parties were said to choose are appropriate to societies where basic material needs can in general be met, implicitly allowing that different principles might be chosen for other circumstances. But little or nothing was specified about the principles which would be chosen to govern inter-societal relations, whether of diplomacy, communications, trade, or mutual aid. Even when, in his final book, Rawls focused on these matters, strong constraints were placed on international aid and obligations of assistance.[9]

The deficiency was, however, attended to by Brian Barry in *The Liberal Theory of Justice*.[10] There it was urged that Rawls's contractors would select rules for international relations which would preempt the need for them to live in an underprivileged society, and which would provide, as far as possible, for basic needs to be met in general in every society. Without endorsing Rawls's fundamental but questionable assumption (the assumption that the rules which self-interested but rational contracting parties choosing behind a veil of ignorance select would be just ones), Barry here points the way toward a development or extension of Rawlsian contractarianism which would cope with international relations and, if implemented, have a world-shaking impact on global healthcare provision.

By contrast the rival theory of justice supplied by Robert Nozick's *Anarchy, State, and Utopia*[11] appears systematically at odds with the kind of redistribution that contractarianism is capable of advocating. This historical theory of justice, with its concern for the upholding of entitlements and with its defense of a minimal, night-watchman state, leaves little room for redistribution within any one society, let alone for international redistribution. It consciously and explicitly rejects appeals to non-historical grounds for redistribution, such as current needs, at least as a requirement of justice.

Admittedly Nozick's theory calls for a revision of holdings where present holdings result from violence or deception in the past, as long, presumably, as the claim that this was so can itself be proved; and certainly there would be a basis here for the advocacy of reparations between societies, as long as present deprivations could be clearly ascribed to past exploitation. But if this were the only allowable basis for obligations of international redistribution, the prospects of poor countries would be poor indeed, granted the scope for challenges to such historical explanations of poverty. As long as needs are not counted as in themselves grounds of obligation, the obligations of rich countries would often be exhausted well before the lack of healthcare resources in poor countries had been so much as alleviated. But the implication that there is nothing unfair or unjust about people in their millions inheriting wretched life prospects which are far worse than those of millions of others, and through mere accidents of birth at that, puts a great strain on the credibility of any theory that carries it. Indeed it puts a great strain on the credibility of Nozick's theory in particular. Nozickians remain free to defend aid to developing countries on a voluntary, charitable basis, but their stance remains inadequate as an account of justice.

This in turn suggests a theory of value which locates high value in the satisfaction of basic needs. States of affairs are here understood to be of value when there are interpersonal reasons for promoting or preserving them. This granted, a theory of obligation and of justice is readily suggested which requires agents to maximize the satisfaction of basic needs (including needs to develop the characteristic capacities of our own species). Maybe it should be said that such a theory is readily suggested unless other goods outstrip the satisfaction of basic needs in point of value, but it is surely implausible that a sufficiently high value belongs to any such other goods. The resulting theory is of the consequentialist type, but is much more plausible than positions requiring the maximization of happiness or the minimization of unhappiness, or again the maximization of the satisfaction of preferences (utilitarian positions which theorists such as Rawls and Nozick understandably rejected). On such a theory, if there are unsatisfied basic needs in one country, however distant, their satisfaction would generally take priority over other goods, even if the other goods were liable to arise much closer to the agent's home.

Further, this form of needs consequentialism can justify obligations to conform to certain rules or practices. These are rules or practices overall compliance with which would enhance appreciably the satisfaction of basic needs, and can do so for the reason that where people act together and conform to such rules, a greater difference is made to the satisfaction of needs than would otherwise be made. (Accordingly this theory is not a version of act consequentialism, or open to the standard objections to which that kind of theory is liable.) Good examples would include rules of trade which take into account the interests of primary producers as well as those of consumers and entrepreneurs; rules such as these would be upheld by this kind of consequentialism, every bit as much as by the extended contractarianism introduced earlier. This point survives objections such as that rules like these would remove salutary incentives. This is because the difference made by such rules to the satisfaction of basic needs will be far greater than the impacts of current rules, which often leave primary producers and the economies dependent on them unable to satisfy basic healthcare needs, whether of the producers or of other members of their societies.

There again, rules requiring reparations on the part of the agents or the beneficiaries of unjustified violence or deception would be upheld by this kind of theory just as much as by historical and libertarian accounts such as that of Nozick. Needs consequentialism can therefore account for justifications of policy such as appeals to reparations, appeals which are apparently a strength of Nozick's theory. (By contrast, Nozick-like theories cannot consistently be revised to find room for non-historical considerations such as needs.) Through combining the justifications of redistribution found in other theories of justice, and through its capacity to appeal without inconsistency to basic needs, consequentialism thus supplies a strong basis for tackling international obligations in the matter of healthcare, deserving thereby to receive a readier acknowledgement of its own intrinsic merits as a theory of obligation and of value. Such a theory (together with an attempt to specify basic needs, including self-respect, and to locate the boundary between acts of obligation and of supererogation) has been given further elaboration and defense in two earlier works of mine.[12] I have also offered a related theory of the nature and limits of supererogation.[13]

4. Some Implications

It follows from such an account of justice that much more effort is called for in forms of treatment and of prevention alike. More doctors and nurses, more hospitals and dispensaries are needed in much of the Third World, but also much more effort should be given to ensuring for people everywhere clean water, adequate sanitation, improved nutrition, better education, and the control of pollution. These issues, indeed, interact with ones of healthcare, and in at least two ways. They are in many cases preconditions of improved health, and, there again, improved health prospects often form a necessary condition of the success of population policies, and thereby of progress in economic and social development in general. This also helps explain the inclusion in the Millennium Development Goals of the aims of reducing infant mortality by two thirds by 2015, and reversing the spread of malaria and other killer diseases by the same date. Such goals are in line with needs consequentialism. They are also likely to require an International Finance Facility on an even greater scale than the fifty billion dollars proposed by UK in 2002.[14]

It does not follow that hospitals and health systems should be transplanted from the more developed countries to the less developed, whether literally or as models. On the one hand the basic needs of people of the former countries matter too, and on the other hand these institutions will not easily transplant, and will not function at all unless supplied with sufficient recurrent resources. Agents have to take account of the world as it is, and only if large numbers of agents or powerful agencies co-operate are the contexts and the limits of possible action likely to change. Until that happens the typical ethical problem confronting agents is how, while resources remain inadequate, to make the most difference to the ocean of unsatisfied basic needs, while fostering self-help among the people concerned, so that the fruits of intervention are multiplied and development becomes self-perpetuating. If the likeliest way of achieving this is through training paramedics and barefoot doctors (rather than, for example, through building modern hospitals), then that is how action should be shaped. The same applies if the likeliest way consists in supporting a new and more just social order, and leaving the citizens of that order to confront their health problems without further intervention.

Yet healthcare is an international project in more ways than this would suggest, and concerns more than the bilateral relations of any pair of countries. Infectious diseases are an international and sometimes a global threat, while much medical research is and perhaps must be of an international character. (This applies also to research into the sociology of medicine, and the study of, for example, why doctors all over the world prefer on average to ply their trade in cities rather than in the countryside, and of how, in the face of such problems, to provide for rural healthcare.) In such matters, whatever the merits of self-help and local autonomy, collaborative effort is often vital, as well as being in the interest of each and every country; and, even if a creaking international bureaucracy must be endured, each of them has an obligation to take part in one way or another. International divisions, barriers, and hostilities obviously inhibit and sometimes prevent such collaboration, but that is just one of the many reasons for eroding them.

5. How Obligations "to Our Own People" Can be Overridden

So far, the activities delineated may suggest that greater effort on the part of (and support for the efforts of) international organizations such as WHO and charities such as Oxfam is the greater part of what theories of justice call for, if supplemented with some amount of aid from governments of the more developed countries. But this is to ignore some of the ethical dilemmas facing individuals and governments alike. For where the same outlay of effort or resources would make more difference to the satisfaction of basic needs if directed to a poor country instead of to your own rich country, consequentialism apparently calls for it to be directed to the former. This holds good of the agency of governments as well as of individuals.

It is widely held that the first duty, whether of an individual or of a government, is to assist our own family, district, or country. And certainly if everyone belonged to a family, district, or country where concerted action was viable and enough people assisted their relations or their fellow citizens, there would be much less call than there is for assistance to strangers and aliens. Someone might here conclude that this is enough to justify prioritizing effort to provide for your own family, district, or country, at least as far as the satisfaction of basic needs is concerned. Yet the world is such that in some countries concerted action, for example in matters of healthcare, is not viable, whether because of famine, poverty, or corruption, and also because, for these or other reasons, not enough local people are capable of showing solidarity with one another. But this suffices to bring out fatal defects in the view that agents may quite generally give priority to their own family, district, or country.

Admittedly the pressures on agents will often be so great that giving priority to the basic needs (healthcare needs included) of faraway people is out of the question. But often it is not. There are governments which would have the support of a sufficient proportion of their electorate to be able to dedicate at least 1% of the gross national product to aid Third World countries, or to negotiate better terms for these countries in international trade, or (for example, through participation in the counsels of IMF or the World Bank) in negotiations to reschedule international debt. And the resulting changes could make enough difference to satisfy unsatisfied health needs on an enormous scale. These governments lack the excuse of inability to act, and should accordingly do so as justice demands, as many individuals and voluntary organizations (such as churches) do already, and as many more individuals and organizations should also be doing.

For some medically qualified individuals, then, this could well mean practicing in the Third World, where the need is great, rather than in the West, where need is sometimes less great. For others, granted their situation, abilities, and the medical needs of their own community it would not mean this, but would mean reviewing intelligently their own sphere of operations from time to time to discover where, in the circumstances, most difference can be made, and their skills and aptitudes best deployed.

6. The Inescapability of Commitment

Those who reject the kind of consequentialism advocated above might be thought to be under no obligation to adopt these conclusions, and free, perhaps, to regard medical ethics as limited to individuals and intrasocial dilemmas rather than to the problems which I have been discussing. Yet any theory which recognizes the importance of the satisfaction of needs, whether consequentialist or not, is likely to generate the same conclusions. There again, any contractarianism which does not insist that the contract is a purely local one is likely to yield them too, as has been seen. Only a theory restricted to the defense of current entitlements and liberties is likely to be able to resist these conclusions. But such theories diverge so far from the widespread moral beliefs of humanity about right and wrong and about justice that theorists who defend them risk loss of credibility and governments resort to them at their peril.

These conclusions are borne out by the widely acclaimed Earth Charter (of the International Union for the Conservation of Nature).[15] The Charter's preamble makes it clear that recognition of universal human rights is indispensable for a sustainable global society, rights that match the basic human needs mentioned above. It welcomes the emergence of a global civil society, so aptly expressed in the medical realm (as it happens) by the name of the humanitarian organization *Médecins sans Frontières* (Doctors without Boundaries). Among the Charter's Principles are included recognition that all human beings have an inherent dignity, and that increased knowledge and power confer increased responsibility to promote the common good. Information of importance to human health is to remain available in the public domain, and not be restricted by patents or intellectual property rules. Safety nets are to be provided for those who are unable to support themselves, and services for those who suffer. Multinational corporations are to act transparently in the public good, and to be held accountable for the consequences of their activities. Women and girls are to be protected from violence against them, and the rights of everyone to bodily health are to be respected. Any credible account of obligations or of justice (one of which the Earth Charter enshrines) upholds the above implications for action, which apply to agents and agencies able to make a difference, whether they recognize them or not.

7. Conclusion

I have argued for the relevance of medical ethics to international and intersocietal issues, and maintained that the most plausible normative theory, a kind of consequentialism, and indeed other plausible normative theories besides, generate far-reaching obligations with regard to meeting the unsatisfied basic healthcare needs of people of all ages in poor countries. Given these obligations, there are far-reaching practical implications for governments, for international bodies, for companies (which often have the power of international bodies), for voluntary organizations, and for individuals. In addition there are special implicit obligations for medical ethicists to ensure that the international aspects of medical ethics are in future much more extensively pursued, and that the practical implications are more explicitly drawn and publicized.

NOTES

1. Robin Attfield, "The Global Distribution of Health Care Resources," *Journal of Medical Ethics*, 16:3 (June 1990), pp. 153–156; Robin Attfield, "The Global Distribution of Health Care Resources," *Ageing, Autonomy, and Resources*, ed. Harry Lesser (London: Routledge, 1999), pp. 131–141.

2. Anonymous, "Thematic Review of Past Issues," *Journal of Medical Ethics*, 15:2 (June 1989), pp. 99–106.

3. Paul Brown, "Global Warming Kills 150,000 People a Year," *The Guardian*, 12 December 2003.

4. Rania Al Abdullah, Mary Robinson, and Jens Stoltenberg, "Vaccinations that Can Save Millions," *The Guardian*, 27 February 2004.

5. Donald A. Brown, *American Heat: Ethical Problems with the United States' Response to Global Warming* (Lanham, MD: Rowman and Littlefield, 2002), p. 93.

6. Sarah Harper, "Ageing Society," *Oxford Today*, 16:2 (Hilary 2004), pp. 16–18.

7. Sarah Boseley, "AIDS Defeating World's Best Efforts as Record Numbers are Infected," *The Guardian*, 7 July 2004.

8. John Rawls, *A Theory of Justice* (New York, NY: Oxford University Press, 1972).

9. John Rawls, *The Law of Peoples* (Cambridge, MA: Harvard University Press, 1999).

10. Brian Barry, *The Liberal Theory of Justice* (Oxford: Clarendon Press, 1973).

11. Robert Nozick, *Anarchy, State, and Utopia* (Oxford: Blackwell, 1974).

12. Robin Attfield, *A Theory of Value and Obligation* (London: Croom Helm, 1987); Robin Attfield, *Value, Obligation, and Meta-Ethics* (Amsterdam and New York: Rodopi, 1995).

13. Robin Attfield, "Supererogation and Double Standards," *Mind*, 88:1 (1979), pp. 48–499.

14. H.M. Treasury, "Special Topics: Poverty Reduction Strategy Papers (PRSPs) and Trade Reform," *International Development Newsletter*, 27 August 2003, p. 4.

15. www.earthcharter.org; Klaus Bosselman and J. Ronald Engel, *The Earth Charter: A Framework for Global Governance* (Amsterdam: KIT Publishers, 2010).

Eleven

THE RIVAL CLAIMS OF CHILDREN AND ADULTS TO HEALTHCARE RESOURCES: IS THERE A NEED FOR GREATER COHERENCE IN OUR VIEW?

Margaret Harris

1. The Work and the Reward

Alex: I wish I'd been quicker off the mark just now, when Alan said he detested children and didn't see why he should contribute to children's services through taxation. I was taken by surprise and a couple of glasses of Prosecco had slowed me down. If only we could play some scenes again!

Nicky: Well, you did point out that he'd been a child himself once.

Alex: Yes, and fortunately you chipped in and said that today's children will be paying for us all tomorrow.

Laurie: He seems to think that a lot more money goes into children's services than into care of the elderly, or into Health and Social Care in general. A woman had just knocked on the door collecting for the National Society for the Prevention of Cruelty to Children, and a neighbor had asked for a contribution for Great Ormond Street children's hospital; so he was feeling provoked. If they gave us the job of allocating resources, we wouldn't ask Alan on to the committee—would we?

Alex: Only if he was well out-numbered!

Alan: I'll be watching the snooker.

Laurie: It must be nightmarishly hard deciding how to share out limited funds. I remember years ago doing an essay on the Children Act of 1989 and thinking then that there was not enough in it which specifically addresses the relationship between children's rights and those of adults, though there have been numerous pieces of legislation defining the rights of children in different contexts. Strange how British kids are now said to be the most miserable in Europe when there have been so many measures taken to protect them. Most parents would give their own lives for their children, and yet we don't seem able to bring them up to be happy.

Nicky: In healthcare children are well provided for, aren't they? Most big hospitals have pediatric Accident and Emergency departments, so that kids get appropriate treatment and have less time to wait. Up until the end of the Second World War, children were treated by practitioners in adult medicine. Around about then, a doctor called Beryl Corner, who died recently (I heard something about her on the radio), introduced neonatology to Bristol's Southmead Hospital and as a result, infant deaths there were halved. Now we take it for granted that children get specialized healthcare. But is it at the expense of adequate provision elsewhere? Do we give children priority? And if we do, is that fair to everyone else?

Laurie: Over the past fifty years, there has been such progress in medicine and surgical techniques that the possibilities for treatment have increased enormously—and so have people's expectations and their feeling of entitlement. Demand for resources is always outstripping supply. Given that there's never enough to go round, someone's going to get the less good treatment, make do instead of mend, cheap medicines instead of more expensive ones. Have you seen that cartoon on the board in the kitchen, of the General Practitioner saying to the patient: "We can't afford to treat you—shall I kiss it better?"

Laughter; more wine is poured.

Nicky: How can healthcare be distributed fairly? Is there a coherent policy and if so, what is it?

Alex: It must be shifting all the time, with demographic changes and new initiatives. We hear often enough through the media about postcode rationing, tight-fisted Primary Care Trusts, ageing population, and so, on but I don't remember ever hearing any evidence of a coherent policy. What does the question boil down to, exactly?

Laurie: We're talking about justice, aren't we? Is justice better served by sharing out resources purely according to need or by taking different claims into account, such as the claims of children, which could be on various grounds, or those of the elderly, on the basis that they have made the greatest contribution?

Nicky: How can resources be shared simply according to need? That raises some questions, doesn't it? To each according to his need is hardly a model for a satisfactory healthcare scheme, unless resources will stretch to answer all needs. The more medical knowledge advances, the more needs pop up; for example, there was no *in vitro* fertilization when I was a kid. Given that resources are limited, there will never be enough to satisfy every need. If we were talking about feeding people, we could distribute the rice and beans in proportion to need, even if in lean years everyone had to make do with less, but health care isn't like that. You can't treat someone with half a course of antibiotics. Ten years' supply of insulin for all diabetics, then off to your long home! While people are allowed to lobby for the claims of different groups, you're going to have competition for resources.

Laurie: That sounds likely to be true. In that case, we should look at the competing needs of various groups. Let's look firstly at the claims of children. Society makes a tremendous investment in them for the first two decades of life, then, as workers, they start to pay back. They need to be as fit as possible in order to make the best contribution and to produce healthy offspring. Children and the present working population have similar claims. There'd be no money for healthcare if no one worked and no future working population if children didn't grow up to have children themselves.

Alex: I'm not sure that the working population have a claim enhanced by the very fact of working: after all, most people get the best paid, most interesting jobs they can, out of self-interest rather than a sense of duty to society. Are we confusing value *to* society and value *by* society?

Nicky: It's in all our interests to keep the working population fit.

Alex: Most people feel that children should come first. Isn't that natural? We're the dry husks that fall away and children burst forth into the future: the consolation of our age and our compensation for putting on our grave clothes. Or do we suppose that to be the natural feeling of adults because in the rich West, the birth rate is low and children are especially precious? And let's not forget that in some countries, there are six boys to every five girls because girls are valued less and some are done away with. How children are valued isn't standardized through time and space. Anyway, how should we sum up the claims of children?

Laurie: You've said that prioritizing children seems to be natural—or, that not to do so could be judged an aberration, the product of cultures some of us don't much like. Not for the way they regard children at any rate! Using them as soldiers and torturers for example, or killing baby girls.

Nicky: I agree that we are not bound to respect practices which are grossly cruel or unjust on the basis that they are somebody else's cultural norm, but that's not what is at issue here. And there's a circularity in that argument which undermines it: I think you're saying that it is natural to value children over adults and that it is proper to do so because it is natural. That assertion leaves out any argument as to whether what is natural is just. It's natural to feel a lust for revenge when one is wronged but that doesn't justify violent reprisals. What we might long for, we might at the same time prefer not to see enshrined in law. Like capital punishment.

Can we make a claim for children on the grounds that they are more vulnerable than adults, or most adults? No, because elderly and disabled people would have to come under the same umbrella. If all vulnerable groups had priority over the healthy workforce, there'd be trouble.

Alex: I can imagine what Alan might say about the claims of children: pots of money going to keep alive some unhealthy babies, who are never going to have useful, gratifying lives.

Laurie: Is there any way of sorting out these problems? Would the Health Service be best left as it is, not rigidly structured and controlled but constantly responding to these competing pressures, so that people have the feeling that their claims are getting some consideration and that compromises are being made which are not beyond challenge and review? That gives some hope for improvement for each need and avoids coming face to face with a hierarchy of deserts, which is bound to seem unfair to many.

How about the elderly? We hear quite a lot about coronary care units which operate an age-related admissions policy, even though two thirds of people treated for heart attacks are over sixty-five. I saw the other day that women over sixty-five are not invited for mammograms, though almost two thirds of deaths from breast cancer occur in this age group. A third of cancers affect people over seventy-five but many clinical trials for cancer exclude the elderly. Admittedly, flu jabs are offered to pensioners, but on balance there seems to be plenty of age-related rationing in the National Health Service. Age Concern claims that eighty per cent of General Practitioners think so.

Nicky: Is there any explanation that might justify the examples you've given of apparent rationing? What do you think, Alex?

Alex: Well, I've read that in May 2005, National Institute of Clinical Excellence government advisors recommended refusing treatments on age grounds. They said it was appropriate when age can affect benefits and risks of treatment. If a treatment benefits a younger more than an elderly person, the younger one should get it. So, if a young person is enabled by treatment to live and work for longer than an older one, discrimination is OK.

Laurie: Where there are insufficient resources to treat everyone, old people are often going to be last in the queue and in some cases, they will die before their number comes up. By that rationale, the ever-thrusting young are very often going to have a stronger claim on resources. That means that the health of the young is more to be prized than the health of the old. There seems to be no way around it—isn't that clearly unjust? What does anyone say about that?

Nicky: Isn't it a way of maximizing good quality life years, rather than prizing the health of the young over that of the old? That takes out the discrimination on age grounds. What's more, when older people run greater risks by having treatment, there is a duty to protect them from treatments where the risks might outweigh the benefits.

Laurie: Wouldn't it be better to explain the risks and offer the treatment, rather than deny it altogether? To find a way of sharing treatments so that older people have opportunities to be treated and can choose for themselves whether to risk it?

Alex: Find a way of sharing! That's the problem. Let's not forget that everybody, old and young, will press their own claims and not everyone will have the same views of how the inevitable rationing should be managed. Most people who aren't suicidally depressed feel that life has a unique value but even so, some elderly people may want to absolve the managers of responsibility and limit their own claim, out of altruism.

Alan: Bloody marvelous! Excuse me while I trudge out on to the moors and hope to be dead by morning!

Nicky: Nicely put, Alan, as usual! Should we connive at this undervaluing of old people by themselves? It's no wonder that some elderly people feel that that they are a burden. This is the message they get from how society treats them. A large proportion of old people are poor, live alone and feel forgotten and a nuisance. Should we cash in on this to help the National Health Service balance the books?

Laurie: It isn't necessarily the case that an elderly person, consciously making a sacrifice, is giving in to pressure to play the martyr or feeling worthless. We should give people credit for generosity, when that's what it is.

Alex: But that's not how it works, is it? Elderly people aren't given the choice: "You could have this expensive treatment but that would reduce the chances of younger people getting what they need." Those choices are made for the population by government advisors; generosity doesn't come into it.

We aren't giving people a choice of who jumps out of a lifeboat. The only choice anyone has is to accept or reject what is on offer, without any explanation of what impact that has on budgeting. How could we educate people to make fair claims for themselves, when there's no consensus about what is fair?

Laurie: People are increasingly conscious of their right to a fair claim; that much certainly seems to be true and it's hardly surprising that there's no consensus. Where have we got to with this? We've found out that there's quite a lot about discrimination in the National Health Service against the elderly. Evidently, these government advisors feel that if something's got to give, it had better be in that part of the Service that is getting more and more demanding, as people live longer and as medicine has more expensive treatments to offer. We haven't thought about how to get the balance right between caring for those older people who have had what you might call a fair innings and younger ones who haven't yet got a good number of years in the bag. How about the claims of children in their own right, not just as the future mainstay of the economy? A young person with life stretching ahead, but in jeopardy from some serious condition, might feel that there's an injustice in giving resources to an older person which could save his or her life.

Nicky: Ill health is hardly an injustice: there is no agency against which a grievance can be directed—it's no-one's fault if a teenager becomes seriously ill, it's just bad luck.

Alex: Yes, but if that young person could be saved and isn't, because a seventy year-old's claim takes precedence (she has been waiting eighteen months for this operation and may die of old age before she gets it), one might feel with the young person that resources haven't been fairly distributed. We're talking about sharing what you might call 'quality years' We might want to choose in favor of the young person because, as the National Institute for Clinical Excellence has said, he will derive more benefit from those resources, given that the older patient has already had seventy years' worth.

Laurie: Funny how cold it sounds from the pen of government advisors but how warmly we feel when contemplating the fate of the young person, denied the years of adult life to which we feel, intuitively, whatever that means, that he is entitled. And yet, why should it be an entitlement, if ill health is not of itself an injustice?

Alex: As Nicky has said, it's not the ill health that would be the injustice. It's the decision to let one kind of ill health take from another, where the benefits of treatment would be greater in terms of time to enjoy improved health. Time is easier to place in an equation than quality of life and the young person might argue that he is entitled to expect that the Health Service will see to it that he gets a good innings, which the seventy year old has already had.

Laurie: But why should time be the heaviest thing in the scales? That old person might say that her life is as enjoyable as anyone else's and should not be devalued because there's less of it left.

Alex: She might, but time and health can be measured objectively. We're talking about the Health Service, not the Enjoyment Service. Happiness is far trickier to evaluate. Do you remember Woody Allen saying in one of his films: "I was so happy this morning!" and someone answers, "No you weren't." "Yes I was," he says "I just didn't know it." Given that there's never going to be a general agreement about whether a short, happy life is to be preferred over a longer, less happy or healthy one, it makes sense to go for those values which can be measured, that is, time and health. It's quite enough that we aim for an evenhanded distribution of healthy years, without bringing in enjoyment to muddy the waters. Anyway, who said that ill health is not an injustice? Ask a young black man who has been diagnosed with a mental illness, following trouble with the police (rightly or wrongly accused), whether or not his ill health is an injustice. Some black men fear the mental health service and think that they might die if they come to the attention of psychiatrists. Someone from Mind said recently that there is a greater likelihood of black rather than white men being detained in psychiatric hospitals and given large doses of medication. He claimed that this results from serious inequalities in the mental health services. A possible instance of ill health being exacerbated by the National Health Service—sounds like an injustice to me.

Nicky: We're getting off the point: is it more just to distribute what resources we have strictly according to need or to operate some sort of apportioning system, responsive to other considerations, for example, the contribution an individual or group is making or has made, or special status such as that of children?

Alex: Haven't we agreed that it would be impossible to distribute according to need, because healthcare isn't like rice and beans? Even if it were, there would never be enough to go around. When the budget is limited, as it probably always will be, it will have to be a case of some getting treatment and others dying on the waiting list; or, people getting treatment but not realizing that something more expensive would have been more effective. What we need to think about is the justice or otherwise of positive discrimination in favor of any group or groups. I think that the most interesting argument is the one which justifies discrimination in favor of those who will benefit most from the resources. On the face of it, it's a strong argument but it will certainly disadvantage the old. It may bring in the claim of dependants too—we haven't touched on that yet. The younger person's life may be bound up with the benefit to children of having a healthy parent.

Laurie: Obviously, if we're giving the greatest value to years of healthy life to come, a child's claim is the strongest.

Alan: (coming in from the shadows) By that argument, resources should be ploughed first into children's services and only when every no-hoper, brain-damaged kid has had every treatment known to man, would the rest of us get a bite at whatever's left. That's the logical conclusion!

Nicky: I don't think any of us has that in mind and I do wish you wouldn't push an argument to extremes, in order to ridicule what you then call the logical conclusion. No one expects you to stop cleaning your teeth in order to save water!

Alan: I'll be in the garden.

Alex: Alan's got a point: there are more children surviving with birth defects and such like than ever before—and rising. That's a whole, very sensitive area of debate. It's not always clear how such babies should be managed.

Nicky: That problem's central to this discussion, isn't it? It's not always clear who benefits most from resources. However, I don't think we can place Pediatric Special Care very easily in the picture, other than to acknowledge that it's an especially heart-breaking area, fortunately fairly small compared to something like Geriatric Medicine. We weren't talking about spending more on damaged babies, rather on prioritizing children on the two grounds we've already mentioned, that is, that the future depends on the good health of today's children, and second, that children have had less of a chance to benefit from life's goods than adults have and therefore have an entitlement to the best we can offer them. After all, they can't make the claim for themselves; we have to make it for them. Isn't that what we've been talking about?

Alex: Those are two strong arguments in favor of children

Nicky: Back to the difficulties of sharing resources: how many departments are straightforward in terms of resourcing? For example, who benefits more from the kidney available for transplant? The person who is doing OK on dialysis and could wait, even though the kidney would prolong her life by maybe twenty years and the longer she waits, the less fit she will be when her turn comes, or the seriously ill patient who, without a transplant very soon, will surely die and even with the kidney, will probably live only half as long as the other? Doctors are making decisions like these all the time and how do they do it? Are we looking for a model to which all decisions can be referred and which would seem just to everyone?

Laurie: Ideally, yes.

Alan: Can you think of any moral problem that has been settled to everyone's satisfaction? Can't be done! Might just as well leave them to it. Let 'em slug it out in the healthcare jungle.

Nicky: You may be right that it can't be done to everyone's satisfaction but we aren't in a state of nature, red in tooth and claw; there has to be some coherence. If there is ageism, then it needs to be challenged or justified. I think we agree that people of all ages are entitled to call their own lives precious and inviolable, in a way that commodities are not. We also think it possible that elderly people themselves would put younger ones first and we see that this is very hard to fit into the equation. We don't want to take advantage of the elderly or discriminate unjustly. From what Laurie has said, we see that there's plenty of discrimination going on. Should we demand that more be given to them and less to other groups? That would lead to some younger people suffering more ill health, possibly even death. Can we take that on the chin?

Alan: I can live with it.

Laurie: It seems that we identify love of justice with egalitarianism. We want to put in what God left out, as much as we can and we don't want anyone to be done out of his or her due, which is the longest, healthiest life available to us, given the need to ration resources. Now we are struggling with the problem of how to acknowledge that life has a special value of its own, which is different to that of any commodity but which is nevertheless vulnerable to the decisions of government advisors. Life is certainly different from income and possessions but any decision making, whether it's about allocating an organ for transplant or making rationing policies is, in effect, treating life as if it were income or possessions, of which some will get more than others. Maybe this acknowledgement of life's unique value is not the province of government advisors, maybe it is more properly treated by Art and Religion.

Alex: I don't want to be left out of this sort of discussion because I never go to galleries and I certainly can't agree that religious people should have a special say when it comes to debating the value of life; no, we should all exercise our right to lobby on issues like this. I'm inclined to say that we shall have to settle for a degree of justice, rather than perfection because of the difficulty of reaching a consensus. The trouble is that age thresholds inevitably lead to clear injustices, if only because people age at different rates: who's to say that a sixty five year old is elderly? The compromise with justice on this point comes when patients are excluded from tests or treatments purely on ageist grounds. Apart from people undergoing those tests which are offered to sections of the public, like mammograms, every patient sees a doctor only when he or she feels the need for treatment, and so an individual assessment is possible in each case. I think that the least unjust system would be to do away with age limits for treatment and rely on doctors' assessments, though they might complain that too much of the burden of tough decision making is loaded on to them. Informing these decisions would be the understanding that not every patient will be eligible for expensive treatment and that quality years ahead come into the assessment: back to the National Institute of Clinical Excellence recommendations of 2005.

Nicky: Someone is going to go short when there's rationing, because life chances aren't as easily measured as beans. I'm leaning toward Alan—for once—that there shouldn't be special pleading for children. I've been struggling throughout this discussion with my parent's-eye view of children as special, but since I can't accept a view that our entitlement to healthcare lessens as we approach old age, I have to conclude that resources should be distributed on grounds other than age. It's life that is special, not any particular group. I'm not quite satisfied with that because it feels like a cop out and goes only part of the way to sorting out the problems.

Laurie: I agree that we shouldn't agree to discriminate against the elderly, though I suspect that many doctors will lean toward the younger patients, both because of the value given to children in our society and because it would lead to less trouble. Aggrieved parents are likely to be more vocal than aggrieved children.

Alan: Seeing children as special is sentimental claptrap—they're people, like the rest of us.

Laurie: If you had some of your own, you might feel more tenderly toward them. I'm sure you won't mind my saying that.

Nicky: I think there's more to be said but I'm not sure what it is. What we should argue for, if anything, is continuing debate.

Alex: We haven't come to very coherent conclusions, have we? Anyone for cocoa?

Alan: I must be off; I've got a face-lift and a nose job on my list for tomorrow and I need my beauty sleep.

2. Epilogue

Apart from Alan, who slept like a baby, the group of friends went to bed dissatisfied with their discussion. They had agreed that rationing would be needed in healthcare for the foreseeable future. It follows from this that not all needs will be satisfied and that some groups of patients will feel aggrieved. The question of how to arrive at justice remains unresolved. Many people feel, perhaps instinctively, that children are more precious than the rest of us, but decisions affecting the well being of millions should not be made on the basis of instinctive beliefs: suppose we share the "instinctive" views of some that women are unclean and cats evil! The friends have struggled with that instinctive feeling that favors children—and there are more considerations in play with resource allocation than the rival claims of young and old. Laurie's point that Alan might feel and think differently if he were a parent prompts the question: in what ways do personal circumstances condition thinking? How many children had Lady Macbeth?

This dialog aims to provoke debate about how life is to be valued when resources are limited, and to set the scene for the papers that follow.

Twelve

SETTING LIMITS FAIRLY: A CRITIQUE OF SOME OF DANIEL CALLAHAN'S VIEWS

Michael Rivlin

1. Introduction

Daniel Callahan published in 1987 an influential and provocative book, *Setting Limits: Medical Goals in an Ageing Society.*[1] Callahan, the author of over twenty books on healthcare ethics, founded the influential Hastings Center in the United States, and was for many years President of it. In this book he argues that the use of age as a principle for the allocation of resources can be perfectly valid, and indeed a necessary and legitimate basis for providing healthcare to the elderly, because there is not likely to be any better or less arbitrary criterion for the limiting of resources in the face of open-ended possibilities for medical advancement in therapy for the aged. He admits this is distasteful, but has said: "If you do not like my nasty solution [to the problem of allocating scarce healthcare resources], what's your nasty solution?"[2]

Callahan's second point is easier to deal with than his first. As I have pointed out in the past,[3] surely it is sufficient to show (for example) that the practice of slavery is immoral, and should therefore be discontinued, even if one cannot offer a substitute economic system to put in its place. Those who criticized the practice of slavery in the US South were not obliged to put forward an alternative strategy which would ensure equal profits for the plantation owners. If the only way of maintaining the cotton plantations were by using slave labor, it would still be wrong to suggest that in these circumstances to continue slavery was morally justified. Similarly, any method of allocating healthcare that depends on discriminating against members of a group solely because they are members of that group, rather than taking into account the particular circumstances of the individuals concerned, is so unethical that it should not be countenanced. Furthermore, if any government increased the money it put into healthcare and spent that money wisely, then the need to consider ageist procedures at all might not exist. Raising the level of taxation, for instance, would be ethical in ways that ageism is not.

Callahan uses three arguments in particular to justify age-based rationing of healthcare (ABR). They are what I will call:

(1) *The "intergenerational injustice" argument.* If unlimited sums are spent on treating the old then this is necessarily at the expense of the young, which is unjust. Therefore, once people have achieved a "natural" lifespan they should not demand further expensive treatment, even though it might extend their lives. Nor is it the duty of the government to give it to them.
(2) *The "accepting death" argument.* Death should not always be fought against. It should be regarded as the final stage of a fulfilled life and not be regarded as an enemy.
(3) *The argument from altruism.* Obligations to the community require that the elderly should willingly give up the chance of expensive life-extending and life-enhancing treatments. Callahan writes, "Individualism should, in sum, give way to a community-based and affirmed notion of the value of the aged in society and with that, an acceptance of limits to healthcare for the aged and medical research of benefit to them."[4]

There are three conditions that must be in place, according to Callahan, before ABR can be justifiably used:

(a) Guaranteed access to a reasonable level of healthcare for all, including the elderly;
(b) Medical care that helps everyone to avoid premature death, if possible;
(c) Greatly improved long-term and home care for the elderly.

It may be thought that once we have heard the above three points, there is little to argue with Callahan about. After all, he is only advocating ABR if and when we are living in a near-utopian (with regard to healthcare) society. But even taking into account that Callahan is only suggesting that ABR should be implemented in such a desirable state, there are still concerns with his views that need to be addressed.

2. Some Criticisms of Callahan's Ideas

A. The "Intergenerational Injustice" Argument

Callahan writes:

> Age and death in old age are inevitable and there should be no unlimited claim on resources to combat them. But premature death and bad schools, and blighted suburban areas of great poverty are not inevitable. The first health task of a society is that the young should have a chance

to become old. That should always take priority over helping, at great cost, those who are already old from becoming older still.[5]

From an economic standpoint this argument simply does not stand up to scrutiny. It is not because we help the old in this way that these problems exist, and if we ceased to help them the money saved would do little to alleviate their problems. Callahan states that it is only the (very) old who should be denied the chance of expensive, high-tech life-extending treatment. He also emphasizes that care and relief of suffering must be given to those who would be refused treatment, and that we should "greatly strengthen long-term and home care support" before any ABR takes place.[6]

I agree with Callahan that alleviation of poverty, good education, and a reduction of the gap in incomes between rich and poor will have a dramatic effect on a nation's health. If we were able to make an improvement in these areas then there is little doubt that the chances of the young becoming old would increase dramatically. However, all these things are hugely expensive to implement. The money saved by not providing elderly patients with some types of treatment would be very small, and tiny in relation to what Callahan wants and expects these savings to do. They would not begin to meet the task of providing justice between generations. If this is the case, then one of Callahan's major justifications for ABR appears to be flawed.

One further problem is that any savings that might be made may in any case not go to the young, but instead to those who are simply less old than the very elderly. Let us assume that it has been decided that no patient over the age of eighty should be treated with high-cost life-saving technologies. The reason for doing so would presumably be to use the funds saved to treat younger patients. But there is a problem that must be faced by those who advocate ABR: if by not treating Mr X, aged eighty-three, the resource would instead be given to Miss H, aged eight, then there may be an argument for saying this should happen. However, the numbers of those who are aged over sixty-five are increasing. So in fact what is likely to happen is that the funds saved by not treating Mr X might be used to treat a patient who is in fact very little younger. The only way to justify such a policy (which is based on the fact that it is only potential life years that count in the allocation of resources) would be if it were stated that only those people who were very much younger would be treated, and that of course would be both absurd and unworkable, even if it were thought ethically supportable. If this is the case, then it is difficult to see how the transfer of resources between generations that Callahan regards as being crucial could be effected, as although young people might benefit from old patients being refused treatment, they would not necessarily do so.

In other words, the fact that there would be a larger cake available for distribution whenever an elderly person refused or was denied treatment, does not in itself mean that the extra cake would be given to those who are most hungry, or even to those who are hungry at all.

B. The "Accepting Death" Argument

In *Setting Limits*, Callahan argues that the elderly should forgo their claim to expensive life-sustaining treatment even if unlimited resources are available and there is no need for rationing. His reasoning is that death should be seen as a natural part of life, and not something to be avoided by use of high technology treatments after people have reached their natural life span. The argument has nothing to do with distributive justice, fairness, or costs, only with the concept of death being an acceptable part of life, and the point that after reaching a certain age, it is not something to be regarded as an enemy.

In later writings Callahan goes even further, claiming "We should instead accept ageing as a part of life, not just a medical obstacle to be overcome."[7] Note the use of the word "ageing" here. It seems that it is not only death that must no longer be thought of as an enemy, but ageing itself. However, even if we agreed with him that death should be accepted, surely ageing is something that not only can be attacked by medicine, but often, though not always, attacked successfully.

C. The Argument from Altruism

Callahan's view that the elderly should refuse treatment is based on the notion that they should be altruistic. He writes, "The primary aspiration of the aged, I have proposed, should be to advance not their own welfare but that of the young and the generations to come."[8] For this to happen depends on altruistic behavior by the elderly. Few would disagree that altruism is to be welcomed; however, the degree of altruism that Callahan expects from the elderly is too much to demand from anyone. Even if we have achieved a long life, this does not mean that we are, or should be, so ready to give up the chance of having more of it. Callahan makes too little of this. Further, to say that even if we do want more of life we should suppress this want in order that others can benefit is stretching altruism to the limit. Also, altruism is not something that can justly be forced on people. Justice may require that people be compelled, by the law or by the workings of the system, to carry out their strict duties, for example to look after small children, but it cannot be just to require them to be positively altruistic, particularly not to this extent.

In seeking to find a role for elderly people, Callahan writes that:

> If the elderly lack an established, coherent and meaningful place in life and society, there is no real rationale for their protection; it merely exists as a kind of sentimental beneficence. We lack, in the end, any penetrating social vision of the place of the aged.[9]

But why does the rationale have to be an altruistic one? There is no reason that the place in society for the elderly cannot be one of further fulfillment for themselves. In any case, in fulfilling themselves they may be helping others. I am thinking here of the development of a relationship between a grandparent and a grandchild, something which could be of great benefit to both. Why should such a relationship be ended earlier than necessary? Of course, there will be some elderly people who have had enough of life, just as there will some younger people, and it is not being suggested that we should insist on treating such patients against their will. For Callahan to assert that the best role for elderly people is to make way for the young is to ignore what other possibilities are available to them. We could also ask: why should the elderly make sacrifices when there are other ways of raising money, such as higher taxation, or prioritizing government spending in a different way?

It may be suggested that the elderly have a duty to refuse medical treatment in order for younger people to benefit on the basis that the elderly have already had their "fair share" of life. I do not accept this argument. Fairness surely depends on more than just one factor, the time one has been alive. It might be argued that if there are two people competing for a bed, one an elderly person who has looked after herself all her life and a young person who has abused herself through her own lifestyle choices, then fairness might dictate that the older woman is treated in preference.

3. Other Criticisms

A. The Problem of Biological versus Biographical Age

In *Setting Limits* Callahan maintains that age is a legitimate basis for rationing because it is a meaningful and universal category, which can be understood at the level of common sense, made relatively clear for policy purposes, and even be of value to the aged themselves if combined with an ideal of old age that focuses on its quality rather than its indefinite extension.

Callahan makes much of the fact that one of the advantages of choosing age as a method of rationing healthcare is that it is easy to establish. However, he emphasizes that it is biographical age that it is of relevance and not biological (chronological) age. But the problem for Callahan is that whereas the latter may be easy to ascertain it is almost impossible to ascertain the former. The following anecdote illustrates well the difference between biographical and chronological age. A friend's very active eighty-seven year old mother had been out for the day. On her return he asked where she had been. She replied, "Looking after an old woman of sixty-five." In choosing biographical instead of biological age as the determinant, Callahan is choosing a marker that is almost impossible to define, and so negates one of his principal justifications for the use of age to ration healthcare.

Callahan acknowledges that biological age tells us little about the outcome of treatment:

> What seems clear now is that age as such is a poor predictor of medical outcome. Determining a priori that a certain form of care is futile or inappropriate is no more rational in the case of the elderly than in any other age group.[10]

Yet he still wants to use age as a criterion for rationing healthcare. Why? His answer may be simpler than might be thought: because he cannot find an easier way of establishing a cut-off point for the denial of treatment. He writes, "Yet I find it hard to know where else we might usefully look."[11]

But the fact that Callahan cannot find something easier to use than age, is not an ethically adequate reason for using it. In looking for a meaningful and universal category as a marker for the allocation of resources, there are better, and fairer, markers to use, the main one being fairness itself. Let me give an example. There are two people, one aged twenty-five and the other aged seventy-five, both requiring treatments. The younger person may have already used up large amounts of National Health Service (NHS) resources due to her reckless lifestyle, whereas the older person may not have used the NHS at all, but, late in life, requires life-saving or life-enhancing treatment. Surely in this case fairness would dictate that the older person be preferred.

I accept that whereas it might be fairer to use fairness as a marker for rationing than age, it would be difficult to implement such a policy. But I doubt if it is any more difficult to use fairness than it is to use biographical age as a method of allocating healthcare. In this context, those who object to ABR must state whether they believe it is ethically supportable but difficult to implement.

So age is not, as Callahan claims, a meaningful and universal category; many things that seem to be common sense, or are intuitively attractive, are not in fact so; and the fact that age can be made relatively clear for policy decisions is not enough of a reason for using it. In any case, none of these is the real reason that Callahan wants to adopt ABR.

After detailing the most common objections to ABR Callahan writes that:

> A standard of allocation rooted not in dehumanizing calculations of the economic value or productivity of the elderly, but in a recognition that beyond a certain point they will already have had their fair share of resources does not degrade the elderly or lessen the value of their lives.[12]

It appears that Callahan's main reason for justifying ABR is actually the "fair innings argument," an argument that can be shown to be flawed, for the following reason, among others.

It surely should be considered unfair that some people who have had a hard life when young should be denied the chance of making up for it when they become old. John Grimley Evans expresses this well with the following example: He writes that:

> An aged and ill, but treatable, patient of mine gazed round her cluttered poky Council Flat and mused that in her days in the Depression and the War, trodden down by a drunken husband and delinquent offspring, she never thought she "would end up in such comfort and happiness" as she was now enjoying. It would have taken a harder-hearted messenger of Fate than I to tell her that she had had her fair innings just when she was beginning for the first time to have some pleasure in her life.[13]

B. Public Policy

Callahan writes that:

> Age is a relevant and conspicuous variable in healthcare costs, and the elderly are more costly as a group than people of younger ages. The fact that many elderly people remain healthy most of their final years—and that there is a heterogeneous pattern of healthcare usage—does not change the fact that the average *per capita* costs are significantly higher than for younger people. Public policy must take account of, and work with, those averages. They are what count in devising programs, in projecting future costs, and in estimating different healthcare needs. Age matters.[14]

There is much to criticize here. First, Callahan appears to be proposing that elderly individuals should be denied treatment just because they are (1) members of a group; and (2) because on average that group uses up more resources than other groups. I accept that some policy decisions have to be made on the basis of averages and projections. For instance, if it were known that the number of those in the age range five to sixteen would decrease in twenty years' time, then it would be reasonable to base the school building and teacher training programs on these figures.

However, the situation with ABR is very different. Here Callahan is arguing that individuals who may be able to benefit from treatment should be refused it solely because they are a member of a group. Whatever definition of fairness we arrive at, this seems to me to be most unfair. Even Quality Adjusted Life Years (QALYs) demand that we should take the benefit that individuals would derive from treatment into consideration when deciding whom to treat.

It would be helpful here to give an example that shows just how unfair it would be to deny elderly people treatment just because they belong to a group. Remember that Callahan states that elderly patients are responsible for the majority of healthcare costs and that as public policy should be decided on averages it is unfortunate, but acceptable, that there might be some individual injustice as a result. Suppose then, because of the expense of administering justice on an individual basis it was decided that all eighteen year olds accused of violent crimes would be jailed without a trial on the basis that statistics showed it was that age group who were responsible for the majority of such crimes. Would we not feel outraged? Why then should we not feel similarly outraged that all elderly people would be disadvantaged just because some within that group use up a large amount of resources? If it is regarded as absurd to deny individual eighteen year olds justice, should it also not be regarded as equally absurd to deny individual elderly people healthcare?

We could also ask why he picks out the elderly as a group. No doubt those in intensive care are expensive to treat, yet Callahan does not mention them. Patients in intensive care are not only very expensive to treat, but a large number of them either do not survive or survive only with a very poor quality of life. There is evidence to show that a large amount of all healthcare funds are spent on treating people in their last year of life.[15] If an aim of denying treatment to elderly patients is to enable those with a longer life expectancy to benefit from the resultant savings, then surely we should instead be refusing to treat those in the last year of their life, or those in intensive care because they use up more resources than elderly patients do. (I accept that some of the money spent on those in their last year is incurred on attempting to save patients whom doctors hope will recover, but who subsequently die.)

There are further points to consider. First, one of the reasons for denying elderly patients treatment is in order for young patients to benefit from the resultant savings. However, the money—resources saved by not giving elderly patients life-saving treatment—may, as was said above, not in fact go to younger patients but instead may remain "in the pot," and may subsequently be used for something far less important than the benefit that would have been obtained by treating the elderly patient in the first place.

Second, in some situations the old can derive greater benefit from certain treatments than the young can. It therefore seems irrational to deny elderly patients who could gain more from a treatment, just because they happen to be old. If those who advocate ABR are to be consistent, they should accept that in many situations ABR would actually exclude the young.

Third, Martin McKee, Elias Mossialos, and Anna Dixon write that:

> Wanless [a former chief executive of Nat West Bank who was asked by the Prime Minister to report on the NHS] dispels much of the mythology

about the cost of ageing populations, showing that disability-free life expectancy among the elderly is increasing and that healthcare (although not necessarily social care) costs are driven more by proximity to death than by chronological age.[16]

C. Is ABR Morally Defensible if Democratically Agreed to?

Even though Callahan states that ABR should never be imposed on elderly people, underlying his views is the assertion that the justice between generations that he wants can only come about if a policy of ABR is implemented. It might be said that there is no problem for Callahan here in that if ABR is not democratically agreed to then it should not be adopted. However, there are insuperable obstacles to finding a method of voting on ABR. Furthermore, even if were able to find a way of doing so, a minority group may be democratically, yet unjustly, discriminated against. Relying on ABR being acceptable only if it is "democratically agreed to" does therefore not let Callahan off the hook. The public might vote to accept many things that are morally abhorrent, or may be unduly influenced, for instance by the way the question is put.

4. Conclusion

T.A. Manolio and C.D. Furburg write that:

> As physicians, we must discipline ourselves to look beyond a patient's age to consider his or her medical condition and potential for benefit, as well as the desires of patients and their families. We should also continually seek the most complete and up-to-date information possible in this under-studied population. Finally, we must apply this information free of misconceptions as to the duration or quality of life that can appropriately be expected at advanced ages. Such is the nature of sound clinical judgement. Not to exercise it in the elderly is to abandon our responsibilities as physicians to the majority of patients under our care.[17]

In this chapter I have tried to give reasons why we should heed such advice, and to show that the arguments for ABR used by Daniel Callahan simply cannot be sustained on either an ethical or a practical basis.

NOTES

1. Daniel Callahan, *Setting Limits: Medical Goals in an Ageing Society* (New York, NY: Simon and Schuster, 1987).

2. Daniel Callahan, Personal Correspondence, 1996.

3. Michael Rivlin, "Protecting Elderly People: Flaws in Ageist Arguments," *British Medical Journal*, 310:6988 (6 May 2005), pp. 1179–1182.

4. Callahan, *Setting Limits*, p. 60.

5. Daniel Callahan, "Setting Limits: A Response," *The Gerontologist*, 34:3 (June 1994), pp. 393–398.

6. *Ibid*., p. 394.

7. Daniel Callahan, "Controlling the Costs of Healthcare for the Elderly—Fair Means and Foul," *New England Journal of Medicine*, 335 (1996), pp. 743–746.

8. Callahan, *Setting Limits*, p. 80.

9. Callahan, *Setting Limits*, p. 32.

10. Callahan, "Controlling the Costs of Healthcare for the Elderly," p. 745.

11. Callahan, "Setting Limits: A Response," p. 396.

12. Callahan, *Setting Limits*, p. 140.

13. J. Grimley Evans, "Age and Equality," *Annals of the New York Academy of Sciences*, 530:1 (June 1988), pp. 118–124.

14. Callahan, "Setting Limits: A Response," p. 394.

15. N. G. Levinsky, "Age as a Criterion for Rationing Healthcare," *New England Journal of Medicine*, 322:25 (June 1990), pp. 1813–1815.

16. Martin McKee, Elias Mossialos, and Anna Dixon, "Paying for the NHS: Are we asking the Right Question?" *Journal of the Royal Society of Medicine*, 95:2 (February 2002), pp. 59–60.

17. T.A. Manolio and C.D. Furberg, "Age as a Predictor of Outcome: What Role Does it Play?" *American Journal of Medicine*, 92:1 (January 1992), pp. 1–6.

Thirteen

SOCIAL INJUSTICE: DISTRIBUTIVE EGALITARIANISM, THE COMPLETE-LIFE VIEW, AND AGE DISCRIMINATION

Richard Wagland

There are "two different kinds of valuable equality" that might be distinguished within contemporary political thought.[1] The first kind is distributive in nature and specifies that justice requires benefits of a certain kind to be distributed equally. Equality of the second kind does not directly specify any particular distribution of benefits, but instead identifies a "social ideal" of "a society in which people regard and treat each other as equals."[2] These two forms of equality can be labeled "distributive equality" and "social equality." It is equality of the first kind that has been the focus of much contemporary liberal political philosophy over the last three decades since the publication of John Rawls's *A Theory of Justice*,[3] and it is that form of equality that is the focus of this chapter.

It might be argued that egalitarians should pursue both conceptions of equality simultaneously, perhaps because one is just an alternative expression of the other. Nevertheless, one of the main claims of this chapter is that these conceptions do in fact conflict, at least when it comes to the treatment of older persons. The reason they conflict is that for a distributive egalitarian theory to be plausible it must ensure that benefits are distributed diachronically between the separate complete lives of individuals, rather than at temporally synchronic moments within their lives. As we shall see, this in turn justifies age-discriminatory policies that are not compatible with the ideal of social equality. Rather they could only exist in a society that does *not* regard and treat all individuals within it as equals.

1. Distributive Equality and the Complete-Life View (CLV)

Although many contemporary political philosophers would describe themselves as "egalitarian" so far as distributive justice is concerned, there are few who would suggest that equality is more important than other things such as providing incentives for the talented to be productive.[4] Non-instrumental egalitarianism, the view that equality is an intrinsic good, is subject to the intuitively implausible implication that it would require us to prefer a society in which everyone was worse off but distribution of resources was more equal, to one in which everyone was better off, but inequality was greater. This is what is known as the "leveling down" objection.[5] Given the opportunity, a non-instrumental egalitarian would reduce the standard of living of everyone in order to create a more equal society. However, there are two possible alternative distributive principles that "egalitarian" thinkers might adopt instead of strict equality: prioritarianism, whereby the worst off in society are prioritized; and the principle of a social minimum (SM), which determines a level of well-being necessary for a decent life below which no-one should be allowed to fall. John Rawls, probably the most prominent of recent liberal egalitarian philosophers, is usually described as a prioritarian rather than a strict egalitarian because his "difference principle" permits inequality insofar as it benefits the least advantaged in society,[6] though it has also been argued that Rawls's methodology would actually only justify an SM.[7]

Whether egalitarians favor strict equality or the priority principle, they must address a second distributive question. This question, described by Larry Temkin as "the unit of egalitarian concern,"[8] involves the making of a decision about whether benefits should be distributed diachronically between the complete lives of separate persons or synchronically at temporal moments within those lives. This question is not relevant to the idea of the social minimum, as I will explain below, because its unit of concern is always synchronic. However, although rarely discussed within egalitarian theory, the issue of whether a synchronic or diachronic unit of egalitarian concern should be adopted is fundamental to distributive justice, because it determines exactly which individuals have claims of justice against the community. It is a question that Derek Parfit briefly addresses in his own discussion of priority and strict equality, where he gives three possible answers to the question of to whom egalitarians should give priority:

(1) those who are worse off in their lives as a whole
(2) those who are worse off at a particular time
(3) those who have needs that are morally more urgent.[9]

Parfit notes that there is often a divergence between (1) and (2), but a convergence between (2) and (3). So, someone who is now among the worst off may have been quite well off in the past, but if someone is worse off at a particular time then her needs are also likely to be morally more urgent. However, despite his insight, Parfit assumes for the purposes of his article that "there is no difference between those who are worse off at a time, and those who would be worse off in their lives as a whole."[10] Parfit therefore assumes what has been referred to as the complete life view (CLV): that egalitarians should ensure benefits are distributed equally or relatively equally to the complete lives of separate individuals.

Nevertheless, his assumption that those synchronically worse off are at the same time also diachronically worse off will often not hold. So the question remains: do the synchronic interests of those who are worse off at a time have a moral urgency that outweighs the moral importance of the CLV? This is precisely what a social minimum, otherwise known as the principle of sufficiency, does claim. The sufficiency principle logically appeals to the concept of urgency and of synchronic need (so, to Parfit's groups 2 and 3), and is not concerned that the shares of separate individuals should be either strictly or relatively equal over the course of people's complete lives. Nevertheless, like Parfit, most egalitarians and prioritarians either implicitly assume the CLV or else explicitly embrace it. Another example is Thomas Nagel, who argues that "the subject of an egalitarian principle is not the distribution of particular rewards to individuals at some time, but the prospective quality of their lives as a whole, from birth to death."[11] So, for distributive egalitarians the question of justice between the complete lives of separate individuals is viewed as a more fundamental issue than their temporal well-being relative to others at a particular time, and as we shall see below, the latter is often framed by the former.

Dennis McKerlie defines the CLV as the normative principle "that different people's share of resources, or welfare, should be equal when we consider the amounts of those things that they receive over the complete course of their lives".[12] While this definition may be applicable to non-instrumental strict equality, Temkin recognizes that the view can also be applicable to the principle of priority, and he therefore defines the CLV as follows:

> *The CLV*: An egalitarian should be concerned about A's being worse off than B to the extent, and only to the extent, that A's life, taken as a *complete whole*, is worse off than B's, taken as a *complete whole*.[13]

If egalitarian distributions are to be maintained over the complete lives of separate persons, then they may also justify significant inequalities between people at a certain time. This means that people can take turns to be rich and poor during their lives and yet be equal over their complete lives. It is in this way that a distributive egalitarianism based upon the CLV would also condone discrimination against older individuals. Geoffrey Cupit, for example, has noted that "the alleged injustice of age discrimination presents a puzzle," because the "standard argument against discrimination—the argument from equalizing benefits—seems not to apply."[14] It does not apply because equalizing benefits over the complete lives of separate persons might actually *justify* age discrimination rather than challenge it. It does this for the obvious fact that nowadays most of us have a turn to be old, and, by taking turns to be well off or badly off, temporal or synchronic inequalities will even out over the course of people's lives. So, Cupit argues that to say something is wrong with age discrimination is to say that there is something wrong with taking turns. If it is fair that we should take turns to be rich and poor at different parts of our lives, why would it not also be fair for those periods of affluence and relative poverty to coincide respectively with youth and old age?

The intuition that discrimination against the old might be justifiable arises from the idea that, in order for each of us to have as good a complete life as possible, benefits should be distributed in such a way that allows more to be consumed during the early part of a life when people are advancing their educational and employment opportunities and raising young families. In contrast, it might be thought that few new long-term projects can be pursued in old age, or indeed that older people would not wish to pursue them, and there consequently seems little point in saving much for that synchronic period of life. Indeed, it is quite possible we will not live to see it anyway. As we shall see below, it might be entirely rational for people to discriminate against their own future older selves. Age discrimination may be said to be fair because it treats everyone the same over their complete lives, and it may be in everyone's interests because it allows the most efficient use of people's equal diachronic shares of benefits.

The implications of the CLV are particularly important in light of the generational equity debate which has been fuelled by organizations like Americans for Age Equity (AGE) over the last couple of decades. It has been claimed by some that those who are currently old are now enjoying more than their fair share of benefits.[15] As a social group the old are perceived to be better off not just than previous generations of the old, and not just better off than the younger age-groups of today, but more importantly to be in addition better off than the next generation of the old can hope to be. If such is the case then the CLV is not currently being respected. Indeed, if the CLV is morally sound then it would require society to restrict the benefits enjoyed by the current old and redistribute those benefits to younger age groups. Moreover, the strict egalitarian version of the CLV would go further than the advocates of generational equity in that it would require this restriction of benefits from the old *even if those benefits could not be redistributed to the young*. The reason for this is that greater complete life equality would be achieved simply by that restriction. As we shall see below, however, distributive egalitarianism and the CLV only justify ageist public policies when they are linked to a prudential analogy (PA). At the same time, however, a PA is necessary in order for a distributive egalitarian theory, based upon the CLV, to provide plausible principles of justice on a societal scale.

2. The CLV and Personal Responsibility

There is of course a very good reason for egalitarian liberals to think it necessary to embrace an exclusive concern for the CLV, which is that it requires individuals to be personally responsible for the success of their own lives. If benefits are distributed on a diachronic basis then individuals must save and invest them wisely in order to ensure a good standard of living throughout their lives. An equal share of a particular benefit, which individuals can then freely dispose of as they see fit, will protect their equal liberty. In this way individuals are assured material autonomy from both other citizens and the state, and they have the equal opportunity to pursue their particular *conception of the good.* Synchronic distributions, on the other hand, would threaten that equal liberty and opportunity, and may seem to reward free riders. If individuals could expect to receive a new share of benefits at each temporal stage of their lives there would be no reason for them to be responsible. They might squander those benefits with impunity. This would have implications for the economic stability of the state, and would also be unfair to those who have been responsible with their share of goods. Responsible citizens would repeatedly find themselves required to redistribute some of that share to prevent the destitution of the imprudent. So, because the CLV obviously prevents free riding, any challenge to it would need at the same time to address this problem of free riding in order to claim any moral superiority.

Distributive egalitarians, or what Elizabeth Anderson has described as *luck* egalitarians, [16] also make a moral distinction between *brute* luck on the one hand, which relates to our unchosen circumstances, and *option* luck on the other, which relates to personal choice. Although Anderson identifies various distributive versions of luck egalitarianism, including "equality of resources,"[17] "equal access to advantage,"[18] "equal opportunity for welfare,"[19] and "equality of fortune,"[20] the fundamental principle underlying each variant is a common conception of fairness. That conception requires that society should compensate individuals for disadvantages for which they are not responsible, but require them to bear the full costs of the adverse consequences of their choices. That is to say, individuals are held personally responsible for the success of their lives. It seems legitimate to do this because each individual then has an equal opportunity to make their life a success. As Gerry Cohen points out, by giving a central role to the ideas of personal responsibility and choice in this way, egalitarians can sidestep one of the most compelling criticisms from the anti-egalitarian right: the criticism that egalitarians wish to equalize the *outcomes* for all persons irrespective of how much effort or personal responsibility they display.[21]

So, distributive luck egalitarianism is based upon two premises: first, that diachronic equality is viewed as the fairest form of distribution; and second, that the cut between choice and circumstance is morally important because it maintains diachronic equality between separate persons. It also has the effect of promoting personal responsibility. The CLV is integral to distributive egalitarianism, because only by giving exclusive concern to the diachronic equality between individuals can it give full expression to these two premises.

3. What Benefits Should be Distributed Over a Complete Life?

A further issue for distributive egalitarians is to determine what should comprise the benefits that are to be distributed over a complete life.[22] This issue refers to the debate between distributive egalitarians as to what standard of interpersonal comparison should be used to identify those individuals who are worse off than others, or how we should operate what Cohen has termed the "currency of egalitarian justice."[23] Because distributive egalitarians are concerned that individuals should have the opportunity to pursue their own conceptions of the good in their own ways, they have tended to embrace currencies such as welfare and resources (or a combination), which are seen either as subjective or as necessary conditions for pursuing any conception of the good, instead of trying to compile an objective list of "goods" for interpersonal comparison.[24] ("Objective list" theorists hold that some goods are intrinsically good or bad irrespective of whether they are desired by individuals, and consequently can be criticized as being "perfectionist" or "paternalist.") The two metrics of welfare and resources differ in many details that cannot be adequately covered here, and for that reason I will mention only the main distinctions between them, and those that have direct implications for the CLV.

Welfare is here understood as the satisfaction of an individual's informed desires. Resources, or the means to achieve our ends, take the form of impersonal goods and money. Welfare egalitarians argue that people only value resources for the welfare they bring, and that resources are merely instrumental goods.[25] However, there are many criticisms of the welfare metric. There are intense practical problems in measuring how much welfare each individual in a society is getting, and in quantitatively or even qualitatively comparing one person's happiness, or desire-satisfaction, with that of others. This would be exacerbated if welfare had to be equalized between the complete lives of separate individuals. The fact that there is some degree of mental and physical decline involved with ageing means that the well-being of people is likely to naturally diminish as people get older. Consequently, older people may require greater resources in order to achieve the same level of welfare as younger people. The changing of a person's conversion ratio of resources into welfare as we age also means that the equality-of-welfare metric would need to find a way of simultaneously comparing the interpersonal welfare between people who are young, middle-aged, and old. However, this process of measuring the respective welfare of people in society would be further complicated because the relative decline that each older individual experiences will proceed at different rates.

Equality of resources, by contrast, would as an administrative task be far simpler to establish and maintain than equality of welfare. Moreover, the use of what might be called a prudential analogy (PA) would allow resources to be distributed justly across lives as well as between them. The PA is a hypothetical thought experiment that requires us to imagine the way in which a rational individual would invest her equal share of complete life resources to pay for insurance against the likely eventuality that she would suffer disability, disease, or accident. This hypothetical insurance scheme would then dictate what levels of resources should be distributed over time to those in society who suffer from such health problems.

Another criticism of the welfare metric is the dilemma it seems to face between expensive and cheap tastes. The criticism is that, since individuals with more expensive tastes require more resources to reach the same level of preference satisfaction as others, welfarism will require people who have cheaper tastes to have fewer resources directed toward them,[26] so that people who have more control over their desires will be required to finance those who are more extravagant. Welfarists will reply that an individual may have expensive tastes for which they are not responsible, such as the desire for mobility among the disabled.[27] They have argued that resource egalitarians are unable to distinguish between the involuntary expensive tastes of the disabled, and the extravagant expensive tastes for which an individual should be held responsible, such as a preference for drinking lots of champagne.[28]

Resource egalitarians, such as Ronald Dworkin, argue that the important moral difference between an individual's expensive voluntary and involuntary tastes can be captured with the distinction between her share of "impersonal" resources, such as divisible goods and money, and "personal" resources, such as her intelligence, skills, and abilities. A just distribution of personal goods can be determined within a resource metric by allowing individuals the freedom to use their equal purchasing power to secure the goods for their preferred conception of the good in a free and competitive market. So, if an individual has tastes that are expensive to satisfy, but for which she is responsible, she may purchase these with her equal purchasing power. If on the other hand that person is disabled, and so has an involuntary expensive taste for mobility, then she is lacking a personal good enjoyed by the able-bodied. A lack of such personal goods can be compensated for using the same hypothetical insurance analogy outlined above. Both Dworkin and Norman Daniels combine the CLV with a PA in order to secure justice across the lives of individuals, and so in effect between age groups. The following two sections briefly critique the PAs of these two egalitarians.

4. Ronald Dworkin's Prudential Analogy

As a resource egalitarian, Dworkin makes a distinction between the impersonal and personal resources that individuals enjoy, and he utilizes what he calls an "envy test" to determine what justice requires. The envy test requires that each person in a just society be satisfied with the level of both personal and impersonal resources they end up with, but also that each person should take responsibility for how her tastes are satisfied. A hypothetical auction divides all divisible goods into separate lots and bundles, and each individual can then bid for those goods with an equal initial purchasing power. Because everyone has equal purchasing power, the particular bundles of goods they end up with will reflect their level of desire for those goods, so that the outcome of the auction is one that satisfies the envy test, because no-one would prefer anyone else's bundle to their own.

However, Dworkin wishes to maintain the distinction between personal choice and unchosen circumstances, and to ensure that his principles of justice are therefore endowment-insensitive. We are not responsible for our abundance or lack of natural talents, or for any natural disability: it is a matter of brute luck. If a distribution is to be endowment-insensitive, a society is required to compensate each individual for shortfalls in their personal resources with a greater level of impersonal resources. To do this Dworkin posits a hypothetical insurance market in which he asks us to think about how much we would insure against being born with handicaps and other natural disadvantages, on the assumption that all are equally likely to suffer from that brute bad luck. The distributive pattern justified by this ideal-world hypothetical thought experiment would then be replicated in the real world of practice by appropriately arranging taxation and public expenditure policies.

The CLV is explicitly embraced within Dworkin's PA. He insists that "we must apply the envy test diachronically"[29] in order that no-one should envy the occupation and bundle of resources at the disposal of anyone else *over time*, even though it is possible that someone may envy another's bundle at a *particular time*. As Dworkin argues:

> If we look for envy at particular points in time, then each envies [Person B's] resources at the end of the year, and the division is therefore not equal. But if we look at envy differently, as a matter of resources over an entire life, and we include a person's occupation as part of the bundle of goods, then no-one envies [Person B's] bundle, and the distribution cannot be said to be unequal on that account.[30]

Dworkin therefore seeks a just distribution of society's goods to the temporal stages of individual lives by combining the CLV with a PA. Some people will wish to work hard and accumulate their resources, while others will wish to enjoy more leisure and consequently fewer resources. For this reason it is viewed as fair to suggest that in order for someone to legitimately envy the bundle of resources of another she would also have to envy the level of hard work that the other person had done in order to accumulate those resources. So, while person A might envy Person B's bundle of goods a year after an initial distribution, she could not envy Person B's complete life and all the work he has had to do in order to accumulate his final complete life share.

Dworkin applies his hypothetical insurance model to the issue of justice in the distribution of healthcare.[31] After equalizing resources along the lines of the CLV, prudential agents are asked whether they would buy in to an insurance plan that would guarantee certain medical treatments and diagnostic procedures but would deny others. Dworkin tries to determine what we would rationally spend on healthcare in competition with the other goods we may wish to purchase, assuming that each person's purchasing power is equal and finite. The idea that shares should be equal and finite means we can measure the cost of any preference we have for one good in terms of the absence of another good of similar value. If individuals would purchase certain healthcare goods (emergency medical treatment) and not others (life-extending treatment when very old), then society should emulate those hypothetical decisions in order to provide a just distribution of healthcare resources. So, the central idea of Dworkin's PA is that we should aim in practice to make collective, social decisions about the quantity and distribution of healthcare so as to match, as closely as possible, the decisions that people in the community would make for themselves in the appropriate conditions.

The first of these conditions is, as already outlined above, that the economic system of society should provide a "fair equality" in the distribution of resources, and Dworkin argues that only by doing so can we treat all citizens with equal respect and concern. The second condition involves individuals having full awareness of the value, cost, and side effects of all medical procedures. The third condition is a type of Rawlsian "veil of ignorance" that hides individual rational deliberators from knowledge of their own probability of contracting any disease or becoming victim to any kind of accident or violent incident. If we could keep as close to these conditions as is practically possible, then the decision that people in the community would have made for themselves would be the ones that the state should emulate on a societal basis.

This, then, is the application of the insurance analogy to the problem of justice of healthcare distribution. However, what Dworkin deems to be just are the decisions that people would make for themselves "if they were looking *from youth down the course of their lives* and trying to decide what risks were worth running in return for not running other kinds of risk."[32] This phrase "looking from youth down the course of their lives" leaves Dworkin's use of prudence open to the criticism that it is ageist. The conditions of Dworkin's PA might be ageist because they are based upon the choices that a young person would make, while aware of her current age and goals, and the result of that choice will consequently be biased in favor of the young and against the old.[33] We might argue that this represents a "tyranny of youth," because the decisions that the younger person makes will limit the opportunities of the same person when they become older.

What, then, does Dworkin believe would be the result of this insurance analogy? He believes that almost no-one would purchase insurance that would provide life-saving treatment once they had fallen into a permanent vegetative state (PVS), and no-one would purchase insurance for expensive medical treatment after they had entered the later stages of Alzheimer's disease. Most contentious of all, perhaps, few would insure for the provision of "heroic medical intervention" that would keep them alive for an additional four or five months or "technology whose main results benefit people in relatively old age."[34] The reason that people would not so invest is that they could better spend those premiums on training, experience, culture, or investment while they were younger. Although Dworkin acknowledges that many people want to remain alive as long as possible, provided they remain conscious, alert, and relatively free of pain, he nevertheless makes the following claim:

> My point is … that they would not want those additional months at the cost of the sacrifices in their earlier, vigorous life that would be necessary if they had to make that choice. They would think the money better spent, earlier, on job-training or education or investment or on something else that would *benefit their lives as a whole* more than just taking on a few months of very limited life at the end.[35]

What this represents, in addition to a tyranny of youth, is a conflict between the synchronic and diachronic interests of a person. The synchronic interests of the older person is to live a few more months, or to undergo certain beneficial treatments, while the diachronic interests of the person is perhaps that the resources be diverted from financing these later benefits and used to provide benefits for the younger self. If we followed Dworkin's reasoning it would mean harming the synchronic interests of our own later selves by allowing the synchronic interests of our younger selves, or what we at any temporal point perceive to be our diachronic interests, to dictate the distribution of a finite share of resources over a complete life. But one might object that there is surely more to what justice requires than the way that prudent people in their youth would determine to allocate a finite set of resources "down the course of their lives." It is plausible to imagine a doctor at a patient's bedside giving the following homily:

> I'm sorry Mrs Smith, but I'm afraid we are going to deny you the medical treatment that would give you five more months of life. The reason we deny you this is because, although you think you want those months of life now, if you were a rational twenty year old deciding how to spend your finite share of goods down the course of your life, you would elect to spend the money that would have paid for this treatment on a youthful culture trip to Italy instead.

It is possible that Mrs Smith would acknowledge the truth of the doctor's words and accept that she must die, but it is not obvious that she would.

5. Norman Daniels's Prudential Analogy

Norman Daniels is another egalitarian liberal who has combined the CLV with a conception of the PA in order to determine the just distribution of goods such as healthcare and income support. There are two assumptions that condition the circumstances in which prudential agents deliberate within Daniels's PA: the standard theory of a maximizing rationality, and the Requirement of Equal Concern.[36] The first of these, the assumption of a maximizing rationality, is based upon the central claim of the classical theory of individual rationality, described by Parfit as the Self-Interest Theory.[37] The central claim is that for each person, there is one supremely rational ultimate aim: that his life go, for him, as well as possible. This central aim involves further claims, the most significant for our purposes being that what it would be rational for anyone to do is what will bring him the greatest expected benefit.[38] Together these two principles are what we can refer to as the maximizing of rationality. Daniels notes that in his conception of the PA, which he describes as the Prudential Lifetime Account (PLA), the greatest expected benefit is to be aggregated over a complete life.[39] That is to say, the prudent deliberators behind Daniels's version of the veil of ignorance will choose the intrapersonal distribution that promises to maximize the greatest expected diachronic benefit. This is important because the intrapersonal distribution that brings about the greatest diachronic benefit may well be that which also creates significant negative benefit at certain synchronic temporal periods.

The second assumption that conditions Daniels's PA, and the decision procedure it involves, is what Parfit has referred to as the Requirement of Equal Concern: that a rational person should be equally concerned about all the parts of her own future.[40] This might also be called the age-neutrality principle because it assumes an attitude of moral neutrality toward the intrinsic worth of the different ages of a life. Such an impartial concern would mean that "a smaller present good is not to be preferred to a greater future good."[41] We must therefore assume that the prudent deliberator is concerned about the diachronic well-being she will enjoy over her complete life, and is not more concerned with the success of one part of that life than with other parts. Given these assumptions, Daniels argues, resources should then be distributed between people of different ages in the way that prudential agents would divide them over the corresponding temporal stages of a single life. Daniels believes that once these two conditions of the PA have been secured regarding the decision procedure, then "[w]hatever is prudent from this perspective constitutes what is just."[42]

So, Daniels assumes for the purpose of his theory that intrapersonal justice is "framed" by the issue of interpersonal justice, and therefore, certain inequalities that egalitarians might otherwise permit in order to maximize the overall social product are not necessary. Therefore, "[i]nequalities in income levels between the stages of life work only as a zero-sum game, making one period of life better off at the expense of another period of life."[43] As a consequence, Daniels believes that "the prudent course of action would be to allocate resources in such a way that income ... would remain roughly equal over the lifespan."[44] If an individual could know that his plan of life contained preferences which at all stages of life would make an unequal distribution preferable, then an unequal intrapersonal distribution would be a better one for that individual. This is what Dworkin's PA allows, but Daniels's does not. The reason that Daniels hides this knowledge from prudential deliberators behind his veil of ignorance is that, as he acknowledges, "we revise plans of life, often in fundamental ways, as we age."[45] It is this fact of uncertainty that leads Daniels to believe the Income Preservation Principle (IPP) would be chosen: a principle that ensured people sufficient resources at each stage of their lives to pursue whatever plan of life they may have at each particular stage.

However, if we accept the CLV, the standard assumption of a maximizing rationality of self-interest, and the conditions of Daniels's PA, it is still arguable that rational deliberators would not in fact decide upon the IPP. In other words, they would not distribute their finite share of resources "roughly equally" across a life. In fact it is possible, as McKerlie has argued, that in order to maximize expected diachronic benefit over a complete life, it may be necessary to allocate disproportionate shares between younger and older selves, and it is consequently quite possible that prudence "would treat the very old harshly."[46]

McKerlie's claim is that, given the goal of maximizing diachronic well-being, people might rationally follow the classical theory of practical reasoning and yet favor a life that did in fact involve synchronic inequalities, *even if by doing so they did not increase the total complete life benefits they could enjoy*. Maximal diachronic well-being might *require* unequal consumption throughout a life. Daniels does in fact point to this possibility himself. He claims some "qualifications" are necessary to the IPP and that income distribution must be adjusted if it is to count as a measure of well-being at different points in the lifespan, because what we are really interested in is a person's "standard of living." But equal income levels at different stages of life may not represent equal standards of living. The example he uses is income spent on raising children, including advancing their educational opportunities. This investment is at least in part inelastic, and if it represents a "durable good" that produces benefits to parents over their complete lifespan, then we should readjust the post-retirement income levels of the parents by subtracting some portion of income to be spent on their children.[47] If we violate the IPP in the way Daniels himself suggests, then this may not be enough to create or justify age-discriminatory policies. But if we combine it with other likely reasons for detracting from the IPP, then the aggregated consequences may result in a significant restriction of benefits from the old.

What then are the other possible reasons that prudential deliberators would fail to preserve sufficient resources for their old age as the IPP suggests they would? First, individuals behind the veil of ignorance do not know how long they personally will live, although they do know the average life expectancy one can expect to enjoy within their society. If that average is something like seventy-five, then they know that although they can expect to reach that age they are far less likely to reach eighty-five, and quite unlikely to make ninety-five. It must seem at least plausible then that rational deliberators, thinking about their own lives, would not save very much for the slim possibility that they might live that long. While it might be prudent to save resources for great age it certainly does not seem *imprudent* to decide not to save the same "roughly equal" share of income at that life stage as every other. To do so would be to risk wasting a significant share of your complete life resources. As McKerlie points out, this consideration does not violate the age-neutrality principle because it is not necessary to assume that the older life segments are of less intrinsic value than any other segment of a person's life.[48] An age-neutrality principle by itself does not therefore prevent age discrimination. For the very old to be neglected it is only necessary to acknowledge that the prudential deliberators, behind a veil of ignorance, would know that they are very unlikely to live long enough to enjoy any benefits set aside for the very old age group.

A second reason that prudential deliberators may not choose the IPP is that people would not necessarily find it imprudent to consume a greater share of their finite resources while young. As we have seen, Daniels stipulates that the budget to be distributed intrapersonally has already been framed by interpersonal justice, and that therefore prudential deliberators could not seek to expand their lifetime share by allocating it in certain ways, perhaps by investing in their human capital while young. Daniels believes that because such a disproportionate youthful allocation would not increase your complete life share of resources, consequently people would not distribute it in that way. However, it does not seem irrational to consume more of your resources while young, either in education or developing yourself in other ways, *even if it does not increase your complete life earning power*. For example, education, cultural experience, and travel may increase your diachronic well-being for psychological rather than merely materialistic reasons, and we might invest in them even if by doing so we would simultaneously reduce our lifetime shares. As we saw in the last section, Dworkin is quite explicit that such considerations would justify restricting resources from the very old. Daniels, on the other hand, seems to deny that such justifications would be considered.

A third criticism, again outlined by McKerlie, is a consequence of the calculations that would be inherent in maximizing rationality: that "prudence will only save for old age if the sacrifice that such saving requires early in life is less than the eventual gain when the resources are used during old age."[49] It is an unfortunate fact that with the onset of old age, our physical and mental powers usually begin to decline and this makes it more difficult to use our resources to improve our lives. It is also increasingly unlikely that we would expect to want to "radically revise" our conceptions of the good life as we grow older. One reason for this might be that we would simply lack the energy and motivation. Another reason is anticipated by Daniels himself in a footnote in which he acknowledges that rationally prudent individuals may well discount their later years from the consideration of the *fecundity* of the benefits they can expect from them, or that fewer opportunities exist for further personal development when we are older. Thus, Daniels recognizes that:

> If this is so, then, other things being equal, a later year is worth less than an earlier one because whatever opportunities for generating further benefits from activities pursued in a later year are less than those generated at an earlier year.[50]

Again, however, it is not necessary that by favoring earlier years in this way we would violate the age-neutrality principle. It would simply not be a prudential calculation to invest as much into later temporal periods of our lives as Daniels's IPP would suggest, given the overall goal of maximizing the greatest diachronic benefit over a complete life.

These considerations suggest that it is quite plausible that given the conditions of Daniels's PA, combined with his commitment to the CLV and maximizing rationality, that prudential deliberators would not choose his IPP. Indeed, rather than saving a roughly equal share of income for each stage of life, it is quite plausible that the later stages will be neglected to some extent. Moreover, while each of these considerations might lead to only a small deviation from the IPP, taken together they may well collectively lead to justifying a certain amount of age discrimination. One of Daniels's fundamental assumptions is that prudence should dictate justice, but if it is not imprudent to leave little for your own very old age, it does not follow that justice does not require society to provide a sufficient income for people who live to the age of ninety-five and beyond. This consideration points to the strong possibility that justice cannot simply be reduced to the prudent decisions that individuals would make about their own lives, irrespective of whether they would, in a hypothetical situation involving an informational constraint, have made provision themselves.

6. A Return to Social Equality

We have seen that there are good reasons for distributive egalitarians to accept the CLV, both because it rewards personal responsibility and maintains "fairness" between separate persons. We have also seen that for a distributive egalitarian theory to provide plausible principles of justice appropriate for societies, rather than just for individuals, the CLV requires the employment of a PA. Different thinkers such as Dworkin and Daniels have deployed different conceptions of the PA, but those conceptions nevertheless involve prudential agents deliberating behind a more or less extensive veil of ignorance, which is designed to ensure that the principles of justice decided upon are disinterested and unbiased. Nevertheless, we have also seen that, even by the conditions of these PAs, the types of policies they would suggest for society might treat the old quite harshly.

McKerlie points out that the combination of the CLV and the PA is reductionist in several ways. It supposes that questions of synchronic distribution between individuals at a time can be reduced to the question of diachronic lifetime distributions. It supposes that interpersonal justice can be reduced to a question of intrapersonal justice. Finally, it supposes that questions about justice can be reduced to a question concerning individual prudence.[51] The first two criticisms refer to the CLV, the third to the PLA. But the use of prudence within the PLA would have no meaning if there were not lifetime shares to prudentially distribute across your life. Contrary to Daniels's defense of the PLA, McKerlie argues that the appeal to prudence is "a kind of trick," and that there are real conflicts between the claims of the young and the old that are "neither transcended nor plausibly resolved" by assuming the CLV and reducing justice to prudence.[52] As we have seen in the previous sections, the CLV and PA combination has implications that are intuitively unacceptable.

The CLV and the PA are integral to distributive "luck" egalitarianism, which remains the dominant position within contemporary political philosophy. Nevertheless, as Samuel Scheffler points out, a "project of critical examination" of that philosophical position has been initiated by Anderson and others.[53] This project questions the distributive egalitarian assumption that egalitarians should focus so extensively on the distribution of divisible goods because it argues that there is something else more fundamental to egalitarianism than simple distribution, for example the social relationships between citizens. This leads us to consider the second kind of "valuable equality" mentioned in my introduction, that of a social ideal in which people regard and treat each other as equals. That equal distribution is not the only important, or even the most important, element of egalitarianism is recognized by Cohen when he acknowledges that "it seems quite unclear that a state which forthrightly refuses to pursue a norm of strict distributive equality *ipso facto* shows failure to treat its subjects with equal respect and concern."[54] Nevertheless, as we have seen above, the state's pursuit of equality or priority over a complete life may well lead to a society that fails to treat its subjects with equal concern and respect.

David Miller believes that the ideal of social equality is more deeply embedded in the contemporary moral consciousness,[55] and, as Timothy Scanlon notes, "the ideal of a society in which people all regard one another as equals … has played a more important role in radical egalitarian thinking than the idea of distributive justice which dominates much discussion in our time."[56] Indeed, both Anderson and Scheffler claim that distributive egalitarianism is not what egalitarian political movements have historically sought to achieve. Instead, they have pursued the social and political ideal of equal social relations between citizens. This is as true for anti-sexists and anti-racists as it is for those who challenge the prejudices and inequalities that disadvantage older people, and it is this *social* form of equality to which anti-ageists should appeal.

A social equality of this kind would have no need for a commitment to the CLV, a PA, or the age discrimination they may justify. Instead, it would be concerned only that relations between citizens remain equal. Integral to such a concern would be the view that the moral force of synchronic interests is greater than any concern for diachronic equality. So, in Parfit's terms, as far as the distribution of divisible goods is concerned both those who are worse off at a time, and those whose needs are morally more urgent, would be given priority over those who were worse off in their lives as a whole (provided the latter were not currently in either of the two former categories). This means that social equality would, at the very least, ensure something like the sufficiency principle. However, as noted above, if we reject the CLV and distribute at least some benefits on a synchronic basis we are faced with the problem of the free rider, and the question of how we ensure that people continue to be personally responsible for the success of their lives. Nevertheless, the following chapter discusses another defense of ageism, the fair innings argument (FIA), which also neglects the importance of the personal responsibility of individuals, although this has not diminished its influence within rationing decisions.

NOTES

1. David Miller, "Equality and Justice," *Ideals of Equality*, ed. Andrew Mason (Oxford: Blackwell Publishers, 1998), p. 23.
2. *Ibid.*, p. 23.
3. John Rawls, *A Theory of Justice* (Cambridge, MA: Harvard University Press, 1971).
4. Derek Parfit, "Equality or Priority?" *The Ideal of Equality*, ed. Matthew Clayton and Andrew Williams (Basingstoke: Palgrave Macmillan, 2002), pp. 81–125.
5. Larry Temkin, "Equality, Priority, and the Levelling Down Objection," *The Ideal of Equality*, ed. Matthew Clayton and Andrew Williams (Basingstoke: Palgrave Macmillan, 2002), pp. 126–161.
6. John Rawls, *A Theory of Justice* (Oxford: Oxford University Press, Revised Edition, 1990).
7. Jeremy Waldron, "John Rawls and the Social Minimum," *Liberal Rights: Collected Papers 1981–1991* (Cambridge: Cambridge University Press, 1993), pp. 250–270.

8. Larry Temkin, *Inequality* (New York, NY: Oxford University Press, 1993), Chapter 8.

9. Derek Parfit, 'Equality or Priority?' p. 101.

10. *Ibid.*, p. 103.

11. Thomas Nagel, *Equality or Partiality* (Oxford: Oxford University Press, 1991), p. 69.

12. Dennis McKerlie, "Equality and Time," *Ethics* 99:3 (April 1989), pp. 475–491.

13. Temkin, *Inequality*, p. 233.

14. Geoffrey Cupit, "Justice, Age, and Veneration," *Ethics* 108:4 (July 1998), p. 702.

15. Henry Fairlie, "Greedy Geezers: Talkin' 'Bout My Generation," *New Republic* 28 (March 1988), p. 19.

16. Elizabeth Anderson, "What is the Point of Equality?" *Ethics* 109 (January 1999), pp. 287–337.

17. Ronald Dworkin, *Sovereign Virtue: The Theory and Practice of Equality* (Cambridge, MA: Harvard University Press, 2000), Chapter Two.

18. G.A. Cohen, "On the Currency of Egalitarian Justice," *Ethics* 99:4 (July 1989), pp. 906–44.

19. Richard Arneson, "Equality and Equal Opportunity for Welfare," *Philosophical Studies* 56:1 (1989), pp. 77–93.

20. John E. Roemer, *Theories of Distributive Justice* (Cambridge, MA: Harvard University Press, 1995).

21. Cohen, "On the Currency of Egalitarian Justice," p. 933.

22. Amartya Sen, "Equality of What?" *Equal Freedom: Selected Tanner Lectures on Human Values*, ed. Stephen Darwall (Ann Arbor, MI: The University of Michigan Press, 1995), pp. 307–330.

23. Cohen, "On the Currency of Egalitarian Justice."

24. Anderson, "What is the Point of Equality?"

25. Arneson, "Equality and Equality of Opportunity for Welfare," p. 237.

26. Dworkin, *Sovereign Virtue*, Chapter Two, Section VIII.

27. Arneson, "Equality and Equal Opportunity for Welfare," pp. 230–231; Cohen, "On the Currency of Egalitarian Justice," pp. 522–523.

28. Richard Arneson, "Liberalism, Distributive Subjectivism, and Equal Opportunity for Welfare," *Philosophy and Public Affairs*, 19:2 (Spring 1990), pp. 190–191.

29. Dworkin, *Sovereign Virtue*, p. 85.

30. *Ibid.*, p. 83.

31. Ronald Dworkin, "Justice in the Distribution of Healthcare," *McGill Law Journal*, 38:4 (October 1993), pp. 883–889.

32. *Ibid.*, p. 888.

33. Richard Posner, *Aging and Old Age* (Chicago, IL: University of Chicago Press, 1995), pp. 266–7.

34. Dworkin, "Justice in the Distribution of Healthcare," p. 890.

35. *Ibid.*, p. 891.

36. Dennis McKerlie, "Justice Between the Young and the Old", *Philosophy and Public Affairs*, 30:2 (Spring 2002), pp. 152–177.

37. Derek Parfit, *Reasons and Persons* (Oxford: Clarendon Press, 1984), p. 4.

38. *Ibid.*, p 8.

39. Norman Daniels, *Justice and Justification*: Reflective Equilibrium in Theory and Practice (Cambridge: Cambridge University Press, 1984), p. 285.

40. Parfit, *Reasons and Persons*, p. 313.

41. Henry Sidgwick, *Methods of Ethics* (Indianapolis, IN: Hackett, 1981), p. 381.

42. Norman Daniels, *Am I My Parents' Keeper?* (New York, NY: Oxford University Press, 1988), p. 92.

43. *Ibid.*, p. 121.

44. *Ibid.*, p. 121.

45. *Ibid.*, p. 120.

46. Dennis McKerlie, "Equality Between Age Groups," *Philosophy and Public Affairs*, 21:3 (Summer 1992), p. 287.

47. Daniels, *Justice and Justification*, p. 162.

48. McKerlie, "Justice Between the Young and the Old."

49. *Ibid.*, p. 160.

50. Daniels, *Justice and Justification*, p. 282, n. 1.

51. McKerlie, "Justice Between the Young and the Old," p. 157.

52. *Ibid.*, p. 158.

53. Samuel Scheffler, "What is Egalitarianism?" *Philosophy and Public Affairs*, 31:1 (Winter 2003), p. 7; Jonathan Wolff, "Fairness, Respect, and the Egalitarian Ethos," *Philosophy and Public Affairs*, 27:2 (Spring 1998), pp. 97–122; Timothy Hinton, "Must Egalitarians Choose Between Fairness and Respect?" *Philosophy and Public Affairs* 30:1 (Winter 2001), pp. 72–87.

54. G.A. Cohen, *If You're an Egalitarian, How Come You're So Rich?* (Cambridge, MA: Harvard University Press, 2000), p. 165.

55. Miller, "Equality and Justice," p. 32.

56. T. M. Scanlon, "The Diversity of Objections to Inequality," *The Ideal of Equality*, ed. Matthew Clayton and Andrew Williams (Basingstoke: Palgrave Macmillan, 2002), pp. 41–60.

Fourteen

A FAIR INNINGS OR A COMPLETE LIFE: ANOTHER ATTEMPT AT AN EGALITARIAN JUSTIFICATION OF AGEISM

Richard Wagland

1. The Fair Innings Argument and the Complete-Life View

The Fair Innings Argument (hereafter the FIA) appeals to the intuitively plausible idea that there is a certain lifespan that we should each reasonably expect to achieve, and that it is unfair if purely because of the structure and arrangements of society people do not enjoy that span of life. John Harris describes the FIA as an attempt to:

> capture and express in a workable form the truth that while it is always a *misfortune* to die when one wants to go on living, it is not a tragedy to die in old age; but it is … both a tragedy and a misfortune to be cut off prematurely.[1]

So the injustice experienced by someone who has not had a good innings when they lose out to someone who has is significantly greater than in reverse circumstances. This greater injustice arguably gives us a normative reason to withhold life-saving medical benefits from an older person, and to give them to a younger one, in situations where both need the same treatment in order to survive, but where scarcity dictates that only one can receive it. Harris therefore outlines what he calls "a reasonable form" of the FIA in the following way:

> *The FIA*: that people who had achieved old age or who were closely approaching it would not have their lives further prolonged when this could only be achieved at the cost of the lives of those who were not nearing old age.[2]

The FIA is a philosophical argument that has obvious advantages for those who must make rationing decisions in the distribution of health services as well as other instances of intergenerational justice involving the distribution of benefits between age groups or generations, and it is unsurprisingly one that has been often used.[3] There is much evidence that discrimination against the old is prevalent within healthcare, and groups such as Age Concern and the King's Fund often claim that this is not so much motivated by notions of fairness as by moral prejudice against the old.[4] It is of course difficult to assess the degree to which those who defend age discrimination on the basis of moral reasons like fairness and justice are in fact motivated primarily by prejudice, but to have a moral reason for doing something that you would like to do for immoral reasons is of obvious benefit to those who are prejudiced. This chapter, however, is not about motives but about the FIA as an argument.

There are obviously strong similarities between this attempt to justify ageism through the FIA and the justification via the complete-life view (CLV) discussed in the previous chapter. At first glance it would seem reasonable to suggest that we could simultaneously support both principles. Ronald Dworkin, for example, is, as we have seen, explicit in his commitment to the CLV within his political philosophy,[5] but he also implicitly embraces the justice of the FIA in his moral theory, when he outlines what he calls the "frustration thesis": the "instinctive assumption of which is that it is a greater tragedy when a young person dies than when an old one dies."[6]

2. Interpreting the Two Views

It is difficult sometimes to determine whether the advocacy of age discrimination in any particular instance is based upon the CLV or the FIA. An example is Daniel Callahan's book *Setting Limits*,[7] which outlines a defense of age discrimination in healthcare based upon the premise that the old should be willing to give up access to life-extending medical treatments so that the young might have the greatest opportunity of becoming old. He argues that "[t]here is nothing unfair about using age as a [discriminatory] category if the purpose of doing so is to achieve equity between generations."[8] However, it is ambiguous as to whether Callahan is appealing to a CLV or an FIA in his defense of age discrimination, or whether he is relying upon some other principle. For example, he appears to be defending the CLV when he argues that beyond a certain point in their lives elderly people "will have already had their fair share of resources,"[9] and will not be entitled to any more resources on the grounds of fairness. On the other hand, he appears to be defending the FIA when he proposes that "[a]fter a person has lived out a natural life span, medical care should no longer be orientated to resisting death," and that it would henceforth "be limited to the relief of suffering."[10] As we will see below, however, these two claims may conflict, and a "fair share of resources" may not have been exhausted by the time a "person has lived out a natural life span."

Both justifications of ageism are concerned with the distribution of some good, and both would seem to be strongly normatively egalitarian. They both hold that if there is something to be distributed then ideally it should be distributed fairly, which is usually taken to mean as equally as possible. As the previous chapter has shown, within the work of egalitarian liberals the CLV is concerned with the distribution of either resources or welfare. While welfare can be understood as an intrinsic good, as an end in itself, resources are viewed as instrumental goods, or the means to achieve our ends. The FIA may also be interpreted in either of two ways. First, it may be a view about the distribution of the instrumental means to ensure the end of a "fair" *duration* of life. If so, the FIA would be a view concerning the means to an end in a way similar to the resource-egalitarian interpretation of the CLV. The difference between the two is perhaps that the means interpretation of the FIA would be more specifically limited to healthcare and medical resources. Understood in this way, the FIA becomes relevant only in circumstances of scarcity, as when only one of two persons can be saved with the limited resources available.

An alternative view of the FIA would be to interpret it as concerned with the end itself, and so be concerned to ensure that each person has a fair or an equal share of life itself. Such an ends interpretation of the FIA would be similar to the welfare-egalitarian view of the CLV. Oliver Leaman is one commentator who has interpreted the FIA in this way and, as he recognizes, there are somewhat implausible implications of this more extreme version of the FIA:

> There are interesting consequences to [this interpretation of] the "fair innings argument." One is that it involves an extreme form of egalitarianism. The fact that someone lives longer than someone else is regarded as patently unfair, and it is just to seek to equalise as far as possible the lifespans of different individuals.[11]

If the FIA is a normative principle that each of us should have equal life spans, then just as it is "unfair" that some people die young, so too would it be unfair that some people live longer than their fair share. The implication is that something should be done to correct this unfairness, perhaps through a policy of enforced euthanasia for all those who have lived beyond the socially determined "fair" innings.

The first interpretation of the FIA identified above, that which identifies it with a view about means rather than ends, does not suffer from this morally implausible implication, and it would remain silent on the issue of the actual life spans that different people achieved above the fair innings. It is silent on this because the view does not concern itself directly with distributing the ends, but only with means. Once the healthcare and medical resources have been directed to ensure everyone has an equal opportunity to reach a fair innings, then the actual innings people enjoy is left unchallenged.

To complicate the issue further, the distinction between whether the FIA distributes means or ends is not the only one that can be made. Like the CLV, the FIA may be interpreted as a principle of strict equality, priority, or sufficiency. As indicated above, Leaman interprets the FIA to involve "an extreme form of egalitarianism," and this implies that its underlying normative principle is that we should each have the same length of life. A world in which everyone had exactly the same length of life would in a sense be fairer than one in which everyone lived to the fair innings but some lived much longer. Such an ideal world of equal lifespans would also be administratively more efficient because we would then be able to allocate exactly the right amount of resources for each life. However, this ideal is not an appealing one, because most people would not find it desirable to know exactly how long they had to live. Arguably what gives life much of its meaning and enjoyment is the very uncertainty of its duration. If we each knew we had an equal life span then as we neared the end of the innings we would become increasingly worried and distracted from the important things in life. Moreover, such a strict egalitarian view of the FIA would be subject to the objection that it was committed to "leveling down" the goods being distributed. If inequality is intrinsically bad and the goods being distributed are life itself, then Leaman would be right in thinking that the FIA would inherently require an older person to give up her remaining years simply because she was older.[12] Therefore, if the basis of the FIA is the ideal that our lives should be of equal length, it is not a plausible argument.

However, Leaman's interpretation is not the only possible one. An alternative interpretation is the *prioritarian* one, that when there are two people who need the same medical resources in order to survive, one of them being nearer "old age" than the other, and only one "package" of resources is available, we should give it to the younger one. But by itself the prioritarian FIA is also implausible. If we are always to prioritize the younger person, we will have to maintain, for example, that it is better to save a thirty year old than a forty year old, or even a thirty-five year old than a thirty-six year old. Harris finds such a choice invidious because neither person has had their fair innings.[13] What is also required, then, is some decision about exactly what length of life is "fair," which can of course only be arbitrary. So, we might more plausibly think of the FIA as a combination of a prioritarian and a *sufficiency* view: the view that people should, as far as possible, be guaranteed a minimum length of life, and that society should prioritize those who have so far not enjoyed that sufficiency at the expense of those who have. This combined view of the FIA would not be subject to the more obvious criticisms outlined above, though it may nevertheless be found flawed for other reasons.

3. The CLV and FIA in Conflict

We can therefore think of the most plausible interpretation of the FIA as being a view that is concerned about means (resources) instead of ends (life itself), and a view that is guided by a principle of priority constrained by a sufficiency minimum (a threshold length of life that is deemed fair). However, although both the FIA in this formulation and the CLV are views about the just distribution of resources that require some of those resources to be withheld from the old (however defined) and given to the young, the two views have different implications. One reason for this is that while personal responsibility is both presupposed by, and a consequence of, the CLV, it is not necessary to the FIA. The CLV requires us to distribute resources so that each person has an equal share over the course of their complete lives, so that the more prudently individuals use those resources the longer they will last. In contrast, the FIA distributes resources only in such a way as to ensure that people have as fair an innings as possible; it is irrelevant how irresponsible a younger person has been about their health, or how prudent an older person has been. The younger person may have smoked and drunk heavily, had a poor diet and taken no exercise, while the older person has lived healthily, but if the FIA merely involves a claim that individuals are all entitled to a certain number of years of life, then it will nevertheless penalize the prudent older person.

In answer to this criticism we might adapt the FIA so that instead of applying to all persons it might instead only be used as a "tie-breaker" between two equally deserving people. If so, then, the level of personal responsibility that each individual had taken within their lives would be relevant. If they were equally deserving then responsibility would not be an issue, because if equally deserving they would have been equally responsible. The tie-breaking FIA would then only be used to discriminate in favor of a younger person in situations where two people, one older than the other, had been equally responsible for their health over their respective lives (always supposing that such a test could be made). However, it might be argued that in such a situation the older person has in fact been the more responsible because they have been so for longer. We can imagine a situation in which a younger person receives a scarce resource instead of the older person because she had at the time been deemed equally deserving and responsible to an older person, but who had then immediately become dissolute. By the time she reaches the same age that the disfavored older person had been when discriminated against, the now dissolute younger individual can certainly not be said to be equally deserving. So with hindsight we see that we ought to have given the resource to the older candidate after all. It does not seem absurd to suggest, therefore, that if to be equally deserving means being equally responsible for your health, then individuals should also be of equal age and so have been equally deserving or responsible for equally long. In such a case, however, the FIA would obviously be redundant because both individuals would have enjoyed an equal innings if not a fair one. The tie-breaking adaptation of the FIA therefore fails, and the criticism that the FIA ignores personal responsibility holds.

A comparison with the CLV, illustrated in the diagram below, expresses this criticism of the FIA. We can use the diagram to imagine two persons of differing ages, A and B, living simultaneously at T4 and both in need of a medical resource to prolong their lives into T5, but which, due to circumstances of scarcity, only one can have. The numbers for A and B at each temporal segment indicate the level of unhealthy living to which they have each subjected their bodies. If we imagine that the higher the number the more unhealthy the lifestyle (the more cigarettes they have smoked, alcohol they have drunk, saturated fat they have eaten, and the less exercise taken) then we can see that person A has been far less responsible in his shorter life than B has been in her longer life. Nevertheless, this is irrelevant from the point of view of the FIA. Any available resources will be directed toward the irresponsible person A to keep him alive as long as possible to ensure he reaches a fair innings, and the fact that B has taken care of her health throughout her life counts for nothing.

	T1	T2	T3	T4	T5	Total life irresponsibility
A		50 (child)	150 (youth)	**150 (middle age)**		**350**
B	50 (child)	50 (youth)	50 (middle age)	**50 (old)**		**200**

A second criticism often leveled at the FIA is that some of the elderly who have perhaps lived hard lives when they were young may have had much less enjoyment in their lives than some younger people have, and could claim in a real sense that they have not yet "had their life" or "their fair share."[14] We can again use the figure above to examine this criticism. In this instance the numbers indicate the quantity of resources that each person has spent or has had spent on them at each temporal period. Person A is only half the age of B but although he is only now coming toward the end of his youth he has used a great deal more resources in his short life than B has in her long life. Person B has therefore had a hard life and in one sense can be said not to have enjoyed as much life as person A. She may nevertheless have another couple of decades of life if she is given the medical resource they both need for survival.

As far as the FIA is concerned the person who has either achieved or is approaching old age should not have her life further prolonged when this could only be achieved at the cost of those who are not nearing old age. So, on the view of the FIA, person A would be saved and B would be sacrificed, even though his complete life share of resources will be far greater, simply because he is not yet nearing old age. By contrast, the CLV requires that the shares of resources that people enjoy over the course of their lives should be equal. As person B has enjoyed significantly less than A in this instance, any further resources should be channeled toward B rather than A. The CLV takes into consideration the past resources that each person has enjoyed while the FIA only counts life time. Moreover, B's claim to further resources would be further strengthened from the perspective of the CLV if we were to consider the projected resources or welfare that each person is likely to enjoy in the next temporal segment (T5). The possibility that A might consume any more resources would mean that the complete life inequality between the two people would be widened further, and this would be unacceptable.

A third common criticism of the FIA is that the old have earned a right to be treated before the young because they will have paid more in national insurance contributions over their lives, and so will have contributed toward both their own old age and those who were members of the old age group before them. Again the FIA is unconcerned about this previous investment and is only concerned with the actual ages of persons, but how is this issue treated by the CLV? At first glance it may seem that the CLV would ignore this issue as well because the view is solely concerned with the fair distribution of resources to the complete lives of individuals, and it stipulates that what people are entitled to is a relatively equal share of these. By itself the CLV would indicate that if someone, like Person B in the above example, distributed their resources in a prudent way over the temporal stages of their lives, then until they had used up those resources, they would always be entitled to further claims irrespective of their age. If I start out with an equal complete life of resources and then invest them carefully, adding to that investment from the income I receive through life, then I will be able to buy significantly more benefits in old age than if I had been profligate. The CLV by itself does not explain how this can be done. For this reason, as outlined in the previous chapter, the CLV has been combined with a prudential analogy (PA) by several political philosophers,[15] and this hypothetical thought experiment is used to show what justice requires society to spend on the well-being of its citizens at the various stages of their lives. The combination of the CLV and a PA is therefore able to address the challenge that the FIA ignores: that the cumulative contributions of people throughout their lives give them certain claims of justice that younger people do not possess.

So, although the FIA and CLV both justify age discrimination, they can each be interpreted in different ways, and the implications of each view might conflict with the implications of the other. However, although the two views differ, a fully adequate anti-ageist argument would need to identify a common reason that accounts for the wrongfulness of both ageist justifications. This is the object of the final section of this chapter.

4. Challenging Age Discrimination

As Geoffrey Cupit notes, "the alleged injustice of age discrimination presents a puzzle," because the "standard argument against discrimination—the argument from equalizing benefits—seems not to apply."[16] It does not apply because, as we have seen, equalizing benefits between the complete lives of separate persons might actually *justify* age discrimination rather than challenge it. It does this for the obvious fact that each of us has a turn to be old, and, by taking turns to be well off or badly off, temporal or synchronic inequalities will even out over the course of people's complete lives. It is this simple intuitive idea that lends discrimination on the basis of age the significant moral plausibility it enjoys. It means that age discrimination can be defended as fair because it treats everyone the same over their complete lives, and it can even be said to be in everyone's interests. It is not therefore surprising that, as Age Concern has claimed, the anti-ageist argument is a position which has "been much less widely articulated or disseminated" than defenses of ageism.[17]

Nevertheless, there have been several attempts to make intelligible the intuition that age discrimination is unjust. Cupit, for example, develops an argument to express the anti-ageist intuition that is based upon the notion of status.[18] He claims that each of us has an equal moral status and that the injustice of age discrimination has its real source in that equal status not being respected throughout a person's life. So age discrimination is not a comparative injustice in the same way as sexism and racism are, and the injustice it involves is not in the inappropriate treatment of some people in comparison to others, but as far as it is comparative, in the inappropriate treatment of people in comparison to their earlier (or later) selves. While defining status is a complex issue, what Cupit's argument implies is that age discrimination is wrong because it treats persons differently at one point in their lives to the way they are treated at another point.

Another defense of the anti-ageist position has been presented by Dennis McKerlie, who attempts to preserve an appeal to the normative principle of equalizing benefits. However, rather than equalizing benefits over the complete lives of separate individuals, McKerlie believes we should, at least on some occasions, seek to equalize as far as possible the synchronic parts of people's lives. In his most recent article McKerlie refines his position from synchronic egalitarianism to a synchronic priority view, and he suggests instead that we should prioritize those individuals who are worst off at the time, irrespective of the level of resources they have enjoyed in the past.[19]

McKerlie supports his position by imagining two scenarios in which he believes it would be morally more plausible to be concerned about the synchronic interests of an older person than a younger one. In the first example, McKerlie believes we would prefer to help an old person who is very badly off instead of someone younger and better off, even if it is clear that the actual benefit for the older person's well-being would be smaller than the benefit to that of the younger person. If one person is presently fairly well off, it would seem odd that we should prefer to give him a larger benefit than to give a poorer person a smaller benefit. The reason it would seem odd must partly be explained by the fact that we can identify with the synchronic interests of the older person who is now in greater need. In a second scenario, McKerlie argues that we would prefer to help an old person who is very badly off rather than a younger person who is badly off, yet not as badly off, even though the older person has already consumed more resources than the younger person is likely to do in his life. When we are dealing with morally urgent claims of justice it does seem plausible that we would not be primarily concerned with the total level of benefits someone has or is likely to enjoy over their complete lives.

Both Cupit and McKerlie are responding to the age discrimination inherent within the CLV. However, John Harris has articulated what is probably still the best "anti-ageist argument" in regard to the FIA, which denies absolutely the relevance of age as a criterion of discrimination within the distribution of healthcare resources.[20] This anti-ageist argument claims that there is something that each of us values equally no matter how old we are, which is to say "the rest of our lives." So long as we do not know the date of our deaths, then for each of us the rest of our life is of indefinite duration, and we each suffer the same injustice if our wishes to continue living are deliberately frustrated. Harris believes that:

> the anti-ageist argument has much plausibility. It locates the wrongfulness of ending an individual's life in the evil of thwarting that person's desire to go on living and argues that it is profoundly unjust to frustrate that desire merely because some of those who have exactly the same desire, held no more strongly, also have a longer life expectancy than others.[21]

Each of these three anti-ageist defenses appeals to the idea that people not only have diachronic interests with regards to a fair lifespan or to an equal lifetime share of benefits or opportunity, but that people also have synchronic interests that are both morally significant and that are not reducible to their diachronic interests. Indeed, the two kinds of interests may conflict.[22] The idea that each person has irreducible and morally significant synchronic interests gives us a reason to be concerned about any policy that leads to differential treatment for the old that is solely based upon chronological age. If each person has the same fundamental synchronic interests that demand equal treatment irrespective of age, then justice requires a balancing of the synchronic interests of different people of different ages on an equal footing. Policies that neglect or violate those interests during any part of a person's life on the basis of something as arbitrary as age are thereby unjust. For Cupit and McKerlie these fundamental synchronic interests would be those that each of us have in enjoying a minimally decent life at each temporal moment of that life. Harris, on the other hand, effectively argues that we each have a synchronic interest in living out whatever life we still have. Looking at the problem from this perspective suggests that the strong plausibility that discrimination against the old seems to enjoy is derived from the assumption that we should give exclusive concern to the diachronic interests of persons: that is to say, to the diachronic interests we each have either to reach a fair innings or to enjoy an equal level of opportunity as everyone else over our complete lives. But this exclusive concern for diachronic interests does not sufficiently recognize the dual nature of our self-interest.

My conclusion, therefore, is that to be effective an anti-ageist argument should appeal to the idea that there are certain synchronic interests that have equal moral value irrespective of the chronological age of the individual who holds them. These interests ought to be protected for each person at each temporal period of his or her life. However, there is an important difficulty that arises from such an anti-ageist defense. If there are two irreducible dimensions to our self-interest, diachronic and synchronic, neither of which is fundamentally prior to the other, then there is no obvious way of determining which has precedence in any particular situation. This means that we would be left with a messy intuitionist balancing of the synchronic and diachronic interests of different people in any rationing decision-making process. And of course the rationing of resources will always be necessary where demand exceeds supply.

NOTES

1. John Harris, The Value of Life: An Introduction to Medical Ethics (London: Routledge, 1985), p. 93.

2. *Ibid.*, pp. 93–94.

3. Alan Williams, "Intergenerational Equity: An Exploration of the 'Fair Innings Argument," *Health Economics*, 6:2 (March–April 1997), pp. 117–32.

4. Age Concern, *New Survey of GPs Confirms Ageism in the NHS* (Age Concern England, Press Release, 17 May 2000); Christine Farrell, Janice Robinson, and Peter Fletcher, *A New Era for Community Care? What People Want from Health, Housing, and Social Care Services* (London: Kings Fund, 1999).

5. Ronald Dworkin, "What is Equality? Part Two: Equality of Resources," *Philosophy and Public Affairs*, 10:4 (Fall 1981), pp. 304–5.

6. Ronald Dworkin, *Life's Dominion: An Argument About Abortion and Euthanasia* (London: Harper Collins, 1993), p. 88.

7. Daniel Callahan, *Setting Limits: Medical Goals in an Ageing Society* (New York, NY: Simon and Schuster, 1987).

8. *Ibid.*, p. 140.

9. *Ibid.*

10. *Ibid.*, pp. 171–173.

11. Oliver Leaman, "Justifying Ageism," *Ageing, Autonomy and Resources*, ed. A. Harry Lesser (Aldershot: Ashgate, 1999), p. 182.

12. Ibid., p. 184.

13. Harris, *The Value of Life*, p. 93.

14. Harry Lesser, "Ageism," *Encyclopedia of Applied Ethics, Volume 1 A–D*, ed. Ruth Chadwick (London: Academic Press, 1998), p. 93.

15. John Rawls, *A Theory of Justice* (Cambridge, MA: Harvard University Press, 1971).; Dworkin, "What is Equality? Part Two: Equality of Resources"; Norman Daniels, *Am I My Parent's Keeper? An Essay on the Justice Between Young and Old* (New York, NY: Oxford University Press, 1988).

16. Geoffrey Cupit, "Justice, Age, and Veneration," *Ethics* 108:4 (July 1998), p. 702.

17. Age Concern England, *The Millennium Papers: Values and Attitudes in an Ageing Society* (London: Age Concern England, 1999), p. 28.

18. Cupit, "Justice, Age, and Veneration," p. 709.

19. Dennis McKerlie, "Justice Between the Young and the Old", *Philosophy and Public Affairs*, 30:2 (Spring 2002), pp. 152–177.

20. Harris, *The Value of Life*, Chapter Five.

21. *Ibid.*, p. 90.

22. J. David Velleman, *The Possibility of Practical Reason* (Oxford: Clarendon Press, 2000), pp. 56–84.

Fifteen

TRIAGE AND OLDER PATIENTS

Harry Lesser

1. The Principle of Triage

The three previous chapters of this book have investigated, and rejected, various alleged grounds for maintaining that in the provision of healthcare, and perhaps of social care in general, some forms of age-based discrimination are just. In this chapter I will consider whether the principle of triage is a possible ground for such discrimination. I will argue that the principle itself is valid, but its application in this way to older patients is not.

We need to begin by explaining the principle, although it is familiar to many, if not most, people. As is well known, its origins were on the battlefield, where it was used by surgeons to decide whom to operate on under circumstances when the shortage of trained doctors, equipment, and time made it impossible to treat all the wounded men before they died. The principle requires the medical staff to make a rapid assessment of those needing treatment, and to assign each of them to one of three groups: those who will probably die, even if treated; those who will probably recover, even if left untreated; and those who, again probably, will live if treated and die if untreated. The first two groups are then put on one side, as it were, and everything possible is done to save as many of the third group as we can. Only when this is done will attention be turned to the other groups, apart from keeping them in the meantime as comfortable as circumstances permit.

The principle is clearly rough and ready. The decisions have to be made at great speed, so that time that could be used for actually saving people is not lost by taking too long to decide whom to save. They have to be based on probabilities: we do not actually know with absolute certainty who will die and who will live. They also have to be arbitrary: there is no exact way of deciding how soon a person must be expected to die in order to be put in the first group, or how long they have to be expected to live to justify their going in the second. But some such principle is presumably needed when resources are limited and time short, and triage does seem to be intuitively right. There is some evidence that in an emergency, such as after a train accident, doctors can find themselves using it almost automatically. But this still leaves three important questions. First, should we trust our intuitions here? Second, if the principle of triage is right, why is it right? Third, should it be extended to situations other than obvious emergencies?

Before we discuss these questions, we should note that the principle itself, though rough and ready, is more complex than this sketch suggests. The fact that treatment will, probably, make the difference between life and death is not always enough to justify putting someone in the priority group. This could be for at least three reasons. One is that it might be possible to save the person from death but only at the cost of a life of great pain or handicap. Another is that the person might already have a terminal illness, so that saving them from one death would not lengthen their life. Third, the time and resources required to save the person might be disproportionate, and require leaving several other people to die. So there have to be the further considerations of whether, on the known evidence, saving a person from this particular death will be a gain for them, and whether saving them is a reasonable use of resources.

2. The Justification of Triage

Given all this, is it right to use the principle, and why? It is commonly thought that the principle is a utilitarian one, that we should use triage because in that way we will maximize the good that we do with the limited resources available—or, at least, maximize it as far as our limited knowledge permits. But is this so? It is true that on the battlefield, or after an accident, use of triage maximizes the saving of life, which is one of the main aims of medicine. But to maximize the saving of life is not the same, always, as maximizing good or minimizing harm. Medicine makes no judgments as to the usefulness to society of the lives saved or the restorations to health. It might be the case that one or more of the people who can be saved are likely to do so much harm, if they live, that from the point of view of benefit to society they should be left to die. Or it might be the case that someone who could be saved, but only by diverting resources from several other people, would nevertheless be likely to do so much good that it would, again from the point of view of benefiting society, be right to save them even at the cost of the lives of these others. Triage is a principle of efficient use of resources, but not a utilitarian principle: it may or may not coincide with what is best from a utilitarian point of view.

To this, a utilitarian may make two replies, not inconsistent with each other. The first is that we simply do not have the knowledge to make judgments of this sort about future usefulness, and therefore ought to make our judgments purely on the basis of the best use of resources. One could maintain this as a weak or a strong principle. The weak principle would be that in practice we seldom or never have the necessary information to justify this kind of conclusion: the best we could have is a suspicion of what might be likely, which is hardly good enough as a basis for giving or withholding treatment, given that our judgments of who is most in need of treatment, though also not certain, are considerably better based. The strong principle would be that it is always impossible to know, or even to assert with real confidence, what a person will do in the future (other than the immediate future, perhaps): we could never do better than a strong suspicion, whatever we knew about past behavior and present intentions. Therefore, the utilitarian can maintain, it is on utilitarian principles that we should opt for triage.

Second, it might plausibly be argued that to require, or even to permit, medical personnel, however well intentioned and upright in character, to choose whom to treat on the basis of their supposed social usefulness would put far too much power into their hands, and in the long term—perhaps not that long—would have harmful consequences from the utilitarian point of view. Even though it would on particular occasions do good, as a policy it would be harmful, if not disastrous; and even occasional use of such a principle would be open to the objection that it might well be the thin end of the wedge. So triage can be justified from a utilitarian standpoint in this way as well.

Nevertheless, triage is not in itself a utilitarian principle. Its use is an example of a common moral phenomenon, that the best consequences are often achieved by operating a system which is overall beneficial, and therefore justified on utilitarian principles, but which operates according to its own principles. Hume pointed this out, in Chapter Three of the *Enquiry Concerning the Principles of Morals*, with regard to promise keeping and respecting private property; and Rawls developed the point, in "Two Concepts of Rules,"[1] with regard to promise keeping and punishment. So a system of punishment may be justified because it discourages harmful activities, but particular punishments are justified by the fact that someone has broken a rule and is receiving the prescribed penalty. Similarly, utilitarianism justifies having a system of triage for deciding who should receive treatment first, but the system itself justifies the choices made.

Moreover, triage can also be justified on grounds of justice. Triage allocates treatment on the basis of the greatest need, bringing those for whom treatment will probably make the difference between life and death to the head of the queue, and only after that dealing with those whom treatment may well not help and those who can probably manage without it. Need is not the only valid principle of justice, even in the allocation of medical care: principles such as desert and entitlement to resources, need also to be taken seriously. But intuitively it seems clear that in the allocation of medical care it is the most important, and that when resources are limited, and some people will therefore not be treated at all, it is the one that should prevail, the others coming in only when needs are equal.

Perhaps this is too strong. The principle that as a matter of justice need is the most important criterion in allocating medical care is one that cannot be proved, and has sometimes been disputed. But it is certainly in line with strong moral intuitions. If two patients cannot both be treated immediately, and it is clear that the life of one is in danger and that of the other is not, the fact that the second patient is ahead in the queue, or can pay for the treatment, or deserves it more, becomes irrelevant: the priority is to save life. This does not apply only to life and death situations. If one patient is in intense pain and another in bearable pain, the first patient has the claim on a painkiller, if it is in limited supply. It could apply in psychiatric medicine, as between a psychotic and a neurotic. It might apply, with regard to help with conception, to a woman near the end of her fertile years with no children as compared with a younger woman with a child already. (This last example is a bit different: it applies if other things are equal, which they are not always). It also can apply to social care, as well as to healthcare, in so far as the two can be distinguished. The need to be saved from a depression that may lead to suicide can be as great as the need for a life-saving operation.

This criterion of need, though it operates widely, is required only when the differences in need are very clear and resources are limited. We expect, for example, that a General Practitioner will normally see patients in the order of their appointments, and depart from this only in a real emergency. On the other hand, we expect assessments of need to be made as a matter of course in an Accident and Emergency Department, where there are great variations in the seriousness of the conditions of those coming in, and often a shortage of time and personnel.

At this point, it might be objected that, while this is what we expect, we need to consider whether we are right to expect it. Can we be so sure that need is the appropriate criterion, as compared with other candidates? To test this, we need to consider other ways of distributing healthcare.

One possibility is to make no judgments at all, and simply to see people in the order they present themselves, or the order in which you come to them. Indeed, as said above, this is how general practice normally operates. But this is something that seems just only when there are no emergencies. In an emergency, whether life-threatening or involving the relief of great pain, it seems entirely just for those in immediate need to be given preference, and it would be very unjust if they were not. Another possibility would be to concentrate on maximizing the amount of good being done, and using some criterion such as Quality Adjusted Life Years (QALYs) to calculate this. Some of the major problems with this procedure have been raised in earlier chapters. Finally, there is the possibility of using merit as a criterion. But, even if one could determine the relative virtue, or social usefulness, of different people, which is in any case nearly always impossible, this is, as regards justice, the wrong criterion for the distribution of healthcare.

However, there are those who would argue that a particular application of the criterion of merit is in fact just. They would argue that those who have brought their illness or injury on themselves do have less claim, if there is scarcity, than those who are ill through no fault of their own. Now this seems to be a fair point if the needs of the two groups are equal; though it may be a purely theoretical point, as a rule, because of the difficulty, unless there is actual and direct self-harm, as in self-mutilation, of determining whether people really have brought their condition upon themselves. But if a person's need for treatment is urgent, then this consideration does not seem to hold. It is very annoying, as medical staff will tell us, to have to give time to people who have deliberately and unnecessarily seriously injured themselves, but no-one thinks it right actually to refuse treatment. The only occasions on which treatment has in practice been refused (and this is rare, but I think not unknown) or where conditions have been made relate not to a person's behavior before they were ill but to their future behavior. So, giving up smoking has sometimes been made a condition of providing an operation or other treatment. But the point here is that if the patient does not give up smoking the treatment will be useless. And to refuse to give useless treatment is exactly in accordance with the principle of triage.

3. Applying the Principle of Triage

So it seems that triage can be defended on grounds of justice, as well as possibly on utilitarian grounds. The question then is: how wide should its application be? I have already suggested that it applies when there is an emergency. But it can well be argued that in healthcare we are always in an emergency situation. Even if we think only of situations where there is a clear and undisputed need for healthcare, it may be said, we do not have the time and resources to help everyone in need. This would be true, moreover, even if considerably more resources were provided, as, in the opinion of many, they should be. So, the argument proceeds, the right and just procedure would be to use triage all the time, in general practice as well as in Accident and Emergency, as being in fact always the fairest system. We should always start by treating those in the greatest need, and work down the list as far as possible.

The possibility that the principle of triage ought to be extended in this massive way raises two big questions. First, would this be practicable? Second, would this be just? As regards practicability, there are two formidable problems. The first is the difference between micro-level and macro-level. When triage is used in a specific situation, such as after an accident, or in running a particular unit, even a large one, assessments are being made between people as individuals. If triage were used across the board, assessments would have to made with regard to types of condition. This would mean that even if assessments were correctly made, there would be some unfairness, even by the criterion of triage itself, because a certain level of need would have to be assigned to all patients with a particular condition at a particular estimated level of seriousness. Constraints of time would make this inevitable. Since in fact these patients would not all be at the same level of need, because of such things as their overall condition of health and their psychological temperament, some patients would benefit and others suffer, and there would be an injustice built into the system, and not simply the result of mistakes.

The second problem would be the weighing up of needs, as more or less serious. In the standard uses of triage, we are dealing—often, at any rate—either with one overriding criterion for treatment, such as whether it will make the difference between life and death, or with one particular type of treatment, for which the need is relatively well-defined. Even here assessments are rough and ready, and subject to error. But with the use of triage across the board we would have to apply it to all health needs. Such needs are of at least three types—the need for life, the need for adequate physical and mental functioning, and the need to be free from serious pain or suffering. Very often these go together, and the provision of medical treatment meets all of them. But this is not always the case, and it is when it is not the case that some of the hardest dilemmas in medical ethics, such as whether to prolong life or relieve suffering, set in. In an emergency it seems to right to concentrate on saving lives. But in formulating general policy things are less clear. A general policy of giving preference to saving life, and then to dealing with conditions which cause the greatest suffering or incapacity, and after that to less serious conditions, would often be right but not always. On occasion it would result in the unnecessary prolonging of suffering or failure to relieve it.

Part of the problem is the impossibility, or at least very great difficulty, of comparing different types of need. If we are dealing only or primarily with threats to life, we can try to assess their relative gravity—how likely they are to kill, and how soon—even if they are very different kinds of threat. But with incapacity and with suffering the problems are much worse. How do we compare physical and mental suffering, or pain and indignity? Is a psychiatric illness more or less disabling than a physical one?

We may therefore say that, even in the standard uses of triage, whether in emergencies or in the allocation of a very specific kind of treatment, there will be arbitrary and rough and ready decisions. If the principle were to be generally applied, so that comparisons would have to be made between radically different conditions, which would also involve decisions about which criteria to use, and how to apply them. There would be as a result so much that was arbitrary that the principle could not be effectively used at all. And then there is the question of justice. In an emergency, what is most important simply overrides what is less important. If the medical staff have got to save a life, people with conditions that are not immediately life-threatening will have to wait, even if they are in pain. But in a normal situation we have to try to meet all claims, including the less important. Suppose, for example, that in a particular medical unit, the person literally or metaphorically at the head of the queue has a painful but not dangerous skin complaint. It is right and just that an emergency case, particularly a life and death case, should overtake them. But it would not be right for everyone with a more serious illness or injury, everyone, let us say, that they themselves would agree was in greater need, to overtake them, with the consequence, very likely, that they were never treated at all. One might make the point by saying that in an emergency some cases have exclusive priority, and if treating those cases makes it impossible to treat others it is nevertheless right to attend to them. But under normal circumstances, even when resources are limited, no genuine need should be excluded from attention. (There is some argument as to what constitutes genuine need, but quite a large area of agreement).

A just health service has to try to provide resources for all levels and types of health needs, as its basic goal, or at least to provide for what are universally or nearly universally agreed to be health needs. It will no doubt be necessary to prioritize, but this is not the same as eliminating some types of care altogether, which is what would happen if a total and consistent use of triage were to be operated. That justice requires some provision for all health needs can be seen if we apply a version of Rawls' "veil of ignorance" test.[2] Consider a person who has no means of knowing what demands they are likely to make on health resources in the course of their life. Probably most of us are in this situation. Such a person would presumably prefer a Health Service which tried to meet all types of health need, even though this meant that resources could not be absolutely guaranteed, over one which absolutely guaranteed that certain crucial needs would be met but altogether failed to meet, or even to try to meet, certain others, admittedly less serious but still needs. A person in this position is a person with no personal axe to grind, since they do not know what they themselves will require from the system. As a result, their preferences are equivalent to the requirements of a fair system. The fairest system is therefore the one that people would opt for if they did not know whether or not it would benefit them personally: the one that can in principle benefit everyone, while giving some priority to those in the greatest need.

4. Triage and Older People

If this is correct, the principle of triage has two proper applications. It provides a rough and ready way of identifying the people with the strongest claim to treatment, both in an emergency and when we are dealing with a relatively specific condition or type of treatment. It also provides a valid reason for withholding treatment, even in emergency—namely, that the treatment will do no good, whether because the patient will die in any event, or because they will not be able to respond. But triage is not a fair principle on which to base an overall system of distributing medical care. It would inevitably lead to ignoring claims to medical care which, although not the most vital, are still legitimate.

What implications does this have for the distribution of medical resources to older patients, or potential patients? Does it give any valid ground for "age discrimination?" The answer is that it does not. If triage is applied, treatment that is in effect useless will not be given. A number of factors can cause this, as we have seen. The patient may be going to die anyway from some other condition; or they may have available only a very low quality of life if their life is saved; or they may be physically or psychologically unable to benefit from the treatment. All these are more likely to occur among the old, and their probability increases with age. But none of them is caused by chronological age alone. There is no point at which we can say that a person is bound to die very soon, or bound to have poor quality of life, or bound to be unable to benefit from a particular treatment. No condition has yet been found which is inevitable after a certain age. So age is simply irrelevant to application of triage. There will of course be more old people who are denied treatment on the grounds of triage than there are younger people. But this should never be on the grounds of age alone, but on the grounds of their actual physical or mental condition.

I have argued (1) that triage is a principle of justice; (2) that it is the appropriate principle to use in an emergency or when we are dealing with a very specific treatment or condition; (3) that it would not be practicable or just to use triage as a principle governing all decisions about the distribution of medical resources; (4) that it can and should be used as a ground for withholding treatment from those for whom it can do more good; (5) that, although a higher percentage of older people will come into this category, with regard to many or most forms of treatment, chronological age cannot in itself be a valid ground for assuming without further investigation that the treatment cannot do any good. We should be tough-minded and unsentimental, and resist the temptation to do things which are useless or harmful because we feel we must do something. But we should not pretend that easing or extending a person's final years, or months, or even days, is doing no good.

NOTES

1. John Rawls, "Two Concepts of Rules," *Contemporary Utilitarianism*, ed. Michael D. Bayles (New York, NY: Doubleday, 1968), pp. 59–98.
2. John Rawls, *A Theory of Justice* (Oxford: Oxford University Press, 1999).

Sixteen

JUSTICE, GUIDELINES, AND VIRTUES

Julian C. Hughes

1. Introduction

Comparing equity and justice Aristotle wrote:

> ... the equitable is just, but not the legally just but a correction of legal justice. The reason is that all law is universal but about some things it is not possible to make a universal statement which shall be correct .... And it is none the less correct; for the error is not in the law nor in the legislators but in the nature of the thing, since the matter of practical affairs is of this kind from the start .... And this is the nature of the equitable, a correction of law where it is defective owing to its universality. (Aristotle, 1980, pp. 1137^b10–1137^b30)

This is an argument for what sounds like a very modern conception of practical ethics, namely that in the application of principles or rules we need to pay attention to the particularities and individual context of each case. But then virtue theory, which derives from Aristotle, has in recent years provided a viable alternative to the influential theories (consequentialism and deontology) that increasingly appear too detached to speak to the realities of clinical practice.

This chapter starts at the coalface with a particular problem: should medication be prescribed to someone, where it might be beneficial and where the risk of adverse effects is low, even though criteria established in national guidelines are not met? To distance ourselves a little from the particular patient, the question concerns the distribution of healthcare resources: if a national regulating body has ruled that a certain medication ought only to be used under specific circumstances, under what circumstances can it be right for an individual clinician to ignore the ruling? The issue is to do with justice and equity.

There is a way to approach the problem of the distribution of scarce healthcare resources so as to make a utilitarian argument seem inevitably compelling. My contention is that virtue ethics allows a more nuanced approach, one that does justice to the reality of the particular clinical encounter.

2. Case Study: Prescribing Anti-Dementia Medication against a NICE Background: *Mr AB*

Mr AB, at the time of his presentation, was a seventy-six year old man who was something of a local celebrity. He came from a working-class background, but had written several books and was frequently asked to speak at public events. His presenting complaint was that, during such a speech, he was interrupted and he then found that he was not able to recall what he intended to say. This led to a general loss of confidence and he started to avoid public speaking so that his life became more circumscribed. His wife said that she found him to be more forgetful and somewhat more emotional.

At the initial assessment he was able to provide a huge amount of detailed history, both recent and remote. Much of this was verified by his wife, but there were some details that were less certain. He said that he had no family history of dementia, but his wife reminded him that his mother had developed Alzheimer's disease. Mr AB's father had been a coalminer, but he himself had won a place at a Grammar School. His later career was mainly clerical, but his contributions to the local community gained him some fame, so that into his later years he remained a well-recognized and respected local figure. Significant features in his previous medical history included angina, hypertension, and a head injury many years prior to his presentation. He took appropriate medications. He had not smoked for many years and his alcohol consumption was minimal.

As regards his mental state, he was animated, intelligent, friendly, polite, and well groomed. His speech was entirely normal. There was no evidence of any marked affective symptoms and certainly nothing psychotic. He had good insight into the nature of his problems. In terms of cognitive function, he was able to recall names. In formal testing he scored twenty-eight out of thirty on the Mini Mental State Examination (MMSE). (Folstein *et al.*, 1975) He had some difficulty drawing interconnecting pentagons and he was two days out for the exact date. He also had problems drawing a clock face, writing the numbers outside the circle, and then circling them, albeit they were correctly positioned. On a test of verbal fluency using the category "animals" he scored twelve in one minute.

It was agreed that further assessment was required. When seen, after a delay, there was little of note on physical examination. More detailed neuropsychological testing demonstrated a global deterioration in both performance and verbal IQ in comparison with his estimated premorbid IQ. His full-scale IQ score was 113, but, at the time of presentation, his actual functioning gave him a full-scale IQ score of seventy-seven (where the 98% confidence interval was seventy-three to eighty-two). A CT scan of the brain showed no ischemic changes, but marked atrophy, with reduced volume of the medial temporal lobes. A SPECT scan showed large ventricles, with reduced temporal lobe uptake, especially on the right, and reduced right parietal uptake.

In summary, Mr AB presented as a seventy-six year old man with a history of problems of recall, which were affecting his functioning and which had caused a noticeable change in his behavior, noted by his wife. Screening tests of his mental functioning had shown only very minimal deficits, mostly affecting executive functioning, whereas more detailed testing demonstrated a more global, but still mild, deterioration in his cognitive function. Neuro-imaging showed atrophy of the medial temporal lobes, which is in keeping with (but not diagnostic of) Alzheimer's disease. The functional imaging was also in keeping with a diagnosis of Alzheimer's disease, although more unilateral than is typical. There were some risk factors for cerebro-vascular disease, but there was no history to suggest transient ischemic attacks or strokes, and no obvious evidence of ischemia on the CT scan.

On the basis of the above findings, a diagnosis of Alzheimer's disease seemed reasonable. Mr AB was expecting such a diagnosis and, indeed, he and his family were keen that he should be started on a cholinesterase inhibitor (an anti-dementia drug). When his case was reviewed, therefore, five and a half months after the initial assessment, the diagnosis of Alzheimer's disease was discussed, a referral to the local Alzheimer's Society was organized, and the use of a cholinesterase inhibitor was considered.

3. A NICE Interlude

The background to the decision concerning whether or not to use a cholinesterase inhibitor (hereafter referred to simply as an anti-dementia drug) is that, having first appeared on the United Kingdom market in 1997, the drugs have been subject to guidance following a technology appraisal issued in January 2001 by the National Institute for Clinical Excellence (NICE). The 2001 appraisal was reviewed in November 2006 and is incorporated in a National Clinical Practice Guideline (National Collaborating Centre for Mental Health, 2007). Having reviewed all the relevant available data, the technology appraisal clearly acknowledged that the anti-dementia drugs have some efficacy in terms of symptom management in Alzheimer's dementia (National Institute for Health and Clinical Excellence, 2006). However, it concluded that the anti-dementia drugs were only cost-effective in the moderate stages of Alzheimer's disease. This was defined in terms of an MMSE score between ten and twenty points. The guidance goes on to say that professionals "should not rely on the MMSE score in certain circumstances"; for instance:

> in those with an MMSE score greater than twenty, who have moderate dementia as judged by significant impairments in functional ability and personal and social function compared with premorbid ability." (National Collaborating Centre for Mental Health, 2007, 7.9.3.2).

The key point for Mr AB is that his MMSE score of twenty-eight puts him significantly above the current cut-off for the use of an anti-dementia drug. Whilst the current technology appraisal allows that judgments might be made that the person is in the moderate stage of Alzheimer's dementia despite scoring above twenty on the MMSE, it would be difficult to argue that Mr AB's general "functional ability and personal and social function" were so impaired compared with his premorbid ability as to place him in the moderate range of a dementia. Consequently, even the "get out" clause does not seem applicable to Mr AB, unless a very broad definition of "moderate dementia" is accepted. The reality was that, at the time of presentation, Mr AB was only in the mildest stages of his condition. The NICE guidelines, therefore, would suggest that he should not have been given an anti-dementia drug.

It is worth noting that NICE guidance contains a general comment, which states that healthcare professionals must take the guidance fully into account "when exercising their clinical judgement"; but it goes on to say:

> the guidance does not, however, override the individual responsibility of healthcare professionals to make decisions appropriate to the circumstances of the individual patient, in consultation with the patient and/or guardian or carer. (National Institute of Clinical Excellence, 2006)

4. Treating Mr AB

The decision, five and a half months after his presentation, was that Mr AB should be started on an anti-dementia drug. After three months of treatment (and therefore eight and a half months after his initial assessment), Mr AB remained mentally and physically active. He still found recall a little difficult, but he was able to enjoy things. On formal screening of his cognitive function using the MMSE he again scored twenty-eight out of thirty. His previous poor drawing of interconnecting pentagons had improved, but his drawing of the clock face was more bizarre. On this occasion his numbering went up to nineteen and he drew lines from the centre of the circle to each of the numbers, which were not equally spaced, and he failed to show the hands of the clock.

It was quite difficult, therefore, to argue that Mr AB had improved since starting the anti-dementia drug. His family, though, thought that things were somewhat better, and they were certainly no worse. After eight and a half months one might have predicted a fall in his MMSE score by at least a few points. However, later on, at thirty months after his presentation, which was roughly two years after starting treatment, Mr AB was doing very well mentally and physically. He continued to take the anti-dementia drug. He was now able to give talks in public, though he was aware that he suffered from a slight tendency to lose the point, especially if there was too much input. His MMSE score was twenty-seven out of thirty. Again, the drop in the MMSE is less than might have been predicted several years after a diagnosis of Alzheimer's disease has been made.

Four years after the diagnosis the anti-dementia drug had to be increased, but Mr AB was still joining in and to some extent leading a discussion group led by the local Alzheimer's Society. He was still able to go out on his own to attend social events, although he was experiencing problems with language expression. Five years after his diagnosis, he remained amiable, continued to live independently with his wife, was occasionally depressed and was somewhat less keen on socializing, but was still getting out. He was also continuing to benefit from and to participate in activities at a day centre. His speech problems were more obvious, but he was able to express his dismay at the new 2006 NICE technology appraisal concerning the anti-dementia drug.

5. A Question of Facts and Ethics

The case of Mr AB raises several questions. There are factual questions, for instance about the certainty (and purity) of the diagnosis of Alzheimer's disease. Nevertheless, the course of his condition over five years has shown a gradual global deterioration, which in most respects looks clinically like the progression of Alzheimer's disease, albeit on a somewhat slow scale. If the clinical impression is true, it might act as a *post hoc* justification for the use of the anti-dementia drug. Although the drugs are mainly regarded only as symptomatic treatments, the suggestion that they might also affect the underlying progression of the disease is one that the pharmaceutical companies would love to establish. The case of Mr AB might demonstrate the benefits of early treatment, which slowed the course of the illness. However, this is precisely the problem with single case histories: they establish little but possibilities. In fact, the truth is we cannot be certain that the anti-dementia drug has been at all efficacious for Mr AB. He and his family are sure it has helped. The clinical impression was that it might have helped, and it certainly seemed reasonable to give Mr AB the benefit of the doubt.

Whatever the factual matters of the case, an ethical question arises. The question has broad applicability, beyond the case of Mr AB or the use of anti-dementia drugs. It is this: can it ever be right and, if so, under what conditions—for an individual clinician to ignore (carefully researched, deliberated, and accordingly authoritative) national guidelines in a particular case?

6. NICE, Equity, and Distribution

Rationing in healthcare is inevitable. In this section I will simply sketch some of the ethical assumptions behind the decision-making of NICE. Theories of rationing in connection with old age are discussed more fully by Tony Hope and Catherine Oppenheimer (Hope and Oppenheimer, 1997) and in Harry Lesser's book (Lesser, 1999). My own inclination is to side with those who hold that, in fact, Quality Adjusted Life Years (QALYs) tend to discriminate against older people because they can expect fewer QALYs than younger people (Harris, 1987). Moreover, some of the assumptions used to calculate QALYs can be doubted. For instance, T.M. Arnesen and O.F. Norheim (Arnesen and Norheim, 2003) argue that the *hypothetical* trade-offs, required to determine QALYs, between the *value* of life lived in different health states and the *number* of life years, are simply not possible.

> It is difficult to conceptualise a trade of lifetime against quality of life because they are so deeply interrelated. Quality and quantity are different dimensions of existence, and neither of them can substitute for the other. (Arnesen and Norheim, 2003, p. 83)

Further, the same authors (Arnesen and Norheim 2003) point to the deep problem of quantifying quality of life, which is especially problematic in dementia (Hughes, 2003). The currency (the QALY) used to allocate resources between conditions is open to the charge that it is not itself fair with respect to age and is therefore ageist. This sort of discrimination "*dis*-values the person *qua* person"; it undermines "the history, values, culture, experience, and agency that help to define older people as persons." (Hughes, 2002, p. 887) Rationing on the basis of age is not fair (Rivlin, 2000) for the same reason that judgments about quality of life for older people as a whole are wrong. In both cases the importance of the individual is subsumed by the group, whereas "older people are a very varied group and, if we are to do the right thing for them, we need to treat them individually." (Hughes, 2007, p. 470)

And yet, at the level of society there is a need to limit the consumption of scarce healthcare resources. In the UK, NICE is the institution intended to give health professionals information that will allow them to provide optimal services. But this involves "judgments both about what is good or bad in the available science (scientific value judgments) and about what is good for society (social value judgments)." (Rawlins and Culyer, 2004, p. 224) NICE operates using the incremental cost-effectiveness ratio, measured in terms of the cost per QALY: "As the incremental cost effectiveness ratio increases, the likelihood of rejection on grounds of cost ineffectiveness rises." (Rawlins and Culyer, 2004, p. 224) In the case of the anti-dementia drugs, therefore, the cost per QALY was thought to be too high, except in moderate dementia. The judgment was that the (undoubted but modest) increase in health that might accrue from treating someone with an MMSE of over twenty was not worthwhile. The fundamental value judgment underpinning such decisions is that, "efficiency in health care involves maximizing the health of the population subject to the resources available." (Rawlins and Culyer, 2004)

Maximizing the health of the population, inasmuch as this allows more people to flourish, would seem to be an undeniable good. Of course, the accusation of ageism is partly a complaint about the manner in which the maximization occurs (by using QALYs). The deeper concern is that there may be no truly fair way to maximize health. Should distribution of resources be according to need or according to the potential to benefit? Should the aim be to obliterate health inequalities or to treat the presenting illnesses as they occur? To accept that health ought to be maximized, by whatever means, is to accept in some form a utilitarian principle. At the societal level, then, health maximization appears to be the morally right course of action.

From the perspective of individual patients, however, the pertinent principle would seem to be that of equity:

> Equity in healthcare requires that patients who are alike in relevant respects be treated in like fashion and that patients who are unlike in relevant respects be treated *in appropriately* unlike fashion. (Culyer, 2001, p. 276)

A presupposition of QALYs is that an extra year to be gained, say, by the dialysis of a fifty year old can be compared to the extra year to be gained by the treatment of a person of seventy-five years with dementia in a manner that does not already undervalue the older person purely on grounds of age.

Maximizing health in a population, therefore, if it is to be acceptable, requires an agreed currency of distribution (the use of QALYs is by no means unchallenged (Quigley, 2007)), and an acceptable policy to ensure equity (but the policies of NICE are a matter of great controversy (Claxton and Culyer, 2006; Harris, 2006)). Anthony J. Culyer (Culyer, 2001) suggested that an equitable healthcare policy might need to be pluralistic: "There may be no single, overriding, equity principle to guide resource distributions." (Culyer, 2001, p. 281)

The conclusion is that the policy pursued by NICE, while in many ways laudable, is open to question because of the value judgments overtly involved in its deliberations and more covertly inherent in its use of QALYs. Nevertheless, the requirement that rationing decisions should be made is inescapable and NICE, at least, presents a more or less transparent mechanism for so doing.

Culyer also recognized that "it is the doctor's obligation to use the available resources in ways deemed best for patients." (Culyer, 2001, p. 277) But he doubted that the individual doctor would be in a position to make the required macro-judgments:

> One doctor may be a good judge of the needs of his or her own patients, but doctors will rarely be in an objective position to weigh either the rival claims of other physicians who make demands on behalf of their patients, or the strength of their own claims vis-à-vis others. (Culyer, 2001, p. 277)

The implication is that individual clinicians must necessarily defer to the macro-judgments of the appropriate authority. This raises two questions. First, under what circumstances might clinicians accept the macro-judgments of the authoritative body that decides on matters of equitable healthcare distribution? It would be possible to put in place some external constraints on physicians' decision-making. But, as Weinstein has acknowledged, this might put clinicians in an untenable position caught between the individual patient and the larger community:

> Patients would lose the undivided advocacy to which they are accustomed, and the pressures on physicians to be responsive would be overwhelming. (Weinstein, 2001, p. 273)

Weinstein's solution is that there would have to be a consensus among all concerned:

> ...a return to unconstrained use of technologies and resources will fail because of the limits at the societal level. The only way out of this dilemma is for citizens and physicians to accept the concept and consequences of resource limits, just as they accept speed limits, zoning laws, and other self-imposed constraints in the interest of the greater good. (Weinstein, 2001, p. 273)

So, the answer to the first question is that physicians might accept the macro-judgment of an authority such as NICE when there are external and internal constraints upon them. As external constraints there might, for instance, be a fixed budget for the use of anti-dementia drugs, or regular audits to check compliance with NICE guidelines. Internal constraints, being optimistic, would emanate from the consensual view that sticking to NICE guidelines was, on the whole, a good thing to do: a way to maintain and maximize healthcare within the population as a whole.

The second question that arises is this: might there be some circumstances under which it is legitimate for the authoritative macro-judgments about equitable distribution to be ignored, as in the case of Mr AB? If so, what would be the ethical justification for breaking the guidelines? My answer is to say that the guidelines should be broken on the basis of micro-judgments made by individual clinicians, and I shall gesture at an ethical justification for such disregard of national guidelines by pointing in the direction of virtue theory. Moreover, I would contend that the sort of consensus that Weinstein was after would be more likely to obtain if the possibility of individual, virtuous disregard of national guidelines were possible. After all, we accept the need for speed limits, but we do not think it is always immoral to drive faster than the limit (even if we mostly obey such limits). As we noted earlier, NICE guidelines themselves contain the caveat that they do not "override the individual responsibility of healthcare professionals to make decisions appropriate to the circumstances of the individual patient ...." (NICE, 2006, p. 2) Indeed, this might carry the implicit suggestion that, under exceptional circumstances, "breaking the speed limit" might not just be optional, but a moral obligation.

7. Virtue Theory

I do not intend to present an account of virtue ethics beyond a few introductory comments. But in one of the best accounts the first premise of virtue ethics is given as follows:

> An action is right iff [if and only if] it is what a virtuous agent would characteristically (i.e. acting in character) do in the circumstances. (Hursthouse, 1999, p. 28)

This immediately implies the need to say more about the "virtuous agent." He or she "has, and exercises, certain character traits, namely, the virtues." (Hursthouse, 1999, p. 29) In turn, this raises a question about what a virtue might be, and (elsewhere) Hursthouse has given the Aristotelian reply that a "virtue is a character trait a human being needs to flourish or live well." (Hursthouse, 1997, p. 219)

Hursthouse makes the point that virtue ethics is *agent*-centered in that it stresses in its first premise the importance of the virtuous agent. This is over against utilitarianism, which emphasizes instead consequences, and deontology, which emphasizes acting in accordance with "a correct moral rule or principle." (Hursthouse, 1999, p. 26) But it is important to see that virtue ethics does not altogether ignore the nature of the act.

> Not only does each virtue generate a prescription—do what is honest, charitable, generous—but each vice a prohibition—do not do what is dishonest, uncharitable, mean. (Hursthouse, 1999, p. 36)

Of course virtue ethics has its detractors and there are internal disagreements between its proponents. For instance, rather than merely allowing that virtue ethics is agent-focused, Slote argues in favor of an agent-based approach. (Slote, 1997) The difference is of some consequence: in the former

(Aristotelian) view, the virtuous individual "*sees* or *perceives* what is good or fine or right to do in any given situation" (Slote, 1997, p. 240); alternatively, agent-based views:

> ...treat the moral or ethical status of actions as entirely derivative from independent and fundamental ethical/aretaic facts (or claims) about the motives, dispositions, or inner life of the individuals who perform them. (Slote, 1997, p. 240)

The difference concerns where virtue resides: whether in the world or within the person's heart. Such weighty matters need not detain us, although they underpin (or undermine) the strength of virtue theory as a whole. Instead, I shall show the usefulness of virtue theory by raising three related issues concerning the breadth of the notion of justice, the unity of the virtues, and the partiality of the virtues.

8. The Breadth of Justice

The first point is a Wittgensteinian one:

> We are unable clearly to circumscribe the concepts we use; not because we don't know their real definition, but because there is no real "definition" to them. To suppose that there *must* be would be like supposing that whenever children play with a ball they play a game according to strict rules. (Wittgenstein, 1958, p. 25)

We are inclined to define justice in terms of distribution or retribution. "Justice as fairness" seems akin to a definition. If, however, we step back from political theory, we can regain a sense of justice as a far broader notion, albeit one that it might be difficult to pin down. In *The Virtues*, Peter Geach, himself an acquaintance of Wittgenstein, wrote:

> Justice is an immensely problematic concept: there are, in old jargon, many parts of justice—there are many strands plaited together, and each strand carries many knotty problems. (Geach, 1977, p. 110)

Geach then devoted his chapter on justice to a discussion of veracity and fidelity, saying that it was too difficult in the current work for him to tackle "the now much agitated topic of justice as fair distribution." (Geach, 1977, p. 129)

The truth is that when we say that someone is just, we impute to the person more than simply the attribute of fairness. The just person will have something to say about the distribution of scant healthcare resources, but he or she will also demonstrate integrity and steadfastness. Indeed, it would be difficult to conceive of a just person who lacked all integrity, but the two concepts are not the same. In turn, integrity implies honesty. So there is, in fact, a network of concepts. The notion of a dishonest judge strikes us, perhaps, as more shocking than the notion of a dishonest estate agent, in part because we perceive a close connection between being honest and being just.

According to Plato's definition of justice, the key does not lie in external action, "but with a man's inward self, his true concern and interest." (Plato, 1987, pp. 43^c^–43^d^) The just person shows a harmony between the elements of the mind. Louden refers to Plato's conception of justice as a "spiritual" virtue, like self-respect and integrity,

> ... traits which do have a significant impact on what we do, but whose moral value is not wholly derivable from the actions to which they may give rise. (Louden, 1997, p. 211)

While expressing matters differently, Aristotle also regarded justice as unique among the virtues:

> And therefore justice is often thought to be the greatest of virtues .... And it is complete virtue in its fullest sense because it is the actual exercise of complete virtue. It is complete because he who possesses it can exercise his virtue not only in himself but towards his neighbour also .... Justice in this sense, then, is not part of virtue but virtue entire ... what, as a relation to one's neighbour, is justice is, as a certain kind of state without qualification, virtue. (Aristotle, 1980, pp. 1129^b^22–1130^a^12)

Older ways of conceiving justice, therefore, emphasize variously its position as (in some sense) underpinning the other virtues, as being an inner disposition that might or might not show itself in action and as being at the heart of a nexus of related concepts, which all pick out a breadth of virtuous dispositions.

9. The Unity of the Virtues

The lack of a determinate definition and the overlapping nature of the relevant virtue concepts call to mind the notion of the unity of the virtues. Although Aristotle recognized that what he termed "natural" virtues might be exercised separately, he regarded this as impossible when it came to the "full" virtues. A natural tendency to be brave might yet allow us to be intemperate, whereas genuine virtues are reciprocal (hence, the "reciprocity thesis": to have one is to have them all). This is possible, according to Aristotle, because each of the genuine virtues requires practical wisdom, but this in turn suggests the other virtues.

> If the reciprocity thesis is right, then we show bravery in circumstances other than those that involve fear and endurance, temperance in circumstances other than those that involve control of appetites, and so on .... The virtues cannot, then, be distributed to different and non-overlapping spheres of action. (Irwin, 1996, p. 53)

Hence, as Hursthouse says, it is for this reason that we are puzzled when someone to whom we have ascribed one particular virtue seems deficient in some other way. Our puzzlement is because attributing to someone virtue in any one particular respect is to say something about them through and through.

> In ascribing to them a settled state of, say, charitableness or honesty, we have thereby ascribed to them at least some possession of all the other virtues as well. (Hursthouse, 1999, p. 156)

A further consequence of the theory is that the virtuous character is precisely that, for he or she cannot avoid those attributes that make him or her into a person whose actions we would wish to emulate inasmuch as we wish to flourish as human beings. The virtuous person, on this view, cannot be both modest and a braggart.

Inevitably, the unity of the virtues is not an idea that goes unchallenged for long. It is easy to argue that sometimes the virtues might tug us in different directions. Indeed, this is most obviously seen in the case of justice, which might well imply the need for punishment, which in turn might go against the disposition to forgive and to be compassionate. Nevertheless, first, it could be argued that Aristotle was pointing to an ideal, where people might genuinely be both just and compassionate; and second, even without the theory of reciprocity, it might still be argued that the notion of justice should involve basic respect and benevolence toward others as individual human agents.

The implication to be drawn from the notion of the unity of the virtues is that, in acting justly (for instance with respect to the distribution of scarce resources) a person will also be acting with courage and charity. The point is not simply that it is possible to act in all of these ways together, which might well be true of anyone with these natural dispositions, but instead that genuine justice must involve the sort of fortitude that constitutes courage and the sort of benevolence that is coterminous with charitableness.

10. Partiality

The point about partiality is that we are naturally inclined to demonstrate virtuous behavior toward those who are close to us. This is regarded as a positive advantage of virtue theory. For instance, Stocker has criticized other ethical theories because they do not show an appropriate regard for the person; instead they are motivated by pleasure or duty or some such.

> What is lacking in these theories is simply … the person. For, love, friendship, affection, fellow feeling, and community all require that the other person be an essential part of what is valued …. The defect of these theories in regard to love … is not that they do not value love (which, often, they do not) but that they do not value the beloved. (Stocker, 1997, pp. 71–72)

Genuine charity, then, embodies a true regard for the person on whom the charity is bestowed. Indeed, to perform a charitable act solely because it is charitable, which would be akin to doing it because it brings pleasure, is to miss the point: genuine charity is aimed at the other person and is good for this reason. Virtue theory stresses the importance of this personal connection or partiality. Moreover, virtue theory recognizes that one way to flourish as a human being is precisely to enjoy personal relationships.

> The development of rewarding personal relationships, which is, in virtue theory, the very core of the good life, requires an emphatically preferential assignment of time and resources to a few chosen individuals—one's close friends and family. (Cottingham, 1996, p. 63)

On this view, human flourishing is seen as being partly constituted by a degree of settled intimacy and regard. Friendships, for instance, not only encourage virtuous behavior, but are also the stuff of virtuous lives. Therefore, the virtuous person is the one who engages in relationships in particular circumstances because such relationships are constitutive of the good life.

> The ethic of the virtue theorist is an ethic for particular individuals, in a particular social setting, whose lives are informed from the outset by an autocentrically determined network of preferential commitments. (Cottingham, 1996, p. 64)

One worry with this view is that it seems to militate against humane treatment of strangers. Slote has argued, however, that his own agent-based approach to virtue ethics can be used to build up an ethic of care that would still allow compassion for the stranger:

> But a partialistic morality that advocated greater concern for near and dear might still deplore *indifference* to strangers, and, if the moral floor of non-indifference, of humane caring, is not set too low, an agent-based morality as caring will be able to treat the usual questions of justice and human rights in a plausible, but highly distinctive way. (Slote, 1997, pp. 257–258).

The "different voice" identified by Carol Gilligan (Gilligan, 1982), which stresses care, interrelationships, and responsibility, as well as the feminist ethic of caring developed by Nel Noddings (Noddings, 1984), has stood against the "masculine" approach to morality, which is said to stress autonomy, rights, and justice. On the whole, there is a natural alliance between the approaches of virtue ethics and the ethics of care, except that virtue ethics emphasizes some special points about justice: it seems to stand over against the ethics of care as well as requiring distinct handling as one of the virtues. Susan Moller Okin makes the point that:

> because of the strong tendency in most people to be partial to those they like or love, it is for good reason that … people are considered virtuous in so far as they treat others impartially—*without* regard to particulars about them. (Okin, 1996, p. 226)

Interestingly, however, in Slote (Slote, 1997; Slote, 2001) we find the notions of care and justice being brought together. For one thing, Slote argues that agent-basing (which looks at the individual's motivation) should look at actions from the perspective of the "agent's total or overall motivation." (Slote, 2001, p. 33) Although partiality is by and large a good thing and constitutive of human flourishing, it might be a bad thing under certain circumstances when there are competing motivations and the overall picture needs to be considered.

Slote considers the example of a father with two children, one of whom has a disability. It would be possible under some conditions, but almost certainly wrong, to argue that the father should devote all of his time and resources to the disabled child in order to maximize utility or to do the greatest good. But the loving father will "*strike some sort of balance*" (Slote, 2001, p. 68) between his love and concern for both children. Slote goes on to argue that a similar sort of balancing can occur when a person has to make a judgment between giving to those who are near and dear, and giving to others (on humanitarian grounds) far away whom one might not even know. It is worth quoting Slote at length:

> The balanced love a father feels toward his children doesn't require explicit moral underpinnings, but neither does it just fall into place out of the blue. It reflects the father's sense of what it means to have a child

> and what it means to a child to have a parent (what it means for people to be close or near or related in this way). Similarly, I want to say that if we understand friendship and kinship relations and really appreciate what it means in our lives to have (the) friends and relations (we do), the force impelling us to be concerned with the welfare of (the whole class of) such people *will not be of a different order* from the impulsion toward general humanitarian concern for others that arises from deeply appreciating our common humanity (our common roots and destiny) and the vastness of human suffering and of human problems worldwide. And this constitutes the kind of rough balance I have been speaking of. (Slote, 2001, pp. 89–90)

Slote argues that for a society to be just, its members must be motivated by the sort of caring ethic that underpins both concern for those near and dear and those far away.

> We thus end up with a view that sees the social virtue of justice as a function of individual virtue(s), that is, of the virtuousness of the individuals who constitute a given society. (Slote, 2001, p. 101)

So, although it seemed as if caring and justice might not be compatible, there is at least an argument that the one underpins the other. This mirrors the argument that justice—in one sense—is required for all of the virtues and, as we saw, according to Aristotle:

> justice is often thought to be the greatest of virtues .... And it is complete virtue in its fullest sense because it is the actual exercise of complete virtue. It is complete because he who possesses it can exercise his virtue not only in himself but towards his neighbour also .... Justice in this sense, then, is not part of virtue but virtue entire .... (Aristotle, 1980, pp. 1129^{b}22–1130^{a}9)

In turn, this reflects the extent to which our notion of justice is broader than the idea of mere distributive or even retributive justice. Instead, justice is quintessentially about our relationships and, *inter alia*, our compassion and our concerned engagement with the world. Thus, Iris Murdoch was able to write, "The love which brings the right answer is an exercise of justice and realism and really *looking*." (Murdoch, 1970, p. 91)

11. Back to the NICE Question

The question posed by the case of Mr AB concerned the ethical justification for disregarding the authoritative macro-judgments made by a body such as

NICE about the equitable distribution of scarce resources. The discussion of virtue theory points in the direction of such justifications.

The truly just doctor will be aware of the requirements for distributive fairness, but we have seen that the notion of justice—at a conceptual level—links to notions such as honesty and integrity, as well as to compassion and concerned engagement. Justice links to and underpins and reflects a raft of virtues. The unity of the virtues is really a statement about our nature as human beings in the world and about how it is possible to flourish. We can flourish in part by being honest, but if we really have and exercise the virtue of honesty then we shall show the other virtues too. It would be a surprise if the honest person were not also steadfast or courageous in the face of an untruth. If, therefore, I am genuinely just, if human nature can ever flourish, then I will also be courageous, benevolent, and charitable. One concept leads to the other and one way of being in the world suggests a whole way of being. So a natural disposition—and a virtuous one—might involve making the decision that, in fairness to this man, the guidelines might be disregarded as a matter of respect and charity, as much as a matter of justice.

This judgment is further supported by the thought that virtues themselves, with justice as an exemplar, should aim *at the person in the context of mutual relationships*. This, virtue theory argues, is the core to the good life. So, the relationship between the doctor and the patient is of central importance. The ethical imperative surrounds a particular individual in a particular social setting. Indeed, it is (arguably) constitutive of human flourishing that such preferential commitments should exist. Within the context of a doctor-patient relationship some sense of partiality would seem to be a *sine qua non.* Furthermore, the care that stems from this individual and partial relationship is a bedrock of social justice, which in turn should nurture compassion. Just as the father has an innate sense of what it means to be a child that requires supportive care, so the doctor appreciates the patient's dependency. Both the doctor and the parent must make balanced judgments, albeit partial, but nonetheless not light-minded.

This is the unspoken background to ethical decisions in healthcare: the nature of interrelationships and the need to make balanced decisions within this context. Such decisions must weigh up the relative expense and the evidence in favor of efficacy, even while alternative dispositions come into play. The doctor's decisions in the context of such a relationship will inevitably be partial and perhaps uncomfortable, because they must be partial toward the person broadly conceived. (Hughes, 2001) Sometimes this might require that the doctor does things the patient is not happy with, which might be required by a commitment to justice and honesty. On other occasions, as in the case of Mr AB, it might be that the courageous and just thing is to risk taking the patient's side in despite of official guidelines or local policies.

12. Conclusion

As Aristotle avowed,

> about some things it is not possible to make a universal statement which shall be correct ... for the error is not in the law nor in the legislators but in the nature of the thing, since the matter of practical affairs is of this kind from the start. (Aristotle, 1980, p. 1137^{b}11–15).

Practical affairs are always particular and in context. The context of healthcare in the UK is governed increasingly by guidelines and targets, which reflect public institutions. So it is pertinent that Alasdair MacIntyre has argued that institutions are prone to a type of corruption because of the nature of the external goods they pursue, which always involve property and possession (in this case of healthcare resources).

> In this context the essential function of the virtues is clear. Without them, without justice, courage, and truthfulness, practices could not resist the corrupting power of institutions. (MacIntyre, 1985, p. 194)

Breaking national guidelines, if these have been developed in an authoritative way, should be unusual. But to deny the possibility of this occurring in individual cases, on the grounds of a defeasible estimation of fairness based on group norms, is a denial of the importance of personal judgment and balance in the context of relationships. So, it is a denial of the possibility of a type of human flourishing and it undercuts true social justice, which is predicated on such manifestations of compassion. Of the greatest importance will be the virtue of practical wisdom, which involves the ability to see what is being aimed at, which should prevent trivial decisions. Of course there must be some balance between the needs of the patient in front of the doctor and the needs of patients elsewhere. But the importance of partiality must be allowed; even if it can be taken to excess, it is the basis of human community.

WORKS CITED

Agich, G. J. (2003). *Dependence and Autonomy in Old Age: An Ethical Framework for Long-Term Care*. Cambridge: Cambridge University Press.

Aristotle. (1980). *The Nicomachean Ethics* (trans. D. Ross, first published 1925; revised by J. L. Ackrill and J. O. Urmson). Oxford: Oxford University Press.

Arnesen, T. M. and Norheim, O. F. (2003). "Quantifying Quality of Life for Economic Analysis: Time Out for Time Trade Off," *Medical Humanities*, 29:2 (December), pp. 81–86.

Ashcroft, R.E., Dawson, A., Draper, H., and McMillan, J.R., eds. (2007). *Principles of Health Care Ethics*. Chichester: John Wiley and Sons.

Claxton, K. and Culyer, A. J. (2006). "Wickedness or Folly? The Ethics of NICE's Decisions," *Journal of Medical Ethics*, 32:7 (July), pp. 373–377.

——— (2007). "Rights, Responsibilities, and NICE: A Rejoinder to Harris," *Journal of Medical Ethics*, 33:8 (August), pp. 462–464.

Cottingham, J. (1996). "Partiality and the Virtues." In *How Should One Live? Essays on the Virtues*, ed. R. Crisp. Oxford: Oxford University Press, pp. 57–76.

Crisp, R., ed. (1996). *How Should One Live? Essays on the Virtues*. Oxford: Oxford University Press.

Crisp, R. and Slote, M., eds. (1997). *Virtue Ethics*. Oxford: Oxford University Press.

Culyer, A. J. (2001). "Equity – Some Theory and its Policy Implications," *Journal of Medical Ethics*, 27:4 (August), pp. 275–283.

Folstein, M. F., Folstein, S. E., and McHugh, P. R. (1975). "'Mini-Mental State.' A Practical Method for Grading the Cognitive State of Patients for the Clinician," *Psychiatric Research*, 12:3 (November), pp. 189–198.

Geach, P. (1977). *The Virtues*. Cambridge: Cambridge University Press.

Gilligan, C. (1982). *In a Different Voice: Psychological Theory and Women's Development*. Cambridge, MA: Harvard University Press.

Harris, J. (1987). "QALYfying the Value of Life," *Journal of Medical Ethics*, 13:3 (September), pp. 117–23.

——— (2005). "It's not NICE to Discriminate," *Journal of Medical Ethics*, 31:7 (July), pp. 373–375.

——— (2006). "NICE is not Cost Effective," *Journal of Medical Ethics*, 32:7 (July), pp. 378–380.

——— (2007). "NICE Rejoinder," *Journal of Medical Ethics*, 33:8 (August), p. 467.

Hope, T. and Oppenheimer, C. (1997). "Ethics and the Psychiatry of Old Age." In *Psychiatry in the Elderly*, eds. R. Jacoby and C. Oppenheimer. Oxford: Oxford University Press, pp. 709–35.

Hughes, J.C. (2001). "Views of the Person with Dementia," *Journal of Medical Ethics*, 27:2 (April), pp. 86–91.

——— (2002). "Ethics and the Psychiatry of Old Age." In *Psychiatry in the Elderly*, eds. R. Jacoby and C. Oppenheimer. Oxford: Oxford University Press, pp. 863–895.

——— (2003). "Quality of Life in Dementia: An Ethical and Philosophical Perspective," *Expert Review of Pharmacoeconomics and Outcomes Research*, 3:5 (October), pp. 525–534.

——— (2007). "Ethical Issues and Health Care for Older People." In *Principles of Health Care Ethics*, eds. R. E. Ashcroft, A. Dawson, H. Draper, and J. R. McMillan). Chichester: John Wiley and Sons, pp. 469–474.

Hursthouse, R. (1997). "Virtue Theory and Abortion." In *Virtue Ethics*, eds. R. Crisp and M. Slote. Oxford: Oxford University Press, pp. 217–238.

——— (1999). *On Virtue Ethics*. Oxford: Oxford University Press.

Irwin, T. H. (1996). "The Virtues: Theory and Common Sense in Greek Philosophy." In *How Should One Live? Essays on the Virtues*, ed. R. Crisp. Oxford: Oxford University Press, pp. 37–55.

Jacoby, R. and Oppenheimer, C., eds. (2nd edition, 1997). *Psychiatry in the Elderly*. Oxford: Oxford University Press.

——— (3rd edition, 2002). *Psychiatry in the Elderly*. Oxford: Oxford University Press.

Lesser, A. H., ed. (1999). *Ageing, Autonomy, and Resources*. Aldershot: Ashgate.

Louden, R. B. (1997). "On Some Vices of Virtue Ethics." In *Virtue Ethics*, eds. R. Crisp and M. Slote. Oxford: Oxford University Press, pp. 201–216.

MacIntyre, A. (1985). *After Virtue: A Study in Moral Theory*. London: Duckworth.

Murdoch, I. (1970). *The Sovereignty of Good.* London and Henley: Routledge and Kegan Paul.

National Collaborating Centre for Mental Health (NCCMH) (2007). *A NICE-SCIE Guideline on Supporting People with Dementia and their Carers in Health and Social Care. National Clinical Practice Guideline Number 42*. Leicester and London: The British Psychological Society and Gaskell. Available at www.nice.org.uk/CG042.

National Institute for Health and Clinical Excellence (NICE) (2006). *Donepezil, Galantamine, Rivastigmine (Review) and Memantine for the Treatment of Alzheimer's Disease. NICE Technology Appraisal Guidance 111*. London: NICE. Available at http://guidance.nice.org.uk/TA111/guidance/pdf/English

Noddings, N. (1984). *Caring: A Feminine Approach to Ethics and Moral Education.* Berkeley, CA: University of California Press.

Okin, S. M. (1996). "Feminism, Moral Development, and the Virtues." In *How Should One Live? Essays on the Virtues*, ed. R. Crisp. Oxford: Oxford University Press, pp. 211–229.

Plato (1987). *The Republic*, trans. D. Lee. London: Penguin Books.

Quigley, M. (2007). "A NICE Fallacy," *Journal of Medical Ethics*, 33:8 (August), pp. 465–466.

Rawlins, M. D. and Culyer, A. J. (2004). "National Institute for Clinical Excellence and its Value Judgments," *British Medical Journal*, 329:7459 (24 July), pp. 224–227.

Rivlin, M. M. (2000). "Why the Fair Innings Argument is Not Persuasive," *BMC Medical Ethics*; 1:1 (December). Available from http://www.biomedcentral.com/1472-6939/1/1

Slote, M. (1997). "Agent-Based Virtue Ethics." In *Virtue Ethics*, eds. R. Crisp and M. Slote. Oxford: Oxford University Press, pp. 239–262.

Slote, M. (2001). *Morals from Motives*. Oxford: Oxford University Press.

Stocker, M. (1997). "The Schizophrenia of Modern Ethical Theories." In *Virtue Ethics*, eds. R. Crisp and M. Slote. Oxford: Oxford University Press, pp. 66–78.

Weinstein, M. C. (2001). "Should Physicians be Gatekeepers of Medical Resources?" *Journal of Medical Ethics*, 27:4 (August), pp. 268–274.

Wittgenstein, L. (1958). *The Blue and Brown Books: Preliminary Studies for the* Philosophical Investigations. Oxford: Blackwell.

ABOUT THE CONTRIBUTORS

Robin Attfield was a Professor of Philosophy at Cardiff University from 1991 to 2010. He was recently awarded a D.Litt. for contributions to environmental ethics and environmental philosophy. The most recent of his numerous monographs are *Creation, Evolution, and Meaning* (2006) and *Environmental Ethics* (2003). His collection of readings *The Ethics of the Environment* was published in 2008.

Beatriz Cardona is a member of the Centre for Cultural Research, University of Western Sydney. Her research areas include education, health, and ageing, and she has published several articles on the cultural context of ageing and the rise of anti-ageing ideologies and practices in Western societies.

Peter Crome is Professor of Geriatric Medicine at Keele University and Honorary Consultant Geriatrician at North Staffordshire Combined Health-care NHS Trust. His other appointments include President of the British Geriatrics Society and Secretary General of the Clinical Section, International Association of Gerontology and Geriatrics, European Region. His current research encompasses dementia, drug treatment in old age, and Health Services research.

AB Dey is a Professor of Medicine and Chief of Geriatric Services at the All-India Institute of Medical Sciences. He trained in Geriatrics at the Royal Victoria Infirmary, Newcastle, UK, and is a past President of the Association of Gerontology (India) and the Indian Academy of Geriatrics. He was involved in the development of age care programs in India.

Caroline Dunn has lectured in Philosophy at Manchester University, and is the author of *Ethical Issues in Mental Illness* (1998).

Andrew Edgar is a Senior Lecturer in Philosophy at Cardiff University, Director of Cardiff's Centre for Applied Ethics, Editor of *Health Care Analysis*, and a participant in the European Union funded project, *Dignity of the Older European.* His research interests are in the philosophy of medicine and modern German philosophy. The most recent of several books on cultural theory and German philosophy is *The Philosophy of Habermas* (2005).

Simona Giordano is a Senior Lecturer in Bioethics at Manchester University. Her research areas are the ethics of psychiatry, and ageism, in which she has published extensively. In particular, she is the author of *Understanding Eating*

Disorders (2005) and *Eating Disorders, Fitness, and Moral Choice* (forthcoming).

Ashish Goel is a Senior Research Associate in Geriatrics and the editor of *Doctors Do Cry*, a collection of real-life stories by doctors from all around the world.

Margaret Harris has worked as a teacher of modern languages, a nurse in two Manchester hospitals, and a teacher of disaffected teenagers. She is currently working on a collection of stories set in a Portuguese village, and on stories based on her experiences with the disaffected.

John Hostler is a semi-retired Research Fellow at the University of Manchester. His working career combined his interests in adult education and in philosophy. His research includes work on ethics and on early modern rationalism in philosophy. He has published two books on the rationalists and several articles on adult education and personal development.

Julian C. Hughes is a Consultant in Old Age Psychiatry at North Tyneside General Hospital, and Honorary Clinical Senior Lecturer at the Institute for Ageing and Health, Newcastle University. He has written and co-edited publications on ageing and on dementia, in particular, *Dementia: Mind, Meaning, and the Person* (2006) and *Ethical Issues in Dementia Care* (2006).

Harry Lesser is, after a career as Senior Lecturer in Philosophy, an Honorary Research Fellow in Philosophy at the University of Manchester. He is the editor of *Ageing, Autonomy, and Resources* (1999), and author of a number of articles on social philosophy and medical ethics.

Michael Rivlin is a Tutor in Medical Ethics and Honorary Fellow of the Centre for Excellence in Teaching and Learning, University of Leeds, as well as Vice-Chair of Leeds West Research Ethics Committee. He is a founder member of the Leeds Teaching Hospital NHS Clinical Ethics Committee. His research interests include healthcare rationing, euthanasia, abortion, and ageism. He has a number of publications on ageism.

Richard Wagland is a Senior Research Fellow in the Faculty of Health Sciences at the University of Southampton, and until 2007 was a Visiting Lecturer in Political Philosophy at Brunel University. Research projects on the well-being of older people in which he has been involved include the Innovation Forum (IF) and the National Evaluation of the Partnerships for Older People's Projects (POPP). He has in particular researched into the expediency and tolerance of ageism in contemporary liberal thought.

Wilma Wilson is a Research Assistant in the Department of Geriatrics, AHMS, and a sociologist associated with Gerontology for the past four years. She is an efficiency trainer with a special interest in the psycho-social development of the elderly, and is currently involved in constructing a web portal for the elderly in India.

INDEX

VIBS

The **Value Inquiry Book Series** is co-sponsored by:

Adler School of Professional Psychology
American Indian Philosophy Association
American Maritain Association
American Society for Value Inquiry
Association for Process Philosophy of Education
Canadian Society for Philosophical Practice
Center for Bioethics, University of Turku
Center for Professional and Applied Ethics, University of North Carolina at Charlotte
Central European Pragmatist Forum
Centre for Applied Ethics, Hong Kong Baptist University
Centre for Cultural Research, Aarhus University
Centre for Professional Ethics, University of Central Lancashire
Centre for the Study of Philosophy and Religion, University College of Cape Breton
Centro de Estudos em Filosofia Americana, Brazil
College of Education and Allied Professions, Bowling Green State University
College of Liberal Arts, Rochester Institute of Technology
Concerned Philosophers for Peace
Conference of Philosophical Societies
Department of Moral and Social Philosophy, University of Helsinki
Gannon University
Gilson Society
Haitian Studies Association
Ikeda University
Institute of Philosophy of the High Council of Scientific Research, Spain
International Academy of Philosophy of the Principality of Liechtenstein
International Association of Bioethics
International Center for the Arts, Humanities, and Value Inquiry
International Society for Universal Dialogue
Natural Law Society
Philosophical Society of Finland
Philosophy Born of Struggle Association
Philosophy Seminar, University of Mainz
Pragmatism Archive at The Oklahoma State University
R.S. Hartman Institute for Formal and Applied Axiology
Research Institute, Lakeridge Health Corporation
Russian Philosophical Society
Society for Existential Analysis
Society for Iberian and Latin-American Thought
Society for the Philosophic Study of Genocide and the Holocaust
Unit for Research in Cognitive Neuroscience, Autonomous University of Barcelona
Whitehead Research Project
Yves R. Simon Institute

Titles Published

Volumes 1 - 209 see www.rodopi.nl

210. Gary G. Gallopin, *Beyond Perestroika: Axiology and the New Russian Entrepreneurs*. A volume in **Hartman Institute Axiology Studies**

211. Tuija Takala, Peter Herissone-Kelly, and Søren Holm, Editors, *Cutting Through the Surface: Philosophical Approaches to Bioethics*. A volume in **Values in Bioethics**

212. Neena Schwartz: *A Lab of My Own*. A volume in **Lived Values, Valued Lives**

213. Krzysztof Piotr Skowroński, *Values and Powers: Re-reading the Philosophical Tradition of American Pragmatism*. A volume in **Central European Value Studies**

214. Matti Häyry, Tuija Takala, Peter Herissone-Kelly and Gardar Árnason, Editors, *Arguments and Analysis in Bioethics*. A volume in **Values in Bioethics**

215. Anders Nordgren, *For Our Children: The Ethics of Animal Experimentation in the Age of Genetic Engineering*. A volume in **Values in Bioethics**

216. James R. Watson, Editor, *Metacide: In the Pursuit of Excellence*. A volume in **Holocaust and Genocide Studies**

217. Andrew Fitz-Gibbon, Editor, *Positive Peace: Reflections on Peace Education, Nonviolence, and Social Change*. A volume in **Philosophy of Peace**

218. Christopher Berry Gray, *The Methodology of Maurice Hauriou: Legal, Sociological, Philosophical*. A volume in **Studies in Jurisprudence**

219. Mary K. Bloodsworth-Lugo and Carmen R. Lugo-Lugo, *Containing (Un)American Bodies: Race, Sexuality, and Post-9/11 Constructions of Citizenship*. A volume in **Philosophy of Peace**

220. Roland Faber, Brian G. Henning, Clinton Combs, Editors, *Beyond Metaphysics? Explorations in Alfred North Whitehead's Late Thought*. A volume in **Contemporary Whitehead Studies**

221. John G. McGraw, *Intimacy and Isolation (Intimacy and Aloneness: A Multi-Volume Study in Philosophical Psychology, Volume One)*, A volume in **Philosophy and Psychology**

222. Janice L. Schultz-Aldrich, Introduction and Edition, *"Truth" is a Divine Name, Hitherto Unpublished Papers of Edward A. Synan, 1918-1997.* A volume in **Gilson Studies**

223. Larry A. Hickman, Matthew Caleb Flamm, Krzysztof Piotr Skowroński and Jennifer A. Rea, Editors, *The Continuing Relevance of John Dewey: Reflections on Aesthetics, Morality, Science, and Society.* A volume in **Central European Value Studies**

224. Hugh P. McDonald, *Creative Actualization: A Meliorist Theory of Values.* A volume in **Studies in Pragmatism and Values**

225. Rob Gildert and Dennis Rothermel, Editors, *Remembrance and Reconciliation.* A volume in **Philosophy of Peace**

226. Leonidas Donskis, Editor, *Niccolò Machiavelli: History, Power, and Virtue.* A volume in **Philosophy, Literature, and Politics**

227. Sanya Osha, *Postethnophilosophy.* A volume in **Social Philosophy**

228. Rosa M. Calcaterra, Editor, *New Perspectives on Pragmatism and Analytic Philosophy.* A volume in **Studies in Pragmatism and Values**

229. Danielle Poe, Editor, *Communities of Peace: Confronting Injustice and Creating Justice.* A volume in **Philosophy of Peace**

230. Thorsten Botz-Bornstein, Editor, *The Philosophy of Viagra: Bioethical Responses to the Viagrification of the Modern World.* A volume in **Philosophy of Sex and Love**

231. Carolyn Swanson, *Reburial of Nonexistents: Reconsidering the Meinong-Russell Debate.* A volume in **Central European Value Studies**

232. Adrianne Leigh McEvoy, Editor, *Sex, Love, and Friendship: Studies of the Society for the Philosophy of Sex and Love: 1993–2003.* A volume in **Histories and Addresses of Philosophical Societies**

233. Amihud Gilead, *The Privacy of the Psychical.* A volume in **Philosophy and Psychology**

234. Paul Kriese and Randall E. Osborne, Editors, *Social Justice, Poverty and Race: Normative and Empirical Points of View.* A volume in **Studies in Jurisprudence**

235. Hakam H. Al-Shawi, *Reconstructing Subjects: A Philosophical Critique of Psychotherapy.* A volume in **Philosophy and Psychology**

236. Maurice Hauriou, *Tradition in Social Science.* Translation from French with an Introduction by Christopher Berry Gray. A volume in **Studies in Jurisprudence**

237. Camila Loew, *The Memory of Pain: Women's Testimonies of the Holocaust.*. A volume in **Holocaust and Genocide Studies**

238. Stefano Franchi and Francesco Bianchini, Editors, *The Search for a Theory of Cognition: Early Mechanisms and New Ideas.* A volume in **Cognitive Science**

239. Michael H. Mitias, *Friendship: A Central Moral Value.* A volume in **Ethical Theory and Practice**

240. John Ryder and Radim Šíp, Editors, *Identity and Social Transformation, Central European Pragmatist Forum, Volume Five.* A volume in **Central European Value Studies**

241. William Sweet and Hendrik Hart, *Responses to the Enlightenment: An Exchange on Foundations, Faith, and Community.* A volume in **Philosophy and Religion**

242. Leonidas Donskis and J.D. Mininger, Editors, *Politics Otherwise: Shakespeare as Social and Political Critique.* A volume in **Philosophy, Literature, and Politics**

243. Hugh P. McDonald, *Speculative Evaluations: Essays on a Pluralistic Universe.* A volume in **Studies in Pragmatism and Values.**

244. Dorota Koczanowicz and Wojciech Małecki, Editors, *Shusterman's Pragmatism: Between Literature and Somaesthetics.* A volume in **Central European Value Studies**

245. Harry Lesser, Editor, *Justice for Older People,* A volume in **Values in Bioethics**

CPSIA information can be obtained at www.ICGtesting.com
Printed in the USA
BVOW080321091012

302195BV00001BA/18/P

9 789042 034907